Tigers, Mountains and Pagodas

The story of a special and adventurous life

The Memoirs of
Lt. Col. Stanley C Robins MBE (military)

(Edited by Philip Robins)

Grosvenor House
Publishing Limited

This book is published by
Grosvenor House Publishing Ltd
Link House
140 The Broadway, Tolworth, Surrey, KT6 7HT.
www.grosvenorhousepublishing.co.uk

A CIP record for this book
is available from the British Library

ISBN 978-1-80381-514-5
eBook ISBN 978-1-80381-515-2

DEDICATION

Editor's note:

The Author provides no explicit dedication for this work but through an example of fortunate serendipity he does provide a very suitable and indeed heartfelt dedication in the last few lines of his memoirs.

"Our task was nearly done and every British officer of the civil service, the army and the other government gazetted services had done their duty to the British Empire and doubly so to India."

(Tigers, Mountains and Pagodas, Chapter 37)

Lieutenant Colonel Stanley C Robins (c. 1941)

CONTENTS

APPENDICES

LIST OF ILLUSTRATIONS

ACKNOWLEDGEMENTS

The first acknowledgement must be to my late father, Stanley, for setting down the details of an extraordinary life and then in his later years, in a state of very poor health, persevering with recording his writing, so that others could have access to the story of the very special and adventurous life that he led during his military career. A career which encompassed desperate action, physical courage and bravery, sacrifice, personal loss and great danger and discomfort but in which he also found time for extensive travel and exploration of the India that had put its "spell" upon him and the interest to acquire a vast knowledge and understanding of its varied peoples, cultures and history and above all to gain an affinity with and expertise about the Indian jungle and its wildlife.

I must also acknowledge the interest, skill and perseverance of my audio transcriber, Deidre Thackray, who over a period of more than 18 months worked hard on converting very old tape recordings into accessible and editable Word text. In addition Deirdre, at her own initiative, followed up likely and often very useful sources of the period; fulfilling an additional role as a researcher for my work.

Also I would like to thank two established authors who, by chance, came to be associated with my father's story. Firstly, the British author and travel writer, Colin Thubron, whose own father was my father's best friend at Sandhurst and who was also his big game hunting companion, as a young officer in India. Secondly, Daniel Ford the American author and researcher; an expert on the operations of the

American Volunteer Group (AVG), in Burma in 1942. The second in command of the AVG (known widely as the 'Flying Tigers'), Major Harvey Greenlaw, and his wife Olga (the AVG war diarist) became good friends with my father and his first wife, Edna, just before and during the Japanese attack on Burma in 1942. On her return to America, Olga wrote a book about the exploits of the 'Flying Tigers' (entitled, 'The Lady and the Tigers', 1943) that has recently been edited and re-published by Daniel Ford. To both authors, who saw relevant sections of the draft text as it progressed, I thank them for their interest, helpful comments and encouragement for the work on my father's memoirs. I also benefited from the advice, comments and experience of another author and academic researcher, Sarah Dietz, especially on some of the chapters about Burma.

Finally, but not least, my great thanks to my heroic proof readers, Sue Robins and Anne Carrick, who brought a 'fresh eye' to the final copy of the text.

Along the way many others generously helped with my enquiries with regard to the use of map resources, including Dr. Hugh Beattie of the Open University, the US Army (Fort Leavenworth, CSI Press) and the library staff of the University of London, School of Oriental and African Studies (SOAS).

PREFACE

To my father serving in the Army in India and Burma was,

> "...the gateway to travel and a special and adventurous life...and although I did not know it...was also to lead to danger, pain and hardship...I was to live and serve with the finest fighting men in the world, to know men who... in later years performed deeds of supreme valour... I was to see many of my brothers in arms resolutely and unafraid meet their death with quiet courage and fortitude."
> (Tigers, Mountains and Pagodas, Chapter 2)

These memoirs were written by my father, when he returned to Britain, after Indian independence in 1947, mainly in the early 1950s but with some later additions right up to the mid 1970s. They describe his life in India and Burma and his Army service on the mountainous North-West Frontier in fierce and deadly action with the tribesmen of that area and also in Burma, in World War II, fighting the Japanese in the jungle in equally fierce and deadly action. On both occasions he was decorated; for gallantry and for distinguished service.

The memoirs were first written in an impenetrable manuscript but fortunately they were later recorded on tape by my father in the later years of his life when he was, sadly, in very poor health. It is from these recordings plus assorted documents and numerous photographs that I have edited his memoirs. Many of the events described were ones that I had heard of, in family conversation as a child, but the memoirs allowed me to place these events in context and in chronological order, and thus to gain a new knowledge and appreciation of my father's love of his, "special and adventurous life" that he felt very privileged to have had the opportunity to live; as well as his fascination with India and Burma and of all things oriental. He possessed an encyclopaedic knowledge of Indian history, life and customs and an enduring love and understanding of the jungle and its wildlife.

My father was married twice; firstly, in 1927, to Edna Parkinson of Preston, Lancashire. This marriage broke up in the mid 1940s but Stanley and Edna had two children; my half brother Brian, born in 1931, and my half sister, Valerie, born in 1933. His second marriage was in 1948, to Mary (Margery) Whelan, from New Ross, Co. Wexford, Southern Ireland. My mother had moved to Britain, in 1942, to train as a nurse to help with Britain's war effort. I was born in 1949, so all (bar one, which is noted in the text) of the family references in the memoirs refer only to my half siblings and to Stanley's first wife, Edna.

The title of my father's memoir encapsulates three great experiences of his life in, "the East". Tiger hunting in the Indian jungle; active service in the mountainous North-West Frontier of India and later active service, in dense jungle, against the Japanese during their invasion of Burma; the exotic land of Pagodas. Despite the privations and dangers of active service in what he calls "trying" circumstances, my father never lost his fascination, admiration and respect for India and Burma or the people, culture and customs he came across over many years.

On numerous occasions his experiences of the nature and circumstances of the people that he met made him feel that he was, "living with history."

My father's memoirs give not only an account of military operations and incidents but also provide an intimate social and cultural record of life lived in British India, including its mores and customs; many far removed from contemporary daily life in the UK or in modern day India and Burma [Myanmar].

Philip Robins (Editor)
Addingham,
West Yorkshire
April 2023

EDITOR'S NOTE

Generally, the chapters in this book are not divided into subsections except in a few instances; where they describe, in the main, sometimes complex, linked and overlapping military operations. The aim is to help the reader follow clearly the events described.

Within the main text, after the Introduction, where rounded parentheses '( )' are used, they include further explanation or clarification from the author. Where squared off parentheses '[ ]' are used, they include further explanation or clarification by the editor.

INTRODUCTION

My father's desire for a "special and adventurous life" no doubt derived from his own father, Frederick, who decided not to follow many generations of his family and become a cordwainer (boot and shoemaker) in Bristol but instead, at 16 years of age, he ran away from home and lied about his age, to join the army in 1897, claiming he was 18 years of age. Frederick did have something of a 'special and adventurous life', as well. In the Army, Frederick served in South Africa, China and Egypt and rose from an ordinary soldier to the rank of Major, becoming a commissioned officer promoted from the ranks; quite an achievement, in those much more class conscious days.

As a result my father, Stanley, was brought up in garrison towns, when in the UK and when abroad would get see far away and exotic lands, that only the wealthy could hope to visit in the early years of the 20th century. Although a child during World War I, he was inspired by the heroic deeds and sacrifices made by British soldiers on the Western Front and also wanted to follow his father and be a British army officer. Stanley was educated at Shrewsbury school and gained a place at the Royal Military College, Sandhurst, which he attended in 1922 and 1923 and was commissioned into the North Staffordshire regiment in January 1924 and then immediately embarked for India; to join his regiment, which had been stationed in India in 1923.

Chapter 1

Early Days and Life at Sandhurst

"We are the Pilgrims, (Master); we shall go
Always a little further; it may be
Beyond that last blue mountain barred with snow
Across that angry or that glimmering sea"

The Golden Journey to Samarkand
James Elroy Flecker (1884–1915)

My earliest memories of childhood are of most intriguing expeditions in company with other four-year olds under the bungalows on the hillside outside of Bloemfontein in South Africa. The bungalows were raised about 3 feet off the ground on wooden balks and the dark spaces under them held endless possibilities for exploration. The spiders, mice, centipedes, big black beetles and a variety of other insect life, which lived in such dark places, had an irresistible fascination for us. Another pleasant way of passing the sunny hours of the day was turning over big stones on the hillside to see what lay underneath them but this game lost its interest when I was stung by a scorpion. It was very painful indeed and I learned my lesson. We also made expeditions to some quarries a few hundred yards away and which were the home of numbers of pretty yellow South African tortoises of which we caught quite a few. Also memories of a small marsh surrounded by bulrushes in which lived huge bullfrogs whose calls and croaks delighted us. They were enormous fellows, about a foot long with green backs and bright yellow underneath.

This vast outside world seemed an intriguing place to a small boy, whether it was the broad green expanse of an English field, with its sheltering hedgerows, or a hot sunny African hillside. In South Africa I knew that I was in a strange land with native servants, such as the huge be feathered Zulus, who pulled the rickshaws. This early experience, I believe, helped to nourish the wanderlust which was within me. Later when my family returned to England, the voyage from the Cape was one long delight; new people and lovely colourful places to excite one as the ship put in from port to port. I remember that when we were in Las Palmas a large whale came into the harbour and tried to upset one of the small tugs lying there. This was quite an unusual event and was very exciting for us to see.

Then came the Great War and although I was only eleven years old, the illustrated papers and stories of the terrific struggle filled my imagination with deeds of heroism and sacrifice, and in due course, when I was old enough, I entered the Royal Military College, Sandhurst to take up the profession of arms, following my father into the Army. I entered Sandhurst in January 1922 and was posted to no 3 company in the new buildings. No 3 company at that time was the 'Champion Company' and had won the King's Banner for three successive terms. Our company commander and lecturer in military history was Lt. Col. H.M. ('Jumbo') Wilson of the Rifle Brigade, later Field Marshal Lord Wilson, and my own platoon commander was Lord Arthur Butler of the 17th Lancers. Many other officer instructors at Sandhurst, during my two years there, were destined to become famous in World War II and render great service to their country.

Amongst them were: Major A.F. Smith, our adjutant, later General Sir Arthur Smith, chief of the general staff in the Middle East, Major G. Le Quesnay ('Q') Martel, who became Lt. General Sir Giffard Martel, Armoured Warfare Authority, Major N.M.S. Irwin, later Lt. General Noel Irwin commanding the 4th Indian Corps and the Eastern Army, Major W.D.S. Brownrigg, later General Sir Douglas Brownrigg, Director General of the Territorial Army.

Looking back over the years, I feel that even as a young cadet one sensed the qualities of leadership, and character and professional knowledge which these officers had, and we were supremely fortunate that our military education and training for leadership were in such able hands. The first year's course at Sandhurst, in the immediate post 1914/18 period, was a most strenuous one. The syllabus included: tactics, military history, organisation and administration, military law, geography, languages, science, mountain warfare, map reading, topography, field engineering and practical instruction in drill, weapon training, riding and physical training. Training in every discipline was, in every way, equal to that taken by the Brigade of Guards and consequently there was never a moment to relax. The first six weeks was a nightmare for the juniors, as we were called.

Every day there were four drill parades of an hour each. The eagle eyes of the drill sergeants noted every slack movement and every sign of lack of attention. These infringements were corrected, with voices of thunder. In halls of study, pages and pages of notes had to be written at breakneck speed and their contents imbibed later in private study. Tailors and boot makers in Camberley had to be visited for the fitting and making of uniforms, riding kit etc., but at the end of a month a remarkable transformation had taken place. The party of nervous youth in civilian clothing had in that short space of time become a platoon of smart, well-drilled, keen young soldiers with pride in their appearance, bearing and movement.

To the juniors, some of the most fearsome figures at Sandhurst were the adjutant, the regimental sergeant major, our own company sergeant major and the company quartermaster sergeant. The adjutant and RSM, to one's relief, we only saw on the weekend parades. But the two other worthies were an ever-present evil. However, as our training progressed, we began to appreciate the efficiency and splendid soldierly qualities that they all had in common. The RSM, a tall but portly figure, was terribly smart, walked with quick short steps and had a high- pitched word of command like a whiplash. He was the subject of humorous remarks and when, at the end of the summer term no 5 coy gave their mock parade at the Garland Ball, the RSM of course was one of the figures of fun.

Hilariously portrayed by General Erskine-Murray with a couple of pillows stuffed under his tunic, a huge bushy moustache and carrying a pace stick, he rushed about all over the parade, bellowing at the top of his voice, telling people to take somebody's name. The parade itself was a really comic spectacle. Uniforms ranged from football kit to Victorian ladies, bathing belles, clowns etc. and one bright youth, attired in huge stockings and suspenders, lady's panties and a clergyman's coat and dog collar, completed the ensemble and received a special ovation. These light moments were few however and the full and strenuous days continued throughout the terms of our course and thus caused them to pass quickly. The culmination of our studies was the examination and the final ceremonial parade, which was the 'passing out' parade for the senior term. This parade finished with the now well-known ritual of the battalion marching up the steps into the old building, to the strains of the tune of 'Auld Lang Syne', followed by the adjutant on his grey charger. This dignified and symbolic ritual was, I am sure, a landmark in the memory of all those who had taken part in it. The more so as the portals through which they went this last time, on passing out of Sandhurst, have been for so many, the gateway to glory and fame and also, for many of one's friends, the pathway that led to the supreme sacrifice on the field of battle.

On Sunday the church parade was held and following inspection by the commandant, the battalion marched to attend divine service in the Royal Memorial Chapel, the pillars of which were covered with panels containing the names of thousands of students who had given their lives for their country. Many officers and their wives from the Staff College, near to Sandhurst, also attended. Among the officers at the time at the Staff College were Major (brevet lieutenant-colonel) the Lord Gort VC and Lt. Col. the honourable Harold R.L.G. Alexander.

After church service it was the custom to walk around the college stables where approximately 100 horses were kept. The stables were a sight worth seeing, the saddlery beautifully polished and burnished and neatly laid out. The horses were expertly and fully groomed and everything was spotlessly clean.

The last parade of each day was roll call in the ante room before dinner. Our mess kit was a blue patrol jacket and a neat shirt. Our platoon dined at its own table in the grand great dining hall, which seated approximately 400. Messing arrangements in each company were under the charge of a butler. Mr. Hopkins, the no 3 coy butler, in those days, was a paragon, ever-watchful for the welfare and comfort of his 'young gentlemen'. His perfection reached its zenith when moving down the table to take orders for drinks he bent over one shoulder and slowly rubbing his hands together said quietly, "And your lordship?". Afternoons and evenings were devoted to games, gymnastics etc. Apart from the inter-company matches and competitions, games and contests were held with the Royal Military Academy, Woolwich, army and university teams and neighbouring establishments including, the Staff College, Wellington College, and Broadmoor criminal lunatic asylum. I remember on one occasion no 3 coy played a team from Broadmoor which was captained by a grey-bearded patriarchal figure who had been the chief actor in one of the most famous post-war murder trials.

Much of our work and training was out of doors and every cadet had to be able to perform proficiently all the duties of a soldier in addition to the training and study required to fit him to become an officer and a leader. He had to be able to handle, in an expert manner, all infantry weapons, be an able horseman, be practised in trench digging and erecting [barbed] wire obstacles. The countryside for many miles around the college was the scene of numerous tactical exercises and practical instructions in field sketching and map reading. Much time was taken up with battalion training and manoeuvres. These were invariably strenuous and in the summer of 1923 on one day's manoeuvre we marched 26 miles and the temperature, at Farnborough, was over 90 degrees Fahrenheit [32 degrees C.] in the shade. Working hard and playing hard, the hurdle of the passing out examination was negotiated [the Author was awarded the course prize for his examination in Organisation and Administration, 'London Gazette', Feb. 9, 1924, p.63] and we all awaited eagerly the announcement in the 'London Gazette' which would notify us of our future postings.

The Author, as a young
boy, with his father,
Frederick (c. 1906/7)

The Author, as a young
man in Preston,
Lancashire (c. 1921)

The Author as a newly commissioned
2nd Lieutenant (1924)

Chapter 2

A Subaltern in India

One morning in January 1924 I received a letter from the War Office informing me that I had been commissioned into the North Staffordshire regiment and posted to the 1st battalion in Secunderabad, India. I was terribly thrilled. My first great ambition had been achieved and the gateway to travel and a special and adventurous life was open to me, and although I did not know it then, it was also to lead to danger, pain and hardship. I was to live and serve with the finest fighting men in the world, to know men who had in later years performed deeds of supreme valour, the story of which will live forever in the history of our nation. I was to see many of my brothers in arms resolutely and unafraid meet their death with quiet courage and fortitude.

I shortly received orders to embark to on the SS *Kaisar-I-Hind* ('Empress of India', in vernacular Hindi) on February 10th 1924 and I was very busy for the next few days visiting my tailors in Saville Row, buying equipment, uniform, mufti, sports gear and bidding farewell to friends and relations. It happened that about 70 fellow cadets of my term were also travelling on the *Kaisar-I-Hind*, to join their regiments in India, which added considerably to the enjoyment of the voyage. One of them was Gerald Thubron, my best friend at Sandhurst, who had also been posted to the North Staffordshires like me. We sailed from Tilbury and after a few cold and blustery days in the Channel and the Bay of Biscay found ourselves in lovely weather off the coast of Spain, and soon came to Gibraltar. The hours ashore were full of interest. The busy and colourful harbour and town bathed with the warm, Mediterranean sunshine was pleasant to see and the towering rock, with its guns in place, dominating the Straits reminded us that this was the most famous of the Empire's outposts.

Our voyage continued to Marseilles where the ship halted for 36 hours and we went ashore and made the best we could of the French cuisine and visited shows of the Folies Bergère type. We sailed on through the straits of Bonifacio, between Sardinia and Corsica, past Stromboli which was erupting, as it nearly always does, but not to any serious extent. Through the Straits of Messina and out into the Mediterranean passing Crete and then onto Port Said, which may really be called the Gateway to the Orient. [Port] Said is a fascinating place and on the many occasions on which I went ashore there in later years, it always held the same interest for me. An emporium had of course to be visited and the numerous small shops with oriental and Egyptian wares for sale were quite fascinating. The peasant vendors of amber beads and necklace trinkets were there hounding us wherever we went. There is a story told of two visitors who were followed for hundreds of yards by one of these gentry and were finally at a crossroads, where an Egyptian policeman stood. One of the visitors turned to the Egyptian and said, "Geroff, or I'll hand you over to that policeman". At which the Egyptian burst into roars of laughter and shouted, "That damn policeman he no good, he my brother!"

When we returned to the ship we were surrounded by hundreds of 'Bum Boats' [small boats used to ferry supplies to ships moored away from the shore], laden with leather pouffes, leather wallets, bags, silk shawls, and other goods of like description and light Egyptian cigarettes and brass. According to established eastern custom, the vendors commenced bargaining by asking five times the price of the article and were quite happy if they got away with a half or a quarter of the original price. If they had no success they shrugged their shoulders and looking up at the deck would say contemptuously, "You're Scots!"

When refuelling was completed the Canal pilot came aboard and we started off on the ever fascinating and restful passage of the Suez Canal. The attractive little canal stations passed one by one, their occupants and local natives standing on the bank waving to the huge liner as it slowly went by. Occasionally a stream of camels came into view treading their silent way over the seemingly limitless golden sands. We came at last to Ismailia and bathers on the pleasant little plages at the edges of the canal waved their greeting. During the passage of the canal our ship was tied up as it halted and pulled in close to the canal bank with huge rope cables, to allow traffic to pass on the opposite direction. Similarly, at other times we passed ships tied up to give us passage. Passing by a homeward bound British liner, we were greeted with the cry "You're going the wrong way!" We arrived at Port Tewfik at the southern end of the canal and having dropped off our pilot, the ship headed south into the Gulf of Suez for its three and half day passage of the Red Sea.

The Red Sea voyage although very hot at most times of the year is not uninteresting. It is a busy shipping lane and there are several groups of islands that are passed, including: the Brothers, Daedalus, and the Twelve Apostles. On this particular voyage, the surface of the Sea was like a sheet of glass and it was possible to see many feet down below the surface, while flying fish played about us. On the second day of our passage through the Red Sea an Indian passenger was taken ill and died. At about 4pm in the afternoon of the same day, a large shark appeared and followed the ship and was still in the vicinity when night fell. This incident brought to mind the mariner's superstition that sharks sense the presence of death and follow the fated ship.

On the fourth day we reached Perim Island and a few hours later anchored in Aden harbour. The ragged lava crags of Aden rock appeared to be boiling in the sun but the small waterfront was crowded with people waiting to welcome the liner. The four hours in Aden allowed a visit to be made to the Arab town in the Crater, with its museum and freshwater reservoirs, said to have been excavated out of the living rock under the orders of the Queen of Sheba. We then headed out to sea and set a course south east, for the 1,600-mile journey to Bombay, our destination. We arrived in the lovely land-locked harbour of Bombay in the early morning. The enormous red sun had risen above the Western Ghats, beyond the waters of the harbour, with vistas of large palm trees and lush vegetation and behind them the mountainsides covered with dense forest. In the harbour Bombay lay shimmering in the sunlight. The Taj Mahal hotel was waiting to welcome us and the great arch of the Gateway of India beckoned.

On 14th March 1924 after a hard but interesting 36-hour journey in the Bombay Madras Mail [train] we arrived at Secunderabad cantonment railway station in the dominions of the Nizam of Hyderabad and I was met by the orderly officer of my regiment. The officer turned out to be Lt. S.R. Harden who, as a child, was one of my playmates in South Africa. This happy incident was the first of many and of which I have found the saying, "the world is a small place" to be very often true. First impressions and experiences in a foreign country often linger and tend to colour the remainder of one's life there, and I count myself lucky that Nizam state was where my life in the East was to begin.

Hyderabad city was then and still is a medieval Indian city and when you passed under the archway of the Charminar (the four minarets) at its entrance, you entered the land of the Mughals; hill forts, palaces, mosques and tombs. The colourful life of the teeming bazaars and the pervading air of feudalism combined to produce the India of the story books and of the imagination, magnificence and splendour, poverty and intrigue all blending to form the unalterable pattern of life of Hindustan. I arrived in Secunderabad at about 8pm and after I had been taken to my quarters in Thimbleby barracks, I deposited my luggage and had a wash. Then my friend and mentor took me over to the officers' mess where dinner was in progress. My memories of that moment many years ago are still bright and clear.

The hot weather had just begun and the dining table had been laid on the hard murram tennis courts at the side of the mess buildings. A lovely frame of forestry formed the background. A bright Indian moon was just rising. Divans, chairs, carpets and rugs from the mess ante-room were also outside.

Dining tables were arranged with a lovely silver candelabra, as a magnificent centerpiece, as well as other pieces of regimental silver. The whole scene portrayed the glamour of regimental life in India and the dignity, good living and tradition in which I was privileged to be included.

Unfortunately, the following day I was taken ill and had to go into hospital, where I spent three weeks suffering some sort of fever. They never told me what it was but I was so ill on one occasion that there were bets being made in the mess as to whether the havildar [Indian sergeant] would have to make a coffin, which was an event that occurred regularly in India. On my return to duty there was quite a lot to be done. The khaki drill uniform which my tailors in London had supplied was the wrong colour and so I had to fit myself out with a uniform of the correct khaki colour and the flannel uniform shirts, which were peculiar to the regiment.

I took over command of my platoon of D coy, was initiated into the duties of the orderly office and soon found myself very busy with the training parades, drills, lectures and various regimental duties. The evenings were spent in playing games with our men, or in tennis and golf at the club. After games at the club we sat round tables in the cool evening air on the club lawn having a 'chota peg' [a small drink, based on whisky] before returning to the mess for dinner. In Secunderabad in those days, a bachelor officer employed a bearer and a dressing boy as his personal servants. As it happened, our adjutant was due to go on leave shortly after my arrival, and passed over his bearer to me. He was a pleasant and industrious little man, who was named

'Baloo' (i.e. the bear), who came from a small village called Ramakrishnapuram and was of course well-trained in his duties, which was a great asset to me.

I was usually woken up by my bearer an hour before the first parade and had a cup of tea, a banana or orange placed on the bedside table. This was 'Chaudhary'. Several subalterns shared the bungalow, which was on the facetiously named 'Bankrupt Alley'. Our beds were placed out in the compound during the fine weather or on the veranda during the rain. One usually regained consciousness to hear a monotonous chant from the bearers, "Five o'clock sahib, all sahibs getting up". Some laggards did not bestir themselves and in due course the chant was changed to, "Half past five sahib, all sahibs getting dressed". And finally, "Quarter to six, sahib, all sahibs going on parade". This final invocation usually had the desired effect. The dressing boys were usually tiny little fellows who did most of the bearer's work for them, except waiting at tables in the mess. They cleaned and polished boots and shoes, Sam Browne belts, buttons etc., took dirty linen clothes to the 'dhobi' or washer-man, ran errands, swept-up and kept the quarters clean. The bearer was paid 20 rupees, or one pound, ten shillings a month and the dressing boys, 10 rupees or 15 shillings.

If a haircut was required, a 'naee' or barber was sent for and the operation carried out in one's quarters. If any sewing or clothing repairs were necessary, the 'dhobi' was sent for. He stayed on the verandah and carried out his work there. Polo was encouraged in all the units and when one purchased a horse a 'saice' or groom was employed to look after the horse, saddlery equipment and also a boy who acted as a grass cutter.

Social life at the station centred on Secunderabad Club. The club was a large spacious building in a lovely garden and had an excellent library, tennis courts and squash courts etc. and in later years a large open air swimming pool. Three dances a week were usually held and a dinner dance on Saturday evenings for special occasions. The Saturday evening dances were formal, requiring evening dress or regimental mess kit.

All officers and their wives and daughters attended and also the nurses from the military hospital. Music was provided by one of the regimental bands. These dances were always very pleasant affairs and enjoyed by all. This was the normal pattern of life in an Indian cantonment, unchanged in many ways from the old East India Company days and the social life in India, as Kipling knew and portrayed it, was very good.

I had from my boyhood days a mission to become a big game hunter and to my delight, I found that Secunderabad and the Nizam state gave excellent opportunities for this, so I promptly provided myself with a 0.45 bore Winchester rifle and a shotgun. I then proceeded to make myself proficient in 'shikar' or hunting and for many years afterwards my leave periods were devoted to this activity, which to me is the most exciting and fascinating of all sports; but more about this later.

A daily routine of parades, lectures, training, musketry etc. kept one busy and being in constant close contact with the men of my platoon enabled me to assess their worth as soldiers and their characters and their individual habits and their reactions to the varying circumstances of a soldier's life. In a few weeks I was assimilated into the life of the regiment, in all its phases. At the same time, as a newcomer I was on trial, as brother officers were studying me. While the men, in a way that 'Thomas Atkins' does, were gauging my worth as their leader.

There was a lot of game in the country around the cantonment. There were also a number of local native Shikaris who endeavoured to inveigle one to go out to shoot a panther, or Black Panther. The countryside was covered with palm groves and areas of fairly thick bush, out of which rose enormous outcrops of granite, with many caves, that provided ideal lairs for panthers. From these, they sallied forth to prey on the village goats, dogs and chickens, and an occasional cow. The Shikari helped to locate a likely panther's cave and then would construct a small hideout, usually made of thorn bushes, in the vicinity and in the afternoon the sportsman would quietly take up position in the shelter. The Shikari would tether a goat about 15 yards away and then depart to a place of concealment to await eventualities. The goat left alone usually commenced to bleat loudly and the sportsman hoped the panther would hear the goat and eventually attack it and give him the opportunity of a shot. This however very rarely worked out in practice.

The panther is a very wily beast, possessed of limitless patience, wonderful eyesight and hearing. In such circumstances it would nearly always listen and watch for perhaps two hours for any sign of movement that might betray the presence of man. In all cases the panther delayed its approach until after dark and should it eventually decide to attack the goat, it would rush in and carry off the goat before the sportsman had time to move. I sat up a number of times for panther but only saw them on two occasions and did not manage to bag one by this method. But disappointing as this was, there was plenty of other excitement and interest. There was always the expectation the panther might come, whereupon the goat would abruptly stop its bleating and birds in the nearby trees would suddenly fly off, calling loudly. These might be the signs that the panther was in the vicinity and excitement grew to fever pitch. The sportsman took great care to make no noise and sound, strained all nerves both to detect the approach of the panther and be ready to shoot as soon as it appeared.

On these trips I learned much of the birds and animals of the jungle. I learned to distinguish the various tracks, how long ago they had been made, whether by a male or a female, learned the different cries and calls of birds and animals, their habits, sounds of alarm and fear. Eventually the jungle became an open book to me, a place of fascination and because of the knowledge I gained of it, in later years it was to become my refuge from the 'human beasts', who would be hunting me.

In those days one resident of Secunderabad, was known as 'Panther Smith', taking his soubriquet from the large number of panthers he had killed. By the time the regiment left Secunderabad for Calcutta in November 1925 he had bagged over 100 panther, and in May 1925 he shot four panthers between seven feet 10 inches and eight feet six inches in length. The last was an enormous beast as big as a tigress and at that time equalled the world record.

Gerald Thubron [later Brigadier Thubron DSO, OBE] was as keen as me on shooting and in April 1925 we took a month's leave together to go after tiger in the magnificent Adilabad forest in the north of Hyderabad state. The 46-hour journey by train took us to the jungle railhead at Balhashar, where we engaged two bullock carts and proceeded to march to our shooting block twenty miles away in the vicinity of the small jungle township, Rajura.

During our march we had to cross the Godavari River which at this ford was about four feet deep and forced us to perch precariously on the top of the bullock carts while the patient bullocks with only their heads visible above the water dragged the carts across the river. Our baggage was carried across on the heads of coolies whose fustian clothing was suitable for such work.

At Rajura we found a nice bungalow in which lived a Mr. Devlin of the Nizam's custom service and his wife, with a year-old baby son. That night sitting near the Devlin's bungalow and over some drinks we learned a lot about the surrounding forest and the game in it from our host. Next day we moved on and continued to an area of forest which evidently contained several tigers, eventually making our camp in a magnificent mixed forest of trees and bamboo groves. The forest had a small lake, which was a favourite resort for the creatures of the jungle and there one morning we saw our first tiger 'pugs' or paw prints. They were in a patch of mud near the edge of the lake and were enormous, almost as large as a dinner plate. It was a great thrill to see them and to know that a tiger was really there. In the evening we set up a 'machan', a platform built in a tree and camouflaged with leaves, over a tethered bullock and although no tiger came we spent an enthralling evening.

As the sun went down behind the trees, bamboo and fronds in a golden glow, a soft evening wind blew out of the jungle and it began to awake. Birds flitted across the water calling to each other. Flocks of green parrots settled in the treetops and had angry arguments. Monkeys sat and chattered in the surrounding trees and then with immense caution a lovely Sambar stag with a magnificent head emerged from the forest and slowly walked to the water's edge. It stood for a few minutes looking and watching and then lowered his head to slake his thirst. Once finished it silently turned to the sheltering trees and was gone. As night fell, the jungle became quiet for a while and then the chirruping of crickets and other insects began and there was an occasional cry from a night bird but these background noises did not seem to lift the brooding silence of both the dark woods all around and the still waters of the pool. Above the trees, the dark dome of the tropic night and the clear bright stars gave the last touch of beauty and mystery to the scene.

At 8am we left our machan and returned to the camp with thoughts of that pleasant and mysterious night at the jungle pool to dwell on. In a few days we moved camp to another valley which, it was alleged, contained wild buffalo and much other game. It was here that we experienced trouble with the local jungle villagers. In the remote jungle the sportsman is dependent on the native villages for supplies of eggs, chickens, milk and country vegetables. Supplies of tinned foods tea, cereal, jams etc are of course taken but to reduce baggage to a minimum the sportsman endeavours to obtain as much local food as possible for his needs and fresh supplies are better for the health when strenuous exertions are called for in a trying climate. The inhabitants of the village we camped by in the valley said they had no milk, chickens, eggs etc.

though we saw the herds of cattle, flocks of poultry and heard them clucking.

Europeans were rarely seen in such remote corner of a native state and we later learned that it was the policy of the state's ministries to discourage villagers and shikaris assisting visitors, so the forest became a preserve for the Hyderabad nobility. Then we moved on into the valley and camped near a jungle stream and there found a village, whose inhabitants after some persuasion sold us the supplies required. In the afternoon I went off into the jungle in one direction and Gerald went in another. I soon came upon a herd of Nilgai. The Nilgai is a large antelope standing 15 hands high and has a good head of speed over the roughest country. There was a fine bull in the herd and taking aim from 150 yards I hit him in the shoulder, and away he galloped despite his wound, and the shikari and I chased after him. It was soon evident the wound was a bad one but he carried on for three miles before we caught up with him and I was able to give him the coup de grâce.

We covered the carcass with grass to hide it from the vultures and returned to camp to find a jubilant Gerald who had bagged a very nice panther, seven feet in length. He had come across it in scrub and had killed it with a single shot. Next day was spent skinning the panther and nilgai and processing the skins with salt. Four more days in the area brought a few heads of black buck and Chinkara. And Gerald also bagged a magnificent Chital (or Axis) deer with a 37.5 inch head. Tigers were elusive as ever. There were no pugs to be found and none of our calves were taken.

It now reached the time when I would have to make the return journey to Secunderabad, partly going through Kasauli and the Shimla hills. Despite having a severe attack of malignant malaria, I travelled through the following night to Rajura, about twenty miles away. I departed at nightfall with the two bullock carts, one of which contained my baggage and I lay on straw placed on the floor of the other one. The forest road climbed a range of hills and then traversed a valley before debouching into the Rajura jungles. By the time we had passed over the hills and into the valley, the full moon had risen and being unable sleep due to the jerking of the bullock cart and my high fever I was restlessly tossing about when suddenly there were shrieks from the bullock cart drivers and Baloo, while the bullocks were snorting and endeavouring to tear themselves away from the yoke. Baloo leaping out of the cart shrieked, "Here Sahib! That is tiger!"

I hoisted my rifle case and put the rifle together but in my excitement, and in the dim light, fumbled, wasting precious time. Once I had the rifle ready, I got out of the cart and walked forward to the leading cart, where the driver had managed to control the bullock, although it was trembling and snorting loudly. About 25 yards away in the middle of the forest road broadside on was an enormous tiger, its head turned in my direction. I knelt down to take aim then with a lazy bound it leapt into the forest and was gone. Nothing more could be done in the circumstances and as soon as I had got back into the bullock cart, the driver took the bullocks to a trot and hurried away from the place. I lay in the bottom of the jolting cart, clutching my rifle and cursing my fate at not getting a shot at the first tiger I had seen but I was beginning to learn that patience is the greatest virtue a shikari can have.

The bullock carts had hardly gone a mile when another outbreak of shouts from the drivers and snorts from the bullocks caused me to leap out of the cart and run forward to the leading one, where the driver was pointing along the road, still shouting in fear as if all the demons of Hades were after him. In the dim light I thought I saw the outline of a large animal but at the same moment it disappeared into the dark jungle. I moved forward and about 50 yards ahead, in the light of my torch; I saw the pugs of large tiger in the fine dust of the jungle road. I did not see the tiger again and the next morning I arrived in Rajura.

I boarded the train at Balharshah that evening and returned to Secunderabad where, not having had enough money left to pay for my ticket when I got on the train, I signed a chit for my ticket to notify the Nizam's railway authorities that I would send cash the next day.

The Hyderabad State army was quite a large force consisting of a battery of horse artillery, two batteries of field artillery, a cavalry brigade and a division of infantry. They also had a personal bodyguard known as the African Cavalry Guard whose adjutant was Captain La Fresnay from a family of pure French blood that had lived in India for several generations. The men of the guard were mostly Nubians together with a large number of Arabs that served in the rest of the state forces. At the New Year's Day [1925] Proclamation Parade, in addition to the Secunderabad Garrison, which is of equivalent size to the State army, the State troops were also on parade, and the line was about two miles long. For the inspection by General Bumataria, there was a march past. It was my honour to carry the regimental colour on parade. Unfortunately a sudden gust of wind occurred and the colour, which was many years old, was ripped from the staff but I managed to retain a grip on it and to march past holding the flag to the poll.

The [Hill] station for troops from Secunderabad was Wellington, in the Nilgiri Hills or the Blue Mountains, at the south of the Madras Presidency and near Uttarakhand. The companies of the garrison relieved each other at Wellington during the hot weather but unfortunately, as my name was not on the roster, I did not see Uttarakhand. This was the only important hill station I did not visit during my service in India.

At this time I was a member of the regimental shooting team and in 1925 we took part in the Southern India Rifle Association championships at Herald camp, Bangalore [Bengaluru]. Teams from all over central and southern India took part, and also many auxiliary force units. Many of them had very romantic names, such as: the Cola Gold Field Battalion, the Nilgiri Malabar Battalion, the Madras & Southern Maratha Railway Battalion, etc. They were all very keen on shooting and put up some wonderful performances. In spite of this stiff competition, my regiment won both the championships, Class I and Class II, a total of 48 cups and spoons. During this 1925 meeting the regimental sergeant major of the Middlesex Regiment obtained a 5-inch group at a distance of 600 yards, an incredible feat, especially for a man in his mid-40s.

The Author (2nd right) with the Regimental Colours, Proclamation Day Parade, Secunderabad, India, Jan. 1925

The Author as a young subaltern in India, 1924

The Author's companion (thought to be Gerald Thubron) in camp on a big game hunting expedition in the Adilabad Forest, 1925

Chapter 3

The Shimla Hills and Calcutta

A week after my return from my shoot I was again on the train on my way to Kisauli in the Shimla Hills to do the physical training course. I awoke in the morning to see the foothills of the mighty Himalayas towering above the railway station at Kalka.

The journey to Kisauli on the little narrow-gauge railway was most interesting, through lovely mountain scenery, and as the train climbed higher it became cooler and cooler and the fragrant odour of the pine trees came as a boon after the blistering heat of the journey on the plains below. I was not destined to complete the physical training course however as after a few days I fell ill with malignant malaria and was very ill for two weeks and a few days after I had rejoined the course, I was involved in a bad riding accident that kept me in hospital for another three months.

I was out riding along the lower mall one evening with several friends when my horse bolted and as I only had a snaffle [light bridle] on the horse I could not control it. The road was cut into the mountain-side, a cliff above the road on the right hand and at some places a drop of several thousand feet on the left side. The horse was going at a full gallop when a hairpin turn appeared ahead of me, with a waist-high railing on the cliff-edge at the point where the road turned. My only hope of avoiding a plunge over the precipice was to throw myself off the horse which I did, putting my left arm behind my head to protect it. I hit the ground with great force and my left arm was badly broken. My left leg had also become entangled in the stirrup strap and the horse dragged me for several yards to the edge of the cliff, where it was pulled up by the iron railing, and after kicking me several times. It galloped around the corner and my leg was freed. I lay dazed for a few minutes but then I got on to my feet and holding my broken left arm in my sound right arm I made my way to a bungalow on the hillside a short distance away where a lady kindly administered to me until the Staff Sergeant arrived 20 minutes later.

I was placed on a stretcher on wheels and taken to the military hospital about two miles away, at the other end of the mountain range, and was soon on the operating table where the anesthetic brought blessed relief from the agony that my mangled arm was now giving me. The arm was broken above and below the elbow and the broken bones were protruding through the skin. I was also badly cut and bruised in many places. The surgical specialist, Major Graham of the RAMC, performed a marvellous operation and after a period of three months I had practically complete use of my arm again.

The days during my convalescence were spent in walks with friends on the top of the mountain range or on the lovely, wooded paths on the mountain side. One of the places we used to visit, was a beautiful spot called 'Lady's Grave'. Here a tombstone in a lovely grove marked the last resting place of an English girl who had died, I believe, in tragic circumstances many years before. She still lies in her lonely resting place there on the mountainside in the Himalayas. Now that British rule in India has ended, pilgrimages of her own countryman to the quiet grave will eventually cease and she will be left in the everlasting peace of Nirvana, which she has surely attained.

Then in November 1925 the regiment moved to Calcutta, to relieve the 1st Battalion of the Cameron Highlanders who were due to move to Rangoon in Burma. The special troop train in which the journey was made took three days to complete the journey to Calcutta, through Mizoram state and thence along the seaboard of the eastern coast of India, through the provinces of Madras, Orissa, and Bengal. The scenery changed and the train left the granite hills and palm groves of the Deccan and made its way along the eastern seaboard. We passed through extensive forest and green rice fields until we reached the heavy tropical vegetation forest of the Ganges Delta. At Calcutta the regiment was located in the famous Fort William barracks on the eastern bank of the Hooghly River, surrounded in all directions by a vast lawn-like park called the 'Maidan'. When we had settled in we merged into the opulent and pleasant social life of that great city.

In January 1926 I proceeded to Ahmednagar to carry out a three-month course on the Vickers machine gun. Ahmednagar has a fine fort which had been built by one of the Moghuls during their conquest and occupation of southern India. The successful assault of the fort in 1803 was the crowning achievement of Sir Arthur Wellesley's army after a march of a thousand miles across India, from Calcutta.

The machine gun course, like all army courses, was very strenuous. Every minute of the day being taken up in gun drills, stripping and assembling, tactical exercises, lectures on the application of indirect and direct fire, the use of the director/field plotter and range finder, firing practices on the ranges and towards the end of course manoeuvres and field firing to test the standard of efficiency, handling and deployment of the weapon.

When I was at Ahmednagar I saw one day the mango tree trick, performed by a wandering conjuror. One evening leaving the officers' mess a number of us were waylaid by the conjuror, who sat down on the bare earth and began to perform several conjuring and juggling tricks which were quite clever and eventually he said he would perform the mango tree trick. His attire was a turban wrapped around and around his head and a loin cloth. The only props were a couple of wicker baskets filled with odds and ends used in his various tricks. He took a handful of earth and put it in a cigarette tin and then put a mango stone into the earth inside the tin. He next placed some water into the tin from a lota or brass pot, covered the tin over with a dirty piece of cloth and commenced to make passes with a hand over it, all the time muttering incantations. After a short time, the cloth began to rise and as it went higher green mango leaves appeared from underneath, the plant continued to rise out of the tin until it was about two feet high and magically appeared before our eyes as a mango tree shrub. The conjuror encouraged us to touch the leaves to convince us it really was there. I pulled some of the leaves off the stalk myself. They were real mango leaves. I do not know what the explanation of this clever trick is. It was performed with none of the equipment that our magicians at home use on the stage and it was performed in the glaring light of the Indian sun with spectators only a few yards away who clearly watched every move the conjuror made.

On return to the regiment in Calcutta I heard the welcome news that Gerald and myself had been granted eight months' leave to proceed to England, and early in April we sailed on the *City of Paris* from Bombay, looking forward eagerly to seeing home again after an absence of two years. The summer months of 1926 passed all too quickly as I was enjoying to the full all of the entertainments and pleasures that London had to offer in those far off days. But when my time to return to India approached I was glad, for India had cast its spell over me. In the days before I sailed, I become engaged to Miss Edna Parkinson, the daughter of Councillor and Mrs T. Parkinson of Broughton, near Preston, Lancashire. We planned to be married in Bombay in October 1927 and Edna was to come out on the *City of Nagpur* at the end of the year.

I sailed from Southampton in October 1926 on the troop ship *Derbyshire* in charge of a draft of 100 men of my regiment. Other than one or two NCOs most of the men had never been East before and all draft-inducting officers were busy attending to these loud and often wayward fellows.

A difficult problem arose, however, during the train journey from Bombay to Calcutta. The men spent some of their time washing their drill uniform, which had quickly become soiled with dust and perspiration. After washing the garments they were allowed to hang them out of the carriage windows to dry and a number of men, as a consequence lost various articles of attire. As the draft had to march through Calcutta, on arrival, headed by the regimental band and some of the men had lost their trousers I was exercised as to what was to be done. Fortunately the quarter master, Lt. Huband, had foreseen this happening and met the train with stock of spare clothing and my worries were over.

As the end of the year came around, I was travelling once more, having been detailed to join the Embarkation Staff in Bombay and I arrived there on 24th December. Arrangements had been made for me to live with the 1st Battalion of the South Staffordshire Regiment which was then in Colaba Barracks, Bombay. Although we were extremely busy with troop ships arriving and leaving Bombay over the whole of the Christmas and New Year period, I was made most welcome in the evenings at parties given by Col. and Mrs Geoghegan, Commandant of Embarkation Headquarters and the other officers of the staff.

The heavy troop ship programme at this time of the year had hardly subsided when one day a landslide of telegrams began to arrive at Bombay headquarters from Delhi. The civil war in China was beginning to have a serious effect on the trade of foreign nations and fears were felt for the safety of their nationals, so much so that various western governments decided to send a military corps to China to protect their interests and citizens.

The British Empire's contribution was two divisions, of which one was a British division and the other a division of the Indian Army. The plan was to embark from Bombay. We received cipher telegrams containing orders for movements and details of arrangements for the provision of shipping etc. Much time was spent in deciphering these telegrams and their orders, given their very sensitive nature and it had to be carried out under the cloak of state secrecy. So I and other officers were very surprised, a couple of days later, to hear the movements of several ships concerned being quite openly discussed by civilians in the Taj Mahal hotel.

One of the regiments being embarked from Bombay was the 1st Battalion of the Gloucestershire Regiment, whose magnificent fighting qualities I was to witness in later years in Burma and which but a few months after these words were written, the regiment was to cover itself in glory again as part of U.N. forces in Korea [Battle of Imjin River, April 1951]. The Gloucestershire Regiment trained in Colaba. It was a splendid battalion. Despite the long and hot journey from central India, the men were clean and smart. As parties they were quickly detailed off and set to various tasks, the orders for embarkation issued by the Embarkation Staff, carried out with clockwork precision. In a few hours the regiment with all its equipment and stores were onboard and the SS Vasna headed out of Bombay harbour on its voyage to Shanghai. Unknown to me, at the same time my father was embarking with the force leaving England and in a few weeks more than half the width of the world separated our family. My father being in Shanghai, I in India and my mother and younger brother Leslie at home in England.

The dispatch of the China force having been completed it was possible in off-duty hours, to take part in the very pleasant social life that Bombay afforded its residents. There were excellent dinner dances held at the Royal Bombay Yacht Club, the Taj Mahal Hotel, the Queen's Hotel, and the Gymkhana Club. Many would spend the day in the fine swimming pool of Breach Candy on the road two miles north of the city or at the lovely Juhu Beach with its four miles of fine sand, fringed with palm plantations. Swimming at night was equally popular when the moon was full. Nothing could be more entrancing than to lie on the sand and listen to the murmur of the phosphorescent waves and swaying palm trees on the hills behind, so good in the soft magic light of the eastern moon.

Race meetings were held at Mahalaxmi. This beautiful and sumptuous racecourse lies in green wooded country, not far from the Breach Candy swimming pool. The lady race-goers, as always, endowed the scene with fashion and elegance, colour and charm. European ladies in their smart race frocks and hats displayed the haute couture of Paris. Parsee and Indian ladies in their lovely brightly-coloured gold and silver spangled saris and Chinese ladies in their beautifully tailored silk dresses completed a picture of beauty and charm, worthy of the sport of kings.

There were also many delightful and interesting places where parties went for picnics, such as Elephanta Island in the middle of Bombay harbour and the beaches at the foot of the hills on the south side of the harbour. Elephanta Island is a jungle-covered hill rising out of the water of the harbour and near the top is an ancient Hindu temple rising out of the rock. There were also statues of a number of Hindu deities, some of which were very similar in form to the statues of ancient Egypt; perhaps indicating a history of seaborne traffic between the Pharaohs and the early kingdoms of southern India. Outside the temple was a freshwater spring bubbling out of the solid rock. This was remarkable enough in itself, as the island is only about 3 miles in circumference and rises steeply out of the water of the harbour to about 500 feet above sea level. The priests say there is a legend that the spring contains the waters of the holy Ganges, which reached the spring by a subterranean channel stretching some 1,000 miles.

Chapter 4

Tiger Shooting in 1927

"The British sportsman of the 20th century was a gentlemanly, refined hunter whose primary characteristic trait was a sense of restraint and a strong sense of ecological awareness."

[Fiona Mani, 'Guns and shikaris:
The rise of the sahib's hunting ethos...
in British India, 1750–1947' (WVU, 2012).]

For two months I was granted privileged leave, from mid-April to mid-June 1927, for the purpose of going on a tiger shoot and had obtained a shooting permit for the Sitanadi block of the Rajput forest basin in the Central Provinces, about 600 miles from Calcutta.

At this point it might be of interest to explain first, how the control of big and small game shooting and preservation of game, was carried out in India in those days. The exploitation of the forest areas and the conservation of each province were the responsibility of the Indian Forest Service (IFS), which drew up regulations for the preservation of all wildlife and the issue shooting permits. The IFS had a number of divisions and in charge of each division was the divisional forest officer. For the purpose of shooting each division was again sub-divided into shooting blocks, which varied in area from upwards of 16 sq. miles

A permit to shoot would specify the number of beasts that were allowed to be shot, together with instructions of the closed season of various animals, birds, and the shooting of females etc.

For a hunting expedition a certain amount of fresh meat could be obtained from local shooting, usually of pheasant, peafowl, pigeon etc. For tiger hunts all shooting had to be reduced to a minimum, so as not to disturb the tigers that might be in the area. As hunters may be alone, many miles from a railhead or anywhere where one can seek medical attention, medical supplies had to be taken. Malaria, dysentery, typhoid and black water fever were endemic in nearly all forest areas and precautions had to be taken against them. Bites had to be guarded against and a lancet and permanganate of potash or a syringe of gold chloride had to be taken. Ammunition had to be tested with each batch of ammunition at 50, 100 and 200 yards to ensure it was absolutely accurate and necessary adjustments made to the rifle, as required.

I travelled to the Princely States of Raipur and there changed to the metre gauge line and travelled south to the railhead of a small gauge township called Dhamtari. At Dhamtari I had to obtain bullock carts to convey my baggage on the 50 mile march to a forest lodge or bungalow at Sitanadi. I had some difficulty in doing this as the local drivers did not relish the idea of travelling so far from their home. However, I eventually obtained a driver and four days later in the evening approached my designated lodge by the forest road, in a valley between two ranges of hills. When I was but a few hundred yards from the bungalow I met a European in the road, followed by several villagers. As he came up to me he said, "Mr. Robins, I presume?" He was Mr. Jenkins, Divisional Forest Officer of the South Raipur Division.

He said, "Get your rifle and climb into the machan". We're going to have a beat and there may be a tigress or panther in it." The beat was put into motion but only a few Chital deer came out during it. Up to the last minute there was a possibility that a tiger or panther might appear, and I was thrilled at this auspicious start of my shoot. After dinner Mr. Jenkins and I sat in long chairs at the front of the bungalow under the stars, drinking our chota pegs and he told me all about the block, the best places to tie up bullocks and gave me much other useful information. Next day he moved on, to inspect another area of his division and I spent it in engaging the village shikari from the small village of Bighan, a few miles away, and I also purchased five bullocks for tying.

While the sportsman-hunter prepared for his pursuit of the tiger, nearby in the forest a tiger would hunt its own prey and proceed carefully and quietly along a forest path, or game paths called lulabegs, walking and listening for its prey. The tiger would choose those routes that it could proceed most quietly along. Upon detecting prey, it immediately concealed itself in the thick cover and very carefully continued to approach until it was in the position to charge and kill the prey. The tiger took enormous care during these movements and would sometimes observe the prey for up to an hour, waiting and watching and looking to ensure its attack would be successful, or to detect the presence of anything suspicious in the neighbourhood. After making its kill the tiger would commence feeding, or if it were suspicious, about any circumstances, it might drag the kill away, up to a mile through dense jungle, before it was satisfied that it could feed undisturbed. The feed commenced with the hindquarters and continued forward to the ribs; unlike the panther the tiger does not eat the entrails. A tiger would feed most of the night during which time it consumed about half of the bullock and then would go to forest pools to drink.

Shooting with a Machan, when hunting a tiger, means a beat area needs to be established. This area will be wide at one end, 'the base', and narrow at the other, as the beaters will try to move any tiger in the area towards a gradually narrowing area near the machan, a platform in a tree where the huntsman awaits sight of the tiger to shoot. At intervals, on either flanks of the base, men are deployed and known as the 'stops'. The stops then converge toward the machan, occupied by the hunter. The main body of beaters, under the control of the shikari, can number anything between 20 to 200 men who form a line at the opposite end of the beat to the machan. They use tom toms, sticks, tin cans etc. to make noise and beat time after the sportsman has entered the machan. The line then moves forward, the beaters shouting to each other and striking the trees and branches with their sticks. The purpose of this is to wake the tiger and make it move forward in the direction of the machan.

If the tiger moves out of the line of the beat, the 'stops' start to tap the trees as it passes them and the tiger will immediately move away from the noise towards the opposite line of 'stops'. Again, it is similarly turned away and will make its way forward, midway between the stops, until it approaches the machan, where this affords the sportsman the opportunity to shoot. For this form of 'beat' hunting to be successful two essential elements are required: firstly, that the area chosen for the beat must include the place where the tiger is lying-up and secondly, the beat must be in the direction that the tiger would take when naturally moving to safety.

Machan hunting can also be used without a 'beat'. In this method of hunting tied-up bullocks are left in the jungle overnight and are visited in the early morning. If a tiger has killed, the sportsman and the shikari withdraw. At midday they return to the scene and locate the kill. This is then dragged in the direction of the planned location of the machan. The machan is then erected quietly in a suitable tree at a height of 15 to 20 feet above the ground and left until the evening. At the time the sportsman wishes to proceed, usually at about 5pm, some fresh green branches are cut at a distance and on arrival the machan is screened with these branches, making it appear as nearly as possible part of the tree. The sportsman then gets inside this construction and settles down to wait for the tiger. He must not make the slightest noise or movement and must be prepared to sit for hours in a cramped position, waiting and watching and ready to shoot with a minimum of movement. For shooting after dark torches are set on the rifle and the best types are ones that light up when the trigger is pressed.

If you happen to shoot tigers on foot, it is usually a purely chance affair because of the habits and highly developed senses of tigers. Normally, tigers are always aware of the sportsman's approach. They may be found on or near the kill when visiting it in the early morning if the approach has been noiseless and along a specially cleared route. Very rarely, they may also be come upon, unexpectedly in a dry riverbed or on a forest road.

On one occasion I had to shoot on foot, after having placed some bullocks tied up near a forest rest house overnight. Just before dawn the following morning I started off with the shikari and two coolies to visit the bullocks and discovered that the first one, having been tied up in sight of the forest bungalow, had been taken by a tiger. The bullock had been dragged off in the direction of the riverbed about 75 yards away, through dense jungle deeply carpeted with dried leaves. Quietly the shikari and I carefully followed the line of the drag and after about 40 yards came across the bullock lying in a depression covered over with dried dead leaves. As we stood looking at the kill a movement caught my eye to my right front and there, about 50 yards ahead, was a small tiger sitting in front of a bush washing its face with its paw. I knelt down slowly and taking a quick aim, fired.

In a moment another tiger or tigress, as it turned out to be, leapt from behind the bush and galloped away in the opposite direction. It was a lucky chance and my heart was pounding with excitement. I could not simply have killed the two tigers charging towards me at the same moment. The first tiger galloped across my front. I swung my rifle onto it and hit it again but it galloped on to the nullah and as it emerged from a pool of water and began to climb the far bank I fired again and it fell over on its side and lay still. With no further movement from the beast, the shikari, I and the coolies made our way to the nullah arriving at high ground on the opposite side, overlooking the place where the tiger was lying. It had not moved and there was no response at several stones thrown at the body. We cautiously moved down to the tiger and found it to be dead. All three shots had hit it, through the shoulder and the chest, but it had still managed to gallop about 75 yards, an example of the terrific vitality and strength of these magnificent animals. The tiger was a three quarter grown cub, seven feet in length, and although I was disappointed at this, I was nevertheless thrilled at my first tiger and to achieve success so quickly.

In addition, I had bagged a tiger on foot, which, as I have said, is a very rare occurrence. A sapling was quickly cut down and the tiger tied to it. With the aid of several more coolies who arrived from the forest bungalow, where a regular hoo-ha had arisen after the shooting, the tiger was carried back in triumph to the bungalow. That evening I got into the machan located over the kill but in rather a pessimistic mood, as it was unlikely the tigress would return to this spot after the incident of the morning. However, at about 8pm, up the valley to the north a tiger started roaring. The roar of the tiger is like a great organ blowing and an impressive sound to hear in the Indian jungles. The tiger roared once or twice and closer to me and about half an hour later I heard roars from the direction of the forest bungalow; which eventually subsided. The tiger come close during the night and shortly before dawn I heard the tiger roar again, further away, higher up the valley. Returning to the bungalow at dawn I found that a tiger had actually been in the vicinity of the bungalow during the night. Baloo, my bearer, the forest guards and the coolies had locked themselves into their 'go-down' and had shouted at the top of their voices to frighten the tiger away, which was why I had heard roars from the bungalow direction during the night.

Later I decided to sit out overnight, with a live bullock tied up in a nullah about one mile north of the bungalow, in the area where I judged the tiger to be when I had previously heard it calling just before the dawn. I got into the machan at about 5:30pm. Shortly before 8pm the tiger roared from still higher up the valley and continued to call as it made its way down the valley, as I judged, on the forest road. I heard it at intervals during the night but my vigil was otherwise undisturbed. As dawn was breaking I heard the tiger grunting not very far up the nullah. The shikaris and coolies arrived a few minutes later and I then stalked up the nullah towards the sound. I had only gone about 400 yards when from an island covered with three-foot high grass in the middle of the dry nullah bed I heard a gruff woof and a tiger stood up in the grass broadside onto me with its head turned in my direction. I took aim in the standing position and fired. The tiger leapt up in the air, turning on its back, and beating the air with its paws it then fell back into the grass and there was no further movement. The shikari and coolies and I then climbed up onto the high ground on the western bank of the nullah and I made my way to a point from which the spot, where the tiger had disappeared, could be observed. There was nothing to be seen, only a number of stones in the thick grass. The shikari and I moved down to the spot and found marks of blood in the grass and a blood trail leading across the sand into the jungle on the opposite bank.

I had hit the tiger and the bullet had passed right through it, as the grass had blood stains on it at a height of three feet on either side of the track made by the tiger. How the tiger had crossed the 500 yards of bare sand between the island and jungle was beyond my comprehension, but it may have done so while we were making our way up onto the high ground after I had shot it. I had now to decide what to do. When a tiger has been wounded in an area, which in time will prove fatal, the correct thing to do is wait half an hour before continuing the follow up as it is probable the tiger will die, and in addition the tiger will not normally move very far. I decided upon this plan, and sent two coolies back to the forest bungalow to collect more men, in the event of having to follow up and bring the tiger down and also to carry it back, should I recover it.

After 15 minutes or so I became impatient and feared that I might lose the tigress unless I followed up quickly. So, with the remaining coolies and the shikari, I commenced to move by bounds on the blood trail of the tiger. A coolie on one flank climbed a tree and from that vantage point of the local jungle area was to give an all clear signal, whereupon the shikari would move forward following the trail and I would move close by him with my rifle at the ready for any instant use. The coolie on the other flank would get into another tree and we would move forward on his signal. We had gone about 200 yards into the jungle in this fashion when to my front, 50 yards away, I saw a large tree stump. It occurred to me that the tiger might be behind the stump and just as the thought entered my mind, a tiger bounded from behind that very tree stump, leaping across my front in the direction of the coolie on my right, who was climbing a tree.

There was a yell of fear from the shikari and coolies and using my rifle in the fashion of a shotgun I swung onto the tiger, shooting it as it was, at the top of its third bound. The tiger fell to the ground and lay still and the shouting coolie fell out of the tree. Picking himself up, he ran like one possessed in the direction of the nullah. I kept my rifle trained on the tiger and after the shikari had thrown several pieces of dried wood at it without response we gingerly approached the tiger and the shikari reaching out his hand pulled the tiger's tail. At this moment the shikari said, "Mar chuka hai, Saahib!" (It is dead, Sahib!). The tension was then broken by the excited chattering of the collies that gathered round the tiger, examining its whiskers, lifting up its paws, making intimations of admiration. This fine tigress was nine feet in length, and was obviously the mother of the cub that I had shot previously and the tiger who galloped off from behind the bush. My first shot had hit the tiger in the vicinity of the kidneys.

The tiger, on the shoulders of eight coolies, was carried down the forest road to Sitanadi where it was received by acclamation by Baloo, my bearer, the forest ranger and other coolies. After I had taken photographs the skinning of the tiger began immediately. This process may take up to three or four hours according to size, and the operation should be supervised throughout by the sportsman.

When the skin has been removed, it is laid on a piece of level ground and a number of men sitting around it stretch it in all directions to obtain the maximum length and width. It is then pegged down with nails and remains in the shade for 48 hours to dry. The skin is then examined to see that there are no soft spots where hair may be falling out and then rolled up to await transport to the taxidermist.

The fat is highly prized by Hindus, as they believe that if used as a body-salve it gives them courage, strength and other attributes of the tiger. By the time skinning is completed it is usual to find all the local headmen and worthies of the district gathered to receive their present of tiger fat. I had distributed baksheesh to the shikari and coolies in the evening when the day's work finished and there was much chattering and drinking of Toddy with the evening meal. The stories of tigers were related and the hubbub went on into the small hours of the morning. I was very elated myself, as I had bagged two tigers so quickly and both in most unusual circumstances, so I also celebrated with a few chota pegs from my small stock of whisky.

The next ten days were uneventful. There were no more kills and there was little else to do than to wait. Meanwhile flocks of the lovely Hariyal, or green pigeon, were numerous but I did not do any shooting, in order to avoid disturbing the jungle. I visited the tied up bullocks early each morning and this required a walk of about ten miles. The animals were watered and fed and then I took a different route back to the forest rest house. The tie-ups were visited again in the evenings and these treks in different directions enabled me to get to know the geography of my block thoroughly and in the process I discover other likely places at which to tie up.

One morning there was another kill. It was only a small bullock and most of it had been eaten. When I got into the machan in the evening I was not very optimistic. I settled down to my vigil but eventually decided to go to sleep and wake up again at midnight. I had developed the faculty of being able to wake up when I wished and so I duly woke at midnight. Twenty minutes later I heard below me the sound of an animal feeding and carefully lined-up my rifle in the direction of the kill. I could not see anything, as there was no moon and the trees added to the darkness. I touched the trigger of the rifle and in the beam of torch light I saw a panther lying beside the remains of the bullock. Two green eyes stared up at me and aiming behind the shoulder I fired. It fell on its side and did not move and I put one more shot into it to make sure it was dead.

I dropped down from the machan at dawn and found the animal was an old female panther; a large one which measured 6ft 10in between pegs. The skin was in good condition despite the age of the animal and was beautifully marked.

Two days later I moved to the southern portion of my block fourteen miles away and made my headquarters at a small forest rest house at a place called Budra [19°46'10.9"N 81°48'39.2"E]. This point marked the border between the south Raipur district and the Indian state of Bastar. Some years later I met the Maharaja and Maharani of Bastar on the voyage to England and with them they had their son and heir, the Rajkumar. After succeeding to the Gaddi [Throne] the young boy was destined to be killed when leading a rebellion of the Goan forest people against the government of India.

In the evening I sat up over a live bullock tied up near a small pool of water only two yards wide, in a depression in the jungle stream. Other bullocks were tied up in various parts of the jungle. The moon in its second quarter had risen and the bamboo groves looked very mysterious and fascinating in the moonlight. About 7pm a bullock, that had been placidly feeding on the fresh leaves placed for it, suddenly snorted and faced in the direction of a spur on my right. Slowly turning my head I saw an enormous tiger, silver grey in the moonlight, moving with long strides towards a bamboo clump behind which it disappeared. For perhaps half a minute there was absolute stillness, then with a great bound the tiger leapt into view, another bound took it over the depression in the ground and at the third it sprang onto the bullock. The tiger placed an enormous paw over one side of the bullock, its other paw on the bullock's muzzle. At the same time he bit the bullock on the back of the neck.

I was already in the aim and placed the shot straight through the centre of the tiger's shoulder lower down, in line with the point of the shoulder. This not only breaks the tiger's leg but also penetrates the lung and is eventually fatal. The tiger fell on its side, lashing about madly with its legs and emitting the most terrific roars. The bullock fell over and lay on its back, also kicking madly and drawing great draughts of air. The tiger had been about to break the bullock's neck by wrenching the muzzle backwards at the moment I fired, but as it happened the tiger had bitten the bullock through the windpipe and it died of asphyxiation.

My torch had gone out with the shock of the discharge of the first shot and I aimed twice more at the tiger in the dim light. It still continued to thrash about and roar fearfully but did not attempt to get up and move off. I then adjusted my torch and fired again into its chest. The tiger roared again and I fired two more shots. My heart was pounding with excitement and I was worried that it might still get to its feet and disappear. After the first of the additional shots, the tiger's movement almost ceased and it lay on its side, with its head still moving a little and the tail twitching. I took careful aim for the centre of the throat and fired a last shot which finally killed the tiger.

Through the rest of the night I was too excited to sleep as I could see it was an enormous tiger and turned on the switch on my light to look at it as it lay there. Dawn came at last and with it the shikari and coolies, who gazed in awe at the great beast. It so happened that this tiger had killed about a dozen people in the past year, in addition to the toll of 100 cattle from their herds, and there was great relief at the end of this affliction.

It was obvious that there were not enough men to carry the tiger back to the camp. Two coolies returned to the village near the rest-house and brought more men. A stretcher for the tiger had been prepared and there were twelve men grunting and groaning at the burden as the tiger was carried back to the rest house. On the way back I noticed several of the junglies who had arrived looking up at a tree and pointing at something. I glanced up and saw an enormous honeycomb attached to a branch of the tree. One of the coolies then broke a leafy branch off a sapling, climbed the tree and made his way to the honeycomb. In the meantime we moved the tiger to a safe distance in the scrub.

The coolie, who was only attired in his pagri [turban] and loincloth brushed the bees off the comb with the branch and then broke it off and threw it down to the ground. We moved on with the tiger to the forest hut and later the junglies arrived carrying the honeycomb. Apparently none of them had been attacked by the bees and this was a normal method they had of collecting honey.

At the rest house I came across a party of villagers who held us up with a rope across the road. Baloo said that they would not let us pass until I had given them baksheesh so having a pocket full of small coins I threw them in the air and the women with shouts and giggles scrambled in the dust for the money. I photographed the tiger. It was laid on his back and bound with pegs from nose to tail. The measurement, between the pegs, was 10 feet 6 inches. I had indeed bagged a magnificent animal as only about one tiger in 200 is more than 10 feet in length.

Most of the day was spent in skinning the tiger and in the evening I went for a walk along the farm line and saw quite a large amount of game. There were several Barking deer, herds of Chital and the sound of pigs. So the next morning I proceeded to visit the bullocks tied up during the night. I first went to the waterhole where a dead bullock was lying and found it was untouched. At that moment, I heard a tiger roaring in the direction of one of the bullocks and quickly and quietly I proceeded to the spot with the shikari and two coolies. A bullock had been killed and dragged away. The trail led up a cart track overgrown with grass. About 30 yards away I found the bullock lying on its side. A tiger had started feeding on the hind quarters and it was obvious it had only just made the kill, because the blood had not yet congealed. Suddenly there was a colossal roar from the jungle ahead of us. A tiger appeared to be about 50 yards away and the jungle rang with the awe-inspiring noise. The coolies were shaking with fright and I motioned them to sit down and be quiet. Then I moved very slowly and carefully forward, followed by the shikari. Two more terrific roars came out of the dense jungle ahead of us and I must admit I moved forward again with some trepidation. We came to the end of the track but the jungle was so dense nothing could be seen. The tiger had stopped roaring and there was no indication as to where it might be.

Rather than disturb it unnecessarily and there being little chance of getting a clear shot, I decided to withdraw and to sit on the kill that night. We approached the junction of the cart track where the bullock had been taken, the shikari glanced up into the trees and there sitting high on a branch were the two men with their arms around each other, still shaking with fright. At midday a machan was erected over the kill and I got into it at 5pm. At about 9.30pm, as I was trying to doze off, I heard the sound of meat being torn off the kill and on my taking the aim, I saw a beautiful panther in the light of the torch lying full length on top of the bullock. The panther looked up at the light and I killed it with a shot through the spine between the shoulder blades. On one or two occasions later during the night there was an animal in the vicinity but if it was the tiger it did not come onto the kill. In the first hours of the daylight I found the panther was a fine young male in his prime, 7 feet 6 inches between the pegs. The handsomely marked skin was of a deep golden-brown colour, which is usually found in animals inhabiting dense forest.

Two days later I returned to the forest bungalow at Sitanadi, which was in quite a lovely spot. It was standing on a bluff overlooking a river below, which in the hot weather had only a few inches of water, with the odd jungle pool in shady areas. From the veranda you could see several miles down the valley to Sitanadi, enclosed on either side by the jungle covered hills. One evening when I was strolling down the forest road the shikari came hurrying towards me and told me news had come of several tiger bullock kills at a village called Umja, about 8 miles away. Immediately we returned to Sitanadi, I picked up my rifle, filled my water bottle, packed up a little food and then started for Umja. Alternatively trotting and walking, I covered the distance in about one and a half hours. On arrival I found that five bullocks had been collected in one place and apparently two tigers had stalked a grazing herd of cattle and after killing the bullocks in a series of lightning attacks, had been driven off by the villagers and so prevented the tigers from feeding on their kills.

A machan was quickly erected in a tree which I later found was the home of a nest of red ants. I had not been in the tree long when I felt the insects crawling all over me and then I received several vicious stings. I folded the sleeves of my shirt down and tucked my flannel trousers inside my socks but I had a most unpleasant night. Nothing happened during the night but before leaving in the morning I looked round and found there were two more bullocks which had been killed by the tigers, and they had been eaten during the night. I was very angry as these bullocks should have been collected in with the rest of the cattle. I had a piece of cloth tied above them to prevent the tigers returning to them. On the way back to Sitanadi I found there was another village that had been visited by two tigers during the night and they had prowled around and had attempted to get into the village cattle kraal. These tigers were almost certainly those also responsible for the killings at Umja.

The unusual behaviour of these tigers was, I believe, because it was mating season, and tigers, like human beings, behave in strange ways in the spring of the year. A few days later a strange and rather alarming incident occurred. A panther frequented the jungles around the Sitanadi bungalow and was quite often seen by the forest guards and bullock cart drivers moving along the forest roads. It had been heard calling in the vicinity of the bungalow for several nights. The sound was like that of a double-handed saw being drawn across a log. My bed was placed on the veranda of the forest bungalow and one night I decided to tether a goat on the end of a rope, about twenty yards long, to one of the legs of the bed. My loaded rifle, a torch attached, was on the bedside table. The idea was that if the panther, in its wanderings, attacked the goat, I would be woken up and perhaps get the chance of a shot. I fell asleep and was woken by my bed moving a foot or so along the veranda. The sound of the wooden legs over the stone floor of the veranda made quite a noise.

I seized my rifle and directed the torchlight onto the goat but it was quietly feeding on some grass. I got out of bed and looked out around the house but there was nothing to account for what had happened. I got back in the bed and hardly had I laid down when the bed moved again. I grasped my rifle, shone the light on the goat but all was in order. I looked around the veranda and as I did so I heard chattering in the servants' quarters behind the forest rest house. Forest guards appeared with hurricane lamps. I asked Baloo what had happened, and he said, "The ground shake up, sahib". Apparently it was an earthquake.

I found out later that this earthquake was felt over a wide area of Bihar and Orissa and there was a great deal of damage. I was relieved that there was some natural explanation for what had occurred but was also amused at the way my unorthodox method at attempting to bag a panther had ended. The following morning a vast swarm of locusts appeared in the valley, coming from the south. The swarm reached a great height and filled the skies in every direction and did not clear the valley until the late afternoon. There is a legend in India that locust swarms must fly to the Himalayan snows to die, and for some months later this legend was the topic of discussion. Newspapers asked readers to report the movement of locust swarms and amongst those traced was the swarm I had seen. It was first observed in Basta state about the time I saw it. Its course took it north across the province of Bihar and it was finally lost trace of in the outer regions of the Himalayas.

A few days later I had a peculiar experience. Bundu, the shikari, told me that a man had just arrived, reporting that in a village, about two miles from Sitanadi, a tiger had attacked a village herd and killed the herd bull. It had dragged the enormous bull across the field to the side of nullah in a bamboo grove and would not leave the kill. All of the villagers had turned out and shouted and banged tom toms. The tiger roared and demonstrated and was still on the kill when the man set out to Sitanadi. Baloo and

I immediately set out for the village and on arrival there found the tiger had just left the kill. After inspecting it, I told the villagers to erect a machan as quickly as possible in a bamboo clump.

It was a less than ideal place to put a machan, as the bamboo considerably interfered with the barrels of the rifle and the machan could only be placed at a height of about 10 feet. Native rope made of charpoy was used to make the machan and it was ready in a short time. Also a bamboo ladder was made to help me get inside. I sent the villagers away and settled down to wait.

The moon rose and bathed the bamboo grove with its soft silvery light, enabling me to see about 20 yards. I had only been in the machan for about 20 minutes when I heard the deep rumbling of the tiger to my rear, and shortly afterwards over my left shoulder I saw it striding along with a beautifully smooth action. The tiger was gliding over the ground. It then disappeared from view behind some bamboo. My senses were alert, my nerves tense as I waited for the next indication of its whereabouts, and then after a minute, I heard a faint noise in the direction of the kill and saw an enormous head as a black silhouette.

One great paw moved forward and it was gone again in the dense shadow. Following a few moments of silence, there was the sound of a heavy body being dragged and a thud as a heavy object hit the ground. Hearing that the tiger was dragging the kill away, I switched the torch on and found the dead buffalo had disappeared. I shone the light in all directions, but saw neither tiger nor kill. Very disappointing, as I was almost certain the tiger would not return again.

However, 20 minutes later I heard an animal galloping towards the machan from my rear and then there was an ear-splitting roar. The tiger bounded past, striking at the bamboo with his paws. I almost jumped out of the machan in sheer fright and with my heart pounding loudly I switched on the torch. I searched the jungle quickly in all directions.

Although the bamboos interfered with the movement of my rifle, they proved to be my salvation. Because of the dense bamboo cover, the tiger could not reach me. I had hardly composed myself after this nerve-wracking incident when with another awful roar; the tiger again came galloping past the machan attempting to strike at me. Quickly I tried to follow him with the light but it was hopeless. Sweating with the nervous tension of the situation, I knew I would have to keep awake all night, but eventually after realising it was difficult for the tiger to claw me out of the machan without gaining an opportunity for a shot, I became almost philosophical about the situation.

The night seemed interminable and when it was half an hour to wait for the dawn, I thought my ordeal was over. At the instant of this thought, I heard a horrible snarling and growling commence in the dark behind me and once more the tiger galloped at the machan roaring like thunder, then withdrew without making a real attempt to molest me. The tiger roared once or twice a few minutes later and then to my relief the dawn came. Soon a crowd of villagers arrived. They had heard what was happening and could not understand why I had not fired at the tiger. Getting down from the machan I found the buffalo lying about four yards from where it originally was, and from the footprints of the tiger and marks on the buffalo I deduced it had seized the buffalo by the head, and with a terrific heave had half dragged and half thrown its kill into a dense patch of undergrowth, where it was not visible to me from the machan.

The strength of the tiger seemed almost incredible as the buffalo was a huge bull and must have weighed nearly a ton. The behaviour of this tiger was unusual, but it seemed it was a vicious beast and was angry at being driven off its kill. I think that it is almost certain that this tiger was the one I shot a year later at the Sitanadi bungalow when my wife and I went down for another shoot. Looking at myself in the mirror at the forest bungalow I was quite relieved to find that my hair had not turned grey after that terrifying night.

By now my leave was at an end and I returned by a small forest tramway, which had been built for the felling of tracts of timber from the vast estate. It consisted of a small engine, a few wooden flat wagons and a small wooden hut which acted as the guard's van at the end of the train. About a 100 or so local Goan villagers and a very obese tehsildar (a local minor magistrate) and his servants came to the small general station in a grove of enormous trees and where there were some enormous honeycombs on these trees. We had only been halted a few minutes when with shrieks and howls of agony everybody in sight dashed into the surrounding jungle. The bees had been disturbed and were buzzing around in the tens of thousands. We were safe inside the guard's house. The tehsildar was far too fat to move and was stung in many places, on the face, arms and legs. The bees went away quite suddenly and I went out to examine the tehsildar who was shrieking with agony. His nose had swelled to gigantic proportions and his eyes were almost closed. The poor old man, apparently, was not popular with the local villagers and there were many sly grins between them and the tehsildar's servants, who controlled their own laughter with difficulty.

Arriving at Raipur I went to the office of Mr. D.J.N. Lee, the commissioner of the division, to be given an award of 50 rupees for each tiger and panther shot. Owing to the number of persons that had been killed by tigers in the Raipur division in the past year, the kills could not be put down to any particular animal, so an award of 50 rupees was given for each animal killed. The reward was welcome, as it defrayed about one third of the cost of the shoot. Afterwards I had lunch with Mr. Duke, the superintendent of police for Raipur, in his lovely bungalow and rested there during the afternoon. Later, I boarded the Bombay-Calcutta mail train to return to the regiment after a most enjoyable shoot and was very well-satisfied with the results.

The forest bungalow at Sitanadi

The Author with the 'Big Tiger' of
Budra, Length 10ft 6ins Girth 52ins

Chapter 5

Tales of Chowringhee (Life in Calcutta), Marriage to Edna

The weather of 1927 passed in the usual way. Most of the European ladies and children left for the cooler climates of Darjeeling, Nainital, Mizoram or Kashmir and their men folk were forced to endure prickly heat, mosquitoes, sand flies, eye flies and the many inconveniences the hot weather brings. The hot weather programme of training, parades and lectures commenced at dawn and ceased at 9am in the open. Thereafter any work required was in the veranda shade followed by a rest period in the afternoon for all ranks and in the evening various games were held.

The three important men's clubs in Calcutta, the Bengal Club, the United Service Club and the New Club were comfortable and excellent in every way. The social and sporting clubs were the Tollygunge Club, which had a lovely golf course and swimming pool and the Saturday Club, the number one social club in India, with its lovely gardens, swimming pool, squash courts and two dinner dances a week.

It was, at the time, for Europeans only and any person wanting to join had also to produce his wife, to see that the lady was also acceptable in every way. The irreverent, younger element of Calcutta referred to it as the Slap and Tickle or briefly the Slap.

I waited impatiently for the hot weather to pass as Edna was coming out to India in October and we were to be married in Bombay, from the residence of

Colonel and Mrs Geoghegan. The Colonel had been the Embarkation Commandant when I was on the embarkation course.

Edna duly arrived, to my great delight, on the *City of Nagpur* in October and we were married at St Thomas's cathedral Bombay on Saturday 22 October 1927. Edna was given away by her uncle, James Gardiner, who managed the Kohinoor mills at Bombay. In addition to many of my own friends, there were a number of friends Edna had met on the journey out.

Lieutenant, later Colonel George McGuiness-Smith MC, senior subaltern of the regiment, was my best man and on the morning of the wedding we received a telegram of best wishes from Colonel Hobson and all ranks of the 64th regiment. Among many lovely presents were a beautiful pair of cut-glass tankards from the members of the Embarkation staff in Bombay, a lovely silver cigar box from the officers of the 64th with the regimental crest in the centre and all their signatures around and a pair of silver entrée dishes from the members of the sergeants' mess. After the reception we proceeded to the Taj Mahal hotel, Bombay where we spent a short honeymoon before returning to Calcutta.

The approach of Christmas was marked by a round of festivities in the regiment, club and town and life was very pleasant. Two cruisers of the Eastern Squadron, *HMS Effingham* and *HMS Cairo*, came up the river Hooghly, anchored off the port and entertained in the way the Royal Navy is renowned for. Concerts held on *HMS Effingham* were most enjoyable and fascinating. The quarterdeck had covered awnings and the dance area was gaily decorated with flags and bunting. In various parts of the ship, cunningly concealed sitting out places were contrived to add to the romance of the occasion. Excellent music was provided by the Royal Marine Band. The blue, red, and green and other coloured mess dress uniforms of the naval military officers, together with the lovely gowns of the ladies, made a most colourful and charming scene.

Ladies' guest night was held in the regimental mess in the port and the evening concluded in the early hours, with a rugger match played by the hilarious teams in mess kit on a football pitch in the middle of the fort, during which, I am afraid, several officers sustained irreparable damage to their expensive attire. The rag was solemnly reported in the statement the next day as an inter-navy and army rugger match. In the British regiments on Christmas Day, the commanding officer and his staff visited all the companies in turn, where their health was drunk. The troops then had their dinner waited on by the non-commissioned officers of the companies and were visited by the company officers and their wives.

At the time I was the only married officer in Headquarters Company and when Edna and I arrived for dinner we saw a blanket at the end table with the greeting picked out in white cotton wool, "A Merry Christmas to All" beneath were two robins on a bough and underneath the words, "Bless 'Em". It was a very nice and touching thought from the men.

The auxiliary force units in Calcutta were the Calcutta Light Horse, the Cossipore Artillery, the Calcutta Scottish, the members of which were British businessmen in Calcutta, and the Bengal Nagpur Railway battalion whose members were British and

Anglo-Indian officials and employees of the Bengal Nagpur Railway. They were all efficient units with splendid *esprit de corps,* who entertained regally during the Christmas period and on many other occasions.

Cossipore Artillery, known facetiously as "the Cossipore Distillery", perhaps because of the outstanding quantities of liquor that these stalwarts could imbibe, concluded their training period with a live ammunition shoot at the Jakpore ranges, 14 miles north of Calcutta. The occasion involved the use of a large shamiana, an awning supported by high posts from which guests watched the shoot and afterwards were entertained to a wonderful lunch with excellent wines.

The culmination of the Christmas festivities was the Proclamation Day parade, which was held on New Year's Day, all over India. In Calcutta it was held on the Maidan between Fort William and Chowringhee, the principal thoroughfare of the city. The great parade was drawn up on the vast expanse of green turf, interspersed with shady copses of trees. The parade consisted of a detachment of sailors and Royal Marines from the naval ships in the Hooghly, the Governor General's bodyguard in full dress, the Calcutta Light Horse and the six battalions of British, Indian and auxiliary force regiments from Calcutta and the neighbouring station of Barrackpore.

There were about 40,000 Bengalis gathered to watch, forming three sides of a great rectangle around the parade as it prepared to march past His Excellency, the Viceroy, the Governor General and His Excellency, the Governor of Bengal.

The trot past of a mounted regiment was followed by the march past of the battalion. It was related that on one occasion, the Calcutta Light Horse set off at too sharp a trot and passed his Excellency at full gallop, finally disappearing into the serried ranks of Bengalis at the other end of the parade and was not seen again that day. Perhaps the Christmas spirit had been transmitted from riders to steeds.

Dinner dances at Flury's and Beleachy's, the two famous restaurants, were excellent affairs. These consisted of eight or more courses. The dishes were beautifully cooked and served and on gala occasions every lady present was given a table doll or a bottle of perfume. Two first class European dance bands played alternately during the evening and the dancing continued until the early hours.

Lt. Stanley Robins & Edna Parkinson, Marriage at St Thomas's Cathedral, Bombay, 22 Oct. 1927

Chapter 6

There's a regiment a-comin' down the Grand Trunk Road

"We're marchin' on relief over
Injia's coral strand,
Eight 'undred fightin' Englishmen,
the Colonel, and the Band;
Ho! get away you bullock-man,
you've 'eard the bugle blowed,
There's a regiment a-comin'
down the Grand Trunk Road;"

Rudyard Kipling (1865–1936), Route Marchin'
(verse seven)

In Kota city, the capital of the native state of that name in Rajputana, no British troops had been seen since the Indian Mutiny in 1857. One morning in January 1928 the inhabitants of the city woke to hear the stirring strains of a British regimental band as the North Staffordshire regiment marched from Kota city station to the campaign ground near the Maharajah's palace five miles away.

When we arrived at the campaign site the Maharajah of Kota and all his court officials, the Kota state army band, and a guard of honour of the Kota state troops were there to welcome us. There was also a pile of Chinkara, Blue Bull, Blackbuck and other venison to provide a surprise luxury for the troops.

In order to implement the relief programme of British troops in 1927/28 the regiment had been ordered to move to Nasirabad in Rajputana to relieve the Royal Welsh Fusiliers. For training purposes and in order to show the flag, the reliefs were often carried out entirely by a march route or part by train and a march route. This move entailed the regiment moving by train to Kota from Calcutta, a distance of 600 miles, and then a march of 200 miles through Rajputana. The advance party with the families of the regiment had left Calcutta on 9 January 1928 direct to Nasirabad, to await the regiment's arrival. Once the troops had settled in, the Maharajah conducted the officers in a fleet of cars on a tour of the surrounding country and the attractive city of Kota. The surrounding country consists of low hills, palm groves and a number of small lakes with islands, with white marble temples at the centre of each island. The pervading atmosphere of feudal tradition had changed little with the years.

Kota is a walled city containing many picturesque Hindu temples and on every dome and buttress there appeared to be a peacock sitting. The drive ended in the Maharaja's private zoo and a delightfully cool and lovely garden. In one cage a full-grown tiger, caught only two days previously in the jungle, was kept. As we gathered around the cage the tiger hurled itself at the bars with a stupendous coughing roar, full of menace. We all instinctively drew back from the cage because it was simply impossible for anyone to face such a demonstration without reaction. When we had recovered ourselves Col. Hobson, still shaken, said, "By gum, I know what young Robins must have felt like in the jungle with nothing between him and a tiger."

After the durbar and the zoo we returned to the palace, where the state officials and several European officers and their wives were waiting to receive us. The rule of an Indian prince is in most cases very paternal and the prince is often affectionately called the durbar sahib by his subjects. We were given drinks and watched the Maharaja play a game of snooker with some of his officers, a game of which he was very fond. We then returned to our mess.

The following morning a duck shoot had been arranged for us, which was very successful and in the evening the regiment and the whole city turned out to watch the final of the Kota State Forces hockey tournament, at which our regimental band played. At the conclusion of the match the Maharaja presented the band with 500 rupees.

Early the next morning we started on our march. It was cool, the sun shone brightly, the band struck up a lively air and flocks of green parrots were flying about in the trees. Peacocks were preening themselves in the fields and many children were gathered in shady palm groves to watch the regiment going by.

The road stretched like a white ribbon, perfectly straight for mile after mile after we had left Kota city, and in the open country we saw on the other side of the road herds of Black-backed, Chinkara and Nilgai antelopes grazing. They pricked ears and looked curiously at the body of men marching down the road. The sun grew hotter during the day and made us perspire freely but in the evening we marched into camp with no casualties other than a few cases of sore feet.

An advance party under one of our subalterns, John Radcliffe, consisting of 40 bullock carts, had left Kota in the very early hours and marched to the camping site with our tents and baggage. When we marched into the camp there was a hot meal waiting for the men, and the tents had been unloaded ready to be pitched. In a very short time the tents were pitched in orderly lines and camp routine put into operation. Inspections were carried out by platoon officers, cases of blisters and so on were tended to and the men made comfortable for the night.

The next day's march took us into the native state of Bundi, where we were met on the border of the state by a person known as the State Liaison Officer, whose duty was to accompany the regiment while it was in the state, ensure our wants were supplied and to liaise with the local, civilian population. We marched by the outskirts of Bundi City and the camp was raised at the state guest house, which had been specially built for the visit of King George V and Queen Mary during the Indian Durbar of 1911. Soon six enormous elephants from the Rajah's stable arrived to take the men for rides round the city.

The elephants did a tour of the city but when they got back to camp, the troops did not want to leave them so the mahouts made the elephants shake themselves which soon got rid of the Tommies. The elephant is a colossal creature and they had difficulty in passing through some of the narrower streets of the city, which must have been very inconvenient on occasions.

Dinner was held for us in the guest house that night, which the Diwan, or Prime Minister of the state, attended. Dinner was magnificent, accompanied by fine champagne and after dinner we were entertained by a troupe of Nauth [dancing] girls from the palace. They were very attractive young damsels in gorgeous dresses and apparently some of the songs they were singing were decidedly naughty, as the Prime Minister in his chair, remarked in mirth that he wished we could understand what the girls were singing.

The next morning a tiger beat had been arranged in some low hills 15 miles from the city and although no tiger came out, a very fine Samba stag was shot by Pat Wharton, our adjutant. The city is dominated by an enormous fort on the hill and lies in a wooded valley with peafowl everywhere.

The reigning Maharaja was an elderly Rajput prince of the old school. Although his state was small, he was very important by reason of his blood and lineage. He lived in seclusion and was not on friendly terms with the Maharaja of Kota in the south and the Maharaja of Kishangarh in the north. The state had its own monetary system, with the coins being irregularly shaped pieces with Hindi characters stamped on them. This state was really quite remote and as there was no industry there, very few Europeans had visited it in the last 50 years of British rule and we were lucky to be able to see this practically unknown but attractive area.

The regiment's march continued. The panorama of Rajasthan, i.e. the land of the Rajahs, unfolding before us and eight days after leaving Kota we marched into the former military cantonment of Deoli. At Deoli there was a unit of frontier constabulary called the Mina Corps, recruited from the jungle tribes in the area. Some miles from Deoli we were met by Major Crisp, the commandant of the Mina Corps, on a beautiful black horse and with the pipe band of the Corps. Unfortunately, the Corps marched as light infantry and for the last three miles the troops had to gallop on at the light infantry pace. This resulted in a barrage of the most uncomplimentary remarks and blue rage from the troops.

The Resident, Colonel McNab, and his wife lived in the residency, which was a very large and sumptuous bungalow with sufficient accommodation to entertain two or three rajahs with their officials at one time. For our two days halt in Deoli we were also guests at the residency for meals.

Col. McNab organised two excellent duck shoots for us and proved to be a splendid shot and charming host. The second day of the stay two maharajas arrived at the residency who were not on speaking terms and the resident had to contrive things so that his guests, although under the same roof, did not make contact with each other. This took the utmost care and diplomacy to achieve.

A few days later, after a 16 mile march, the regiment swung down the mall in Nasirabad, to the strains of our lovely regimental march, "The Days we went a-gipsying" [used as the regimental quick march of the North Staffordshire Regiment]. Small station residences were there to accommodate us. Only one man had become a casualty during the march, he had contracted dysentery, but the rest of the men looked splendidly fit as they swung down the mall.

The march however had been pretty hard for the band and most of them had quite badly blistered lips. For me, however, it had been a most interesting and pleasant experience. We had traversed a fascinating part of India, rarely visited by Europeans, and had added to our store of knowledge of the mode of life of the simple peasants. We lived again a life led by Kipling's soldiers and I was glad of the opportunity to have this experience which had been afforded to me.

We were also pleasantly surprised to find that Nasirabad was one of the best small game shooting stations in India. There were Sambars in great numbers and partridges, quail, pigeon and pea fowl were also numerous. In the many jhils or small lakes dotted round the countryside were many varieties of duck and teal and snipe were quite numerous in the marshy ground around.

A flourishing gun club was formed, which enabled officers, most of the troops and also interested ladies to indulge in the sport and to spend each weekend shooting, until the hot weather and the closed season arrived. The Nasirabad garrison consisted of a battery of gunners, the training centre of the 6th Rajputana Rifles and us, the North Staffords. The cantonment itself was little more than one road, the mall, on either side of which there were the widely spaced officers' bungalows, to the north the barracks of the British troops and to the south the southern bazaar and the Rajputana training centre.

The small club was very popular and when the shooting season was in progress one could go up to the club bar and see up to half a dozen generals gathered. During this period the generals somehow found an excuse for inspecting Nasirabad. Then during the Easter weekend 1928 a tragedy occurred, which affected me personally.

Fifteen miles from Nasirabad was the sacred Hindu city of Ajmer. Built round the banks of a pretty lake called the Anasargar were some popular bathing places. One day a party of troops from the regiment went over at Easter to bathe. There were a lot of weeds growing along the bottom of the lake and they came to within four feet of the surface. It was necessary to take great care not to become entangled in the weeds when swimming. Unfortunately two of my men, Lance Corporal Wyatt-Merri and Private White, became entangled in the weeds, were gradually pulled under and were drowned before anyone could get close enough to rescue them.

The bodies had not been found by nightfall and it was two days before they were recovered. They were buried with full military honours in the small cemetery at Nasirabad.

Chapter 7

The Honeymoon Tiger

It was a year since I had been in the jungle and I had a strong desire to go once again in quest of a tiger. Edna, who was enjoying every moment of the life, was also very eager to see the jungle. I was fortunate enough to obtain the Sitanadi block again and we left Nasirabad on a month's leave in mid-March 1928. We drove to Kota in a hired car, along a road up which the regiment had marched. From there we continued our journey by train, arriving two days later at Raipur. During this journey we passed through the finest shooting areas in the Central Provinces, including, "Seonee" (Seoni) the scene of 'The Jungle Book'.

From Raipur we travelled to Kurud by the small forest tramway which went down to Basta State. When we were at Kurud the Hindu festival of Holi was being held. At this festival both sexes of all ages throw liquid dyes of all colours over each other and their clothing and get themselves into a dreadful mess. Quantities of 'Toddy' [palm or coconut wine] were drunk and several parties were waiting to splash us with their dyes but I firmly refused to permit this.

We brought a bicycle with us, as it was quite practical to ride along the forest roads and game paths, making it possible to visit distant parts of the block more frequently. Edna had also brought her small pet, a Bengal monkey, with her. In the afternoon, by a little tramway, we reached a forest camp and then we marched the 16 miles to Sitanadi, where we were welcomed by the forest range officer and the shikari, Bandoo.

On this evening I decided that Edna and I should sit up over a bullock tied up in the nullah not far from where the two tigers had killed the bullock the previous year, and a machan was put up at a height of about 25 feet. We entered the machan at 5pm and spent an interesting hour and a half before nightfall watching the jungle birds and creatures. Before sighting any animal, a noise would first be heard and until the animal or bird making it was actually identified there was always the possibility that some big game might appear in those marvellous jungles, such as a panther or tiger.

The noise of a displaced dry leaf would be heard once or twice, and then through the bushes below us would come a beautiful jungle cock and several hens, its sharp eyes alert for danger between each peck on the ground. Another noise would be followed by the appearance of a mongoose, that most inquisitive of all creatures, poking its noise into every bush or patch of dried leaves. Then at intervals it would sit upright on its haunches and look around quickly in all directions, before continuing its explorations.

As the hours passed it got colder and colder. When I was at Sitanadi the previous year the hot weather had been well-advanced and, while we were not actually shivering, we felt very cold indeed, most probably as we were only lightly clad. We decided it was best to leave the machan and return to the bungalow, which meant a walk of 300 yards in the darkness through the jungle. Our only illumination would be the electric torch fitted to my rifle. As we were discussing this, noises in the darkness below indicated that some large animals were about.

The bullock snorted and the animals making a noise moved away. We waited another half hour and then decided tiger or no tiger we would return to the bungalow. We had to use a rope to get out of the machan. Edna slid down the rope first and I wound the rope back quickly and let the rifle down to her, and then pulled up the rope again and followed as quickly as I could myself.

As we walked down the forest road I shone my torch at intervals into the jungle. It was an eerie experience but we reached the bungalow without mishap. The next morning at the bungalow the shikari reported that two large bears and two cubs were the animals responsible for the noise we had heard during the night and it was fortunate that we had not come across them in the dark.

The Indian sloth bear is one of the most unpleasant animals of all that you can come upon in the jungle. Its eyesight is not very good and they will normally go bull-headed for anything that they think is disputing their way. As a consequence, a sight commonly seen in the jungle is people with dreadful scars on their faces from such encounters.

A cushion placed on the cross-bar of the bicycle enabled Edna to come with me on my inspections of the jungle. It was not a particularly comfortable way to travel but it enabled us to visit lots of areas which otherwise we would not have been able to see.

On one of these trips we visited Budra in Basta state, where I had shot the enormous tiger the previous year. Edna was the first white woman that villagers in such a remote area had seen. At the time there was a small pool of water in the nullah bed only about 100 yards from the bungalow and round it were the tracks of many animals, Chital, Barking Deer, Bison, wild pig, pea fowl, jungle fowl and panther.

In the evening I decided to stalk the pool and see if I could get a pea-fowl. I carried my shotgun and a coolie carried my heavy rifle behind me. We made a careful stalk down the small side nullah, to a point where it turned right into the main nullah just by the pool. There lapping the water was a fine panther. I beckoned frantically to the coolie to hand me the rifle but as I did so the panther looked round, his great yellow eyes opening wide and like lightning he ran up the bank and disappeared in the jungle. Thereafter I always carried a lethal bullet in the cylinder bell of the shotgun in case such an eventuality should arise again.

In the morning, as I started off to visit the tie-ups, I passed the bungalow vegetable garden and in it I found a herd of seven bison that had had a good feed during the night on the cabbages.

Later I found that the bullock which had been tied up near the pool had been taken. There were pug marks of a large male tiger, which had dragged the bullock across the nullah and 300 yards straight up the steep hillside opposite covered with heavy jungle.

I came across the kill lying in a small water course on the hillside, a few feet wide and about six feet deep. A machan was put in the tree about midday and I returned at about 5pm to begin my vigil. I was not at all hopeful the tiger would return as the machan was very obvious in the small tree and only the shoulders and head of the bullock remained, which did not provide an adequate meal for a tiger.

During the night I heard a noise to my left, high up on the hillside and heard an animal approaching making quite a lot of noise, so much so that I thought it could not be the tiger but probably a bison or Samba. It came on towards the kill and as I judged, right up to it and then after a few seconds I heard a tiger eating. I pointed my rifle in the direction of the kill which I could not see at all in the dark. I switched on my torch and there crouching on the ground directly facing me was a large tiger. His enormous head almost masked his body and his great big eyes glowed green in the light as he looked up at me. I aimed directly between the eyes and fired and as I did so the tiger leaped in the air and then the torch light went out.

I hurriedly adjusted the torch but when I turned it on again there was no sign of the tiger and no blood marks. At that very moment only 200 yards away in the forest bungalow Edna was having dinner and as the shot rang down the valley, the shikari and Baloo ran into the room and said, "Memsahib the sahib has killed the tiger". Apparently they had great faith in my marksmanship.

I searched the jungle in all directions with the torch, but the tiger had disappeared and as I knew that I had hit the tiger, I had the prospect of following up a wounded tiger on the hillside in the morning. There was the distinct possibility that I might even lose the animal altogether and feeling very disappointed, I eventually fell asleep. I was woken up at daybreak by people talking below and to my horror I saw Edna and the shikari and bearer and a number of coolies below me.

I told Edna not to go down the hillside but take half a dozen coolies as quickly as possible and make her way to the bungalow without halting. At this she promptly hurried away. I quickly explained to the shikari what had happened. A line was formed and we moved slowly forward. I had given my bearer a shotgun to carry and we had only moved a few yards when both barrels went off with a roar, and the bearer shrieked, "Tiger, sahib!" I went over to him and there lying at the bottom of the water course was a fine tiger. Making sure it was dead I dropped into the water course and found that my bullet had struck it between the eyes and entered the brain.

The water-course was deep and narrow and had concealed the tiger when it had rolled into the water after I had killed it. The dead tiger was not visible when I searched the jungle with my torch. All the men available were needed to hoist it out of the nullah and it was taken back on a stretcher to the Sitanadi rest house.

Edna was thrilled with her first sight of a jungle tiger, especially as the drama had occurred so close to the forest bungalow and it was an experience that very few European ladies would have had.

After photographs were taken, the tiger was laid between pegs and was found to be 9 feet 6 inches in length, an average length for a tiger and in prime condition. Operations were in hand for the rest of the day and in the afternoon we were pleasantly surprised by the arrival of Mr. Malcolm, conservator of forest for the United Provinces and Mr. Jenkin, the Divisional Forest Officer.

Mr. Jenkin was intrigued at the way I had bagged the tiger as it was well-known to the local jungle villagers that he had tried to bag it himself on a number of occasions. Individual tigers can be accurately identified by experienced shikaris by the size of their pugs [paw prints], occasional peculiarities of the pug marks and the particular area where the tiger is looking for prey at the time. When a tiger arrives at a particular area of jungle and as long as food and game is plentiful, they will usually remain there and visit the villages in rotation, to attack the village herds or if they are man eaters, travel the same valleys, forest roads and paths in search of their human prey.

In the cool of the evening the four of us sat in long chairs in front of the bungalow drinking chota pegs, talking of life in the jungle when up the forest road from the nullah below came two great Forest Department elephants which the forest officers were using on their tour. Directed by their mahouts the elephants quietly padded along and were brought to a halt facing us. The mahouts then put down two baskets in front of the elephants which were filled with a mixture of wheat and maize flour, and damping it rolled it into balls.

Then knowing what was in hand the elephants stood with their trunks curled up, their mouths wide open to receive the balls of flour that were thrown into their mouths by the mahouts. This went on until their rations were consumed, the elephants being obviously very fond of this food. The elephants were then ordered to salaam and curling their trunks upwards, they bent their forelegs and then lowered their heads towards the ground. They were then ordered to rise and were led away by the mahouts to be tied up for the night. This interesting little ceremony is performed as a matter of routine by the elephants whenever they accompany the forest officers on tour.

After dinner a couple of hundred villagers from the shikaris' village assembled in front of the forest bungalow and round a great log fire performed some jungle dances in our honour. The dances were very intricate and were accompanied by tom toms and lengths of hollow trunks beaten with sticks. Some dances were performed by men and others by women, and one or two by a line of men facing a line of women.

A number of clay jars filled with 'Toddy', provided by the largesse of the two forest officers were just off-stage and the dancers imbibing freely, were very soon in a most hilarious mood. As the excitement grew, couples broke off and went into the surrounding jungle near the bungalow, where they began love-making in honour of Krishna the god of love.

The following day we had a lazy day in camp and during the morning walked down to Sitanadi to see the elephants have their bath in a shallow stretch of water under the bluff on which the forest bungalow stood. The creatures lay on their sides making rumbling noises of content, while their mahouts scrubbed them with what appeared to be a large piece of pumice stone. Once one side was completed they were given a word of command and getting up into a kneeling position, they flopped over onto the opposite side and were duly scrubbed again. The gargantuan toilet completed, the elephants walked to the soft damp sand near the water and kicked up small quantities with their forefeet into the curl end of the trunk. They then threw the damp earth over their back and continued doing so until they had covered most of their back and sides. It was done to ease the irritation caused to the elephant by the many flies and insects with which the jungle abounded.

In the event, the forest officers very kindly made the elephants available for us to go for a 'Ghum', that is a walkabout in the jungle. Large pads or mattresses were strapped to the elephants' back and we climbed on and sat astride behind the mahouts, who sat in their usual positions immediately behind the elephant's ears. The mahout guides the elephant by the pressure of his toes behind the ears and goads from the ankus, a large iron instrument about 15 inches long with a spike and a steel hook in the end. The noise made by the ankus striking at the top of the elephant's head is sometimes alarming but the elephant is usually only controlled with this when it is necessary and in the majority of cases a great affection and understanding exists between the mahouts and their great charges. The jungle was quite thick and as the object of our wandering was to watch game, the elephants were ordered to go quietly and they moved indeed like great grey shadows, making only the slightest noise even though they were walking on a carpet of dried leaves. In addition, they took care to avoid large over-hanging branches which would have struck us and on occasions when it was difficult to bypass some branches, would hold them carefully above us with their trunks. If they came across a tree or bush which was edible, a bunch of leaves was quietly pulled off and tucked into their mouth.

We soon came across a herd of Chital that merely interrupted their feeding for a few seconds to stare closely at the elephants and then continued feeding. In this way we were able to get within 40 yards of them and were able to enjoy the sight of these lovely creatures feeding. Wild animals know of course that the elephants are of the jungle but it is curious that they do not become unduly alarmed at human beings on the elephants' backs. Passing the herd of Chital we moved on and came across a Barking Deer [Muntjac] that, after a stir of mild alarm, carried on feeding. This pretty and noisy little deer would, in any other circumstances, have started barking very loudly and then made itself scarce. The noise made by this deer is very like the bark of the dog and is a note of alarm and is consequently a signal to all animals within hearing.

On the homeward journey we saw several Sambars and a number of pea-fowl and jungle fowl rooting amongst the leaves for their food. When there was no need for further care the elephants were ordered to relax and they ploughed their way through the jungle like two tanks. Once a branch had been diverted from us it was seized and torn off and thrown away. The elephants negotiated all varieties of terrain with the utmost ease and were as sure-footed as goats.

The most interesting and amusing incident of the evening was at a place where elephants had to make a steep descent to a nullah bed about sixteen feet below. The elephant punched the lip of the bank away with its forefeet making a small chute. Then sitting on its large stern proceeded down into the nullah and was duly followed by the other elephants.

We reached the forestry rest house just before nightfall having thoroughly enjoyed the ride through the jungle and our first experience of the sagacity, versatility and strength of the elephants. Over the years that followed I had many opportunities of studying elephants working in the timber industry in the forest and using them on shooting expeditions. They were a source of never-ending interest and like all who have been in constant contact with them I developed affection for them, above all other creatures.

The feeding ceremony and the salaam ended a pleasant and interesting day. The following day Mr. Malcolm and Mr. Jenkins started their return journey to Raipur by car and kindly gave Edna a lift, and I made my own way by bike as there was no room for it on the car. During our stay in Raipur we were Mr. Jenkins' guests and after dinner one night he took us to the Chhattisgarh club. Chhattisgarh means '40 forts' and covers a remote area, with only a handful of European officials to administer it.

We had a very pleasant evening in the club and amongst the people we met there was a Mr. Smith-Pierce, the principal of the Raj Kumar College in Raipur. The Raj Kumar College is for the sons of maharajas and large estate owners.

The trip was now over and as it was the first journey where we had been alone since we were married, we regarded it as our honeymoon and I named my trophy the 'Honeymoon Tiger'.

Three days later we were back in Nasirabad and once more the regimental routine began.

Chapter 8

Heading towards the Khyber

"As Cairo, Fez and Isfahan, Bangkok and Singapore, there's Trebizond and Teheran, there's Rio and Lahore. About the name of each there clings enchantments' golden vale, the wonder of strange folk and things, the glamour of the trail!"

Berton Braley (1882–1966), Names of Romance

Life in the [British] Indian Army, with its prospects of active service on the northwest frontier and wonderful opportunities for sport of all kinds, was all I could desire and I applied for transfer. In September 1928 I left Nasirabad for Rawalpindi, where I was to undertake a mechanical transport (MT) course and an animal transport (AT) course. I left my regiment with many regrets because its traditions and all that it stood for had become part of my life. I especially regretted leaving my small command of British troops but I was to realise the same qualities are to be found in all good soldiers wherever they are based.

Moving northwards and the change in the countryside and the physical characteristics of the inhabitants and their dress was immediately apparent. The tall well-built men, with their well-oiled black hair cut in the bobbed fashion, were as different from the smaller, darker Hindus and the aboriginal inhabitants of the southern forests as of a European. Also, because Mohammadism was the predominant religion, a great percentage of the women wore a burkha. Otherwise, they were attired in long coats and trousers that distinguished them from their Hindu sisters in the south.

The Punjab, except for the mountainous area of the Himalayas, is not a heavily forested province, and between Lahore and Rawalpindi much of the land is badly marked with soil erosion and presents the appearance of a miniature grand canyon of Colorado. The vistas of barren, stony ground are very grim and unlovely. Rawalpindi, however, has quite an attractive setting with the 7000 foot Murree hills lying 15 miles to the east and behind them, the snows of the Pir Panjal range at 15000 feet.

The cantonment is a large one and the main road, the mall, passes through its whole length, being part of the grand trunk road, the great strategic military road which links Peshawar, at the end of the Khyber Pass, with Calcutta 1500 miles away, and which has been immortalised in the novel 'Kim' and many of the poems of Rudyard Kipling.

The mall is lined with trees and flowerbeds and the western side of the road has a ride following its length, on which, in the morning and evening, the charming equestriennes of the station could be seen. There is a shopping centre which, in addition to having a large European and a number of Indian stores, had shops full of Kashmiri wares which were very interesting to new arrivals.

Piles of furs, at what seemed to be ridiculously low prices, were for sale. Snow leopard skins, stone marten, silver fox, red fox, lynx. There were beautifully carved wooden screens, chairs, cigar boxes and lovely examples of the world-famous painted papier mâché work. The colours and artistry of these goods were a delight to the eye.

The life of a large Indian cantonment is quite of its own. On cool early mornings, the clear notes of the bugles and trumpets of the regimental lines can be heard as one rides or walks past them. Military activity is noticeable everywhere. Squads are performing exercises on the playing fields, drilling on the parade grounds and in the cavalry lines, mounted drills are taking place for the animals, being trained and schooled in the paddocks.

In the mountain artillery lines, the burly gunners are carrying out gun drills, with the gun parts taken off the magnificent Argentine mules that carry them and the gunners then assembling 3.7 inch howitzers in the matter of a little over a minute. A regiment headed by its band may be seen swinging down the road on a route march. In the shady gardens of the club, the nurses and ayahs [nursemaids or nannies] gather to gossip, while the happy laughing children play, until the great heat of the sun makes it necessary for them to return home.

Bugle calls at intervals mark the progress of the day's activities for cook houses, orderly sergeants, fall-in officers, porters etc and at nightfall the lovely notes of retreat are heard, when the flag is hauled down and the rifle reports are handed in by the orderly sergeants, on the staff parade, to the battalion orderly officers.

The plaintive notes of the last post are heard in the quiet night at 10pm and at 10:30pm lights out marks the end of the soldiers' day.

As it was probable that I would be posted to a frontier station where families could not be taken, after I completed my course, we decided that Edna would return to England early in February 1929.

One evening towards the end of January we were having drinks with some friends in their room in the Kashmir hotel, where we were also staying. Conversation covered many topics, amongst them being those of earthquakes. During this Edna said, "I will be leaving for home in a few days now and I haven't experienced an earthquake". As these words were uttered I saw our host staring at a standard lampshade in the corner of the room. The shade was shaking and on his cry, "It's an earthquake", we all rushed outside into the open air.

As we stood there in the darkness the ground was rising and falling under our feet, just as if we were standing on an enormous rubber ball. It was an eerie sensation but in a minute or so the tremors began to subside, and we returned to the room to drink and talk about the strange coincidence that had occurred.

The next morning when we woke we saw that there had been quite a heavy fall of snow. This was the first snowfall that Rawalpindi had had for nearly 40 years. Thus, these two very unusual incidents had occurred together.

A few days later I bade farewell to Edna as she left in the Bombay Mail and was not to see her again until November. It was the first of many long partings, which circumstances in our service life were to have in store for us.

Both courses kept me very busy and I used to do the MT driver's training in convoys going up to Murree, the beautiful hill station, 34 miles from Rawalpindi, 7000 foot up on the Himalayan ridge.

It was excellent and demanding training, as for 20 miles the road climbed tortuously through the mountains with hairpin bends every few yards, and often a drop of 2000 feet or more on the edge of the road.

One afternoon, when returning from one of these sessions, driving a 13 cwt lorry with another officer student in the cab beside me and also the driving instructor, I decided to pass the vehicle in front of me. After blowing my horn and making sure all was clear behind me, I indicated a signal to the right and pulled out into the road to pass. A staff car appeared from behind me and as it went by at high speed, grazing the side of my vehicle and badly damaging the door, I saw that the brigadier commanding the station was in the car.

His headquarters were only a short distance away and I was flagged down and instructed to report to him. Brigadier Henry Rowan-Robinson was really a charming gentleman and told me off in no uncertain fashion, but it was obvious it was his driver's fault and that the Brigadier had ordered the driver to pass me, although I was already passing another vehicle. For the edification of the rest of the students, my companion and I were told to make up an accident report, and a homily was delivered on careful driving, although it was quite clear that the brigadier's vehicle was really to blame and the matter was gracefully allowed to fade out.

I heard later that the Brigadier had been invited to a cocktail party that evening but he wrote a letter to his hostess expressing his regret that he could not attend "as he had been knocked for six by one of his officers".

On the completion of the mechanical transport course in March I considered I was a competent driver and knowledgeable mechanic and so I bought a second-hand Chevrolet touring car. The urgent call of the jungle decided me to take two months' leave, May and June of 1929, to go after tigers. I obtained permission to shoot in the Kanger Valley, a large estate in the south Raipur district.

I was posted from Rawalpindi to the reserve based at Peshawar and motored there eager for my first glimpse of the premier city of the north-west frontier. Peshawar was the city beloved by the wild Pathan tribesmen of the frontier, where they came in between their blood feuds and raids to endure the soft pleasures of dancing girls and the 'daughters of joy', to bargain in the myriad shops of the bazaars for knives, axes, cheap gramophones, silk and cloth. Great caravans arrived outside Peshawar, the camel caravans from Afghanistan, through the Khyber Pass and the pack mule trains from the remote highlands of central Asia, through the Manawa Pass. With them came the fierce straggling men of high Asia, Afghans, Kashgaries, men from Tashkent and Samarkand, Tartars and Kurds to sell their wares and merchandise, and doubtless think of the plunder that raids into the lush, rich vale of Peshawar would give them.

The native city of Peshawar lies to the south of the grand trunk road and just beyond it is the military cantonment. The cantonment is very attractive, its roads bordered by great shady trees and flowerbeds and the gardens of the bungalows, at the beginning of the hot weather, a mass of flowers and golden fruits on the orange trees.

The inevitable mall traverses the length of the cantonment and from it the road through the Khyber Pass to Kabul in Afghanistan continues. The cantonment is enclosed completely in a high, thick barbed-wire fence, the gates of which are closed at nightfall and only opened again at dawn. Military patrols guard it throughout its length, for only a few miles to the south lie the barren, jagged hills of the Khyber and Tirah where the Afridi, Orakzais, and Chamkarni tribesmen overlook Peshawar and beyond the wire no man's life is safe.

Life however went on in Peshawar in the same happy, vivacious way as in the peaceful cantonments of southern India. The weekend dances at the club were packed. Sports and games occupied every evening. The chief commissioner held dances and dinners at Government House, but at any moment it was possible for some incident to turn the cantonment into a besieged fortress and indeed within a year Peshawar was beleaguered and military operations lasting nine months were necessary to enable a line of forts to be built in the Khajuri Plain beneath the hills, to prevent attacks by Afridis, that had become particularly troublesome.

Just at that time a former ditch-digger and water-carrier, named Bachai Sakao, raised a band of Afghan tribesmen who were bitterly opposed to the westernisation policy adopted by King Amanullah Khan. After several weeks of fighting, Amanullah was obliged to flee from Afghanistan and the erstwhile water-carrier proclaimed himself Emir, taking the name of Habbibulah Kalikani.

At the end of the First World War Afghanistan was, as it had always been, one of the forbidden countries of the world. With the usurpation by Bachai Sakao, the veil of secrecy became even more impenetrable. For a year the caravan trade of the

Khyber ceased, and even we on the Indian frontier could only hazard a guess as to what grim happenings were taking place in that wild land. However Bachai Sakao's venture had a ghastly ending, of which I have more to tell later.

"On the completion of the mechanical transport course in March I considered I was a competent driver and knowledgeable mechanic and so I bought a second-hand Chevrolet touring car."

[Purchased in 1929 and shown with the Author's wife, Edna, in the front passenger seat. Note the car's registration plate, 'FP', standing for 'Frontier Province']

Chapter 9

Motoring across a Continent

Loaded with baggage and tent, I and my Hindu bearer, Mulchan, were bowling along southwards again down the Grand Trunk Road. It was the last week in April with the sun blazing down. Whenever I passed another car or bus, clouds of dust completely obliterated the road and got into one's eyes and throat. But I had to press on as fast as I could because my destination was Kanger, over 1,400 miles from Peshawar and I did not want to take up more time than was necessary out of my leave in getting to and returning from my shooting block. I had planned a route and timetable which I hoped would enable me to do 350-400 miles each day, but because of the great heat, dust and bullock-cart traffic on the roads, it was obvious that I would have to drive at least 14 hours a day or more to cover such a distance.

In order to avoid the heat as much as possible, I intended to drive through most of the night but for the same reason, the bullock-carts also travelled at night and considerably impeded one. They would very often take fright at the sound of the motor-horn and as their drivers are normally asleep in the cart, they career about in all directions, completely out of control, and it is only possible to move on when the carts have been taken off the road into the fields or jungle. This was very exasperating and combined with the heat, dust and other attendant discomforts of the hot weather, nerves become frayed and tempers short. On one occasion, seeing a single cart about half a mile ahead of me, I sounded my horn continuously in order to produce some sign of animation in the driver but to no avail. When my car was within a matter of yards of the cart, the bullocks began to kick and snort and zigzag across the road and at last the driver awoke but I had to stop the car. I was really angry at this and leapt out the car to give the driver a good dressing down. Seeing what was obviously a very angry sahib bearing down on him, the driver jumped out of the cart and ran for his life across an open field, yelling at the top of his voice, and finally disappeared in the jungle beyond. I gave up the chase and returned to the road, where the bullocks had commenced feeding on leaves. Then turning them around, I gave them a pat and sent the cart off in the opposite direction to that it had been proceeding in, hoping that it would be many miles before the driver caught them again.

The drive from Peshawar to Kanger was across about two thirds of the length of the Indian sub-continent from north to south and passed through many places of great interest which of course I had not previously had the opportunity or time to see, to areas very rarely visited by Europeans. Over the years, my travels in India were the foundation of a very extensive knowledge of the country, that I had the good fortune to acquire. Thus, during my military service, I travelled far more widely than the majority of British officers in the Indian Army.

The first 516 miles of my route were through Jhelum, Lahore, Amritsar, Jalandhar, Loharu and Bali, in the Punjab, to Delhi, the capital of India. Then going south to Agra and on through the native states of Dholpur and Gwalior, and continuing on to Jhansi and Lalitpur in the United Provinces, a total distance of 318 miles. After Lalitpur, the remainder of the journey was through the hill and jungle country of the Central Provinces, through the great tiger forest of Seoni, of Jungle Book fame, and Balagarh and the vast forests of Rewa state, the home of the white tiger.

From there I would take the east-west trunk road of the central provinces, through the lovely Sal forests of Bandeau and Drew to Raipur, a further 450 miles. The final stage of the journey was 170 miles over an appalling dirt track road to Kanger.

I managed to make a flying start to my leave, driving through to Rawalpindi the previous evening from Peshawar and staying at Flashman's Hotel. Staying in the hotel was R.W.B. Robins of the Kings Own Royal Lancs. Regiment who had been at Sandhurst with me and Mrs Catherine Jones, a lovely and charming American lady who was married to an officer on the Embarkation staff when I was in Bombay. We spent a very convivial evening together and I left Rawalpindi at 5am, driving as fast as I could and keeping the speedometer needle between 50 and 60 mph. As I have said, the unpleasant driving conditions, together with the presence of numerous herds of cattle, buffalos, sheep and goats on the road greatly impeded me, but I reached Jalandhar 250 miles away at about 1pm.

The car had started misfiring and I had to delay in Jalandhar to have it repaired, before starting off on my journey again. The herds of cattle were not so numerous and I made good progress reaching my next stop at 8:30pm where I had my dinner in reasonable comfort in a restaurant at the railway station, during which I imbibed vast quantities of iced drinks. I started again at about 10:30pm on the road to Agra but I soon felt very tired and on arriving at a small township called Palwal, 36 miles south of Delhi, I decided to stay the night at a Dak Bungalow [buildings serving primarily as a post-house of the Indian postal service, also used as lodging by itinerant British officials and other travelers]. I had been driving for 19 hours and covered about 480 miles. Quite a good distance in the circumstances and it compensated me for my exertions.

After an early breakfast the following morning, I drove on to Agra and then to Delpore the capital of the state of that name. There I crossed the river Chambal by means of a bridge of ropes. Such bridges, which were very common in India, have to be negotiated very slowly and carefully and often the roadway will sway in an alarming manner, with the weight of the car. When the monsoons arrive and the rivers become swollen the bridges are dismantled and traffic is taken across them on ferries which are rowed or punted or pulled across by means of a rope.

At 1pm I reached Kalyani and had lunch in the railway station, and then on to Jhansi in Uttar Pradesh state, where, in later years, my brother was Superintendent of Police and where in the surrounding jungles, Wingate's Chindits did their preliminary training. During this portion of the journey, the road ran through low hills covered with scrub and I came across dozens of covers of partridges on the road, busy pecking at the straw, grain, etc that had dropped from bullock carts. On a couple of occasions I bagged two partridges, which provided a tasty meal that night.

The temperature was 117 degrees Fahrenheit [47 degrees C.] when I entered Jhansi and I was glad to break my journey for an hour in the cool retiring room [a room where passengers can rest, including sleeping, while in transit] at Jhansi railway station. Having rested and refreshed myself with a cup of tea, I drove on to Lalitpur, the most southern district of the United Provinces and halted for the night at the dak bungalow there. Edna and I were to visit Lalitpur in 1935, when my brother was Superintendent of Police.

This leg of the journey was through the hill and jungle country of Central Provinces, referred to earlier. This is perhaps the sporting province par excellence of India, whose lovely valleys and vast jungles have been immortalised in Rudyard Kipling's stories in the 'Jungle Book'. I came around a spur in the hills and there several hundred feet below me lay the white gleaming bungalows of Saugor, on the edge of a lake in rows of trees. It was at that time a location of the School of Equitation of the Army in India and was a very popular hunting ground in those days.

The Central Provinces, Hyderabad state and the Southern United Provinces had for centuries been the chief hunting ground of the Thugs [members of the Thuggee cult, operating as organised gangs of professional robbers and murderers], during which time hundreds of thousands of travellers had been murdered by these villains. It so happened that during my travels and my shoots, I passed through most of the places mentioned in the famous book, 'The Confessions of a Thug' and I must have walked over the graves of hundreds, if not thousands, of their victims.

Shortly before arriving at the central station of Narsinghpur, I had to cross the river Nerbudda by ferry. This river is one of the holiest in India and my bearer, Mulchan, being a devout Hindu asked me to halt while he did his puja, or prayers, to the river. He then removed all his clothes except his loin cloth and immersed himself in the river and spent 15 minutes in saying his prayers and performing his ritual ablutions, after which we proceeded on our way.

At Narsinghpur I stayed at the circuit house. These houses are comfortable places, well-furnished and have a small staff of servants. They are for the use of the governor and high officials of the province, when touring in the district, and when not occupied by the high officials are permitted to be used by gazetted army officers, who may have occasion to stay there.

The rasoiya, or cook, of the circuit house gave me an excellent brunch and moving on I arrived at the forestry house at Seoni in the late afternoon.

Seoni; what a spell that name had cast over me and still does. Although it was only a typical small, simple station in the heart of vast jungle it was here that Kipling received the inspiration to write 'The Jungle Book', and in the actual setting every word rang true. Going into the dining room of the bungalow I found two other sportsmen there. They were Capt Cave and Lord Garmoyle of the Rifle Brigade, who I learned were going on a tiger shoot in a block in south Raipur, which I knew well from my shoots at Sitanadi. I gave them all the information I could about the block which they were very pleased to have. Such information could save a lot of time to sportsmen who have not previously been to a particular shooting block.

I never saw either of them again and Lord Garmoyle went to a gallant death in Libya in 1942. I did hear, some years later, that they had to abandon their car in the remote southern Raipur jungles, as an axle spring had been broken on the atrocious bullock-cart tracks there.

As the moon was nearly full at the time, I decided to leave at 8pm for Balaghat another small township 40 miles away, and perhaps the finest tiger jungles in the Central Provinces. The road from Seoni to Balaghat was through the Mahadial Hills, which were covered with fine sal and bamboo jungle, and there was a possibility that I might see some game on the road.

The road climbed up and down one ghaut, [steep sides of a ravine], after another and the bamboo forest was very lovely in the soft moonlight. I had just begun the descent of a ghaut when I had a puncture, so I started to change the wheel with the aid of a hurricane lamp. While I was doing this, a tiger's roar from the hilltop on the other side of the valley reverberated up and down hillsides. Poor Mulchan trembled with fright and quite unnecessarily said, "Tiger, Sahib!" Again the great ringing organ note echoed down the valley. The awe-inspiring sound resounded on several more occasions before I had changed the wheel, and Mulchan by that time was in a state of abject terror and helplessness.

No further incidents occurred during the remainder of the journey and after an hour's driving through the mysterious moonlit forest, I reached the forest rest house at Balaghat.

Continuing my journey on the East-West trunk road, I arrived at Raipur the following day at 1pm. I had a lot of stores to buy and enquiries to make. During the final portion of the journey to Kanger in 1929, I saw preliminary work to extend the railway line to Negapatam on the Madras coast. This was a distance of 400 miles, the whole length of it being through practically unbroken forest. There was no other railway within 300 miles of this route and the whole area was again mostly fine jungle.

The next morning I left Raipur and after about 25 miles I came to the Mahanadi River, where on the right of the river I saw a fine bungalow in a tree-shaded compound. I drove to the bungalow and was greeted by two charming ladies, a Mrs Perry and her 17-year old daughter, Kathy. Mrs Perry's husband was the engineer of the construction of a large railway bridge over the Mahanadi which was to carry the Raipur Negapatam line. The bungalow had been built for them as their residence while the bridge was being completed. They had already been there three years and expected to be there another year.

Mr. Perry arrived for lunch and gave me much useful information about Kanger and the remaining 80 odd miles of the track. I was pressed to stay for the night, which invitation I gladly accepted. In the evening Mr. Perry suggested we should go and sit up on the edge of a jungle tank, which was about 10 miles away, which he and I and Miss Perry did.

We saw a lot of animals in the few hours spent on the edge of the forest lake. We of course saw many birds and heard the usual jungle noises. Saying farewell to my kind host and hostess, I started the next morning to Kanger. I knew the bullock-cart track, for it was no more than that, would be bad but the reality was far worse than the imagination.

The ruts made by the bullock-carts were very deep and a high mound of earth was left between them. These mounds were so high that the car had not the clearance to drive in the wheel ruts and so had to be taken with one set of wheels on the mound and the other on the edge of the track. If this cannot be done, then the mound in the centre has to be excavated until there is clearance for the car. Sometimes it is possible to find a route in the jungle between bad sections of roadway but progress in these circumstances is very slow.

The Kanger track was however quite the worst I had ever seen. Enormous potholes every few yards, as much as two feet deep, took up the width of the track. And where there were no potholes, the cart mound was too high for my car to proceed. In places boulders also covered the centre mound and a breakdown in such conditions would mean the complete loss of the car, so I had to drive very cautiously and did not average much more than five miles an hour.

By exercising much care, I arrived in the outskirts of Kanger at about 5pm and there come upon a large bungalow. I made my way there and found it was the home of an American missionary and his family. I was covered with dust and very weary but the missionary kindly invited me to have a meal with them and said that afterwards he would take me along the jungle forest road to see the local 'Raja'. These two kind people gave me a good dinner and I gathered in conversation that they found the going very hard in this remote area, owing to strong religious beliefs and opposition from the high caste Hindus.

Arriving at the fort where the 'Raja', as his tenants called him, resided we were informed by some ancient retainers, holding themselves up on still more ancient muskets, that the 'Raja' was indisposed but the lal sahib, the Raja's brother, would call and see me later at the rest house to discuss details of the shoot.

Having thanked the missionary for his help I made my way to the rest house which was nothing more than a single-roomed hut. Shortly afterwards, a retainer of the estate arrived with baskets of fruit and vegetables, a present from the lal sahib.

One of the things that happened to me here, looking back on the event, seems to have no logical explanation, but at the time my feelings permitted no other course. Since Edna had left for England, I had been fully occupied with my duties in moving to Peshawar, the final preparations for the shoot and then the long journey I had just completed. I had not realised how long I had been without her and I yearned for some human companionship. I also thought, perhaps wrongly, that there was local opposition to my shooting on the estate and I decided I would return the next day to Raipur and see if I could get a government forest block, have a couple of week's shooting and then spend the rest of my month's leave with my brother Leslie.

He had been gazetted into the imperial police service in 1928 and having been posted to the united provinces was at that time carrying out his training at the police training school at Moradabad.

The lal sahib called to see me later. He was very charming and assured me that there were lots of tiger in the Kanger forest and also said I would be able to bag any number of bison I liked on the magnificent plateau which lay in the state.

Leaving a brief note of explanation for the lal sahib I left the next morning and spent the whole day on the dreadful track back to the Mahanadi River. I again spent the night with the Perrys, who also had staying with them a Mr. Wainforth, a young engineer on the Bengal Nagpur railway who was engaged to Miss Perry. We chatted and drank into the small hours and I began to feel more settled under the influence of these kindly people.

Before I left for Raipur the next morning Mrs Perry handed me a long telegram to send off to Calcutta for her, in connection with the purchases for her daughter's trousseau. Miss Perry had to prepare this under somewhat exceptional circumstances, right out in the wilds, 700 miles from the nearest European shop.

At Raipur I got a permit for a block 35 miles south of Bandhavgarh and I proceeded there the same day. After a few days I realised that the chances of bagging a tiger were not good, as there had been a lot of tree-felling in the area and where sawing work would be going on for several months.

I decided to move onto Moradabad immediately. The journey there necessitated me retracing my route as far as Delhi and then going due east for a hundred miles, crossing the great river Ganges at Allahabad [now Prayagraj]. Here there were several waterways divided by islands, linked together by a plank bridge.

The plank roadways took the road from island to island until the far bank was reached. There were two narrow runways of wooden sleepers to take the wheel tracks of vehicles and this continued for two miles through fine grey sand, until the firm high ground was reached. Hundreds of bullock carts gathered at each end of the crossing and traffic of course could only move in one direction at a time. Delays of several hours often occurred as there was no system of traffic control. After an hour's wait I started to cross the river and all went well until I reached the wooden runway beyond the start of the boat pitches [pontoons] when, owing to driving the car too fast, I ran off the planks and immediately sank up to the axle in the fine sand.

It was impossible to get the car moving again and eventually I collected a number of coolies passing by and having unloaded the car, had it lifted back bodily onto the ramp. I ran off the runway once more before reaching the far bank and had to have it lifted on again. It was hard work in the blistering, searing heat of the riverbed but it taught me to proceed with the greatest care in the future when making such river crossings.

I continued the journey to Moradabad and at intervals whenever a road crossed the route on which I was proceeding, there was a policeman who would solemnly wave me straight on. I arrived at Moradabad later in the evening and was welcomed by my brother, Leslie, and some of his friends.

The Police Training School was a very busy establishment and one of the biggest operations in India for police training. Police officers had to undergo two years' training in their police duties and also learn Urdu and the other main important languages of the United Provinces. After completing their training, they were posted as assistant superintendents of police in the district and also did three months' attachment to British Cavalry and Infantry regiments.

In the evenings if we were not taking part in games with the men, my brother and I and his friends would go riding or fishing, and at the weekends have a small game shoot. It was fine riding country and had a lot of pig. The world famous, premier pig-sticking event, the Kadir Cup, was held annually in the area. I had some wonderful rides on my brother's grey Arab mare during these jaunts. On one occasion, however, the mare took fright at a buffalo and raced back, causing me to slide under her neck but I somehow managed to regain my seat. The spectacle was, I gather, quite a comic one.

On another evening, when quietly hacking back to the lines, my mare began to get restive and kept turning her head around. Looking back, I saw a large elephant belonging to a local landowner emerging from a patch of jungle. The mare then flattened her ears and taking the bit in her teeth bolted for her life and did not stop, until she had reached the stables.

The commandant of the Police Training School was a Mr. Dickie Powell, a very well-known and very fine member of the Indian Police Service.

I returned to Peshawar in mid-June. My plans had certainly gone awry and the shoot had not been a success, but the long journey had allowed me to be acquainted with vast areas of India that I might not otherwise have seen and had added to my store of knowledge of the great sub-continent and its varied peoples.

The hot sticky months of the monsoon passed slowly and there occurred one of the tragedies that were so typical of the Indian frontier. Lieutenant Hawks, a young sapper officer, was stationed at Landi Khotal in the Khyber Pass, where his brigade was located. He was in charge of one of the sections of the road through the Khyber and one day had lunch in Peshawar Club with me and several other friends. After lunch he had to return to Landi Khotal and as he left, he said he would see us again at the weekend.

Hawks was murdered during the night in his quarters in Landi Khotal fort and the members of the lunch party attended his funeral early the following week. The body had been found at dawn with several stab wounds, lying in the garden in front of his quarters. The electric light was on in his room and his pistol was lying on the ground.

When the full story of the tragedy became known it appeared that a Shinwari tribal contractor on Hawks' section of the road had not been carrying out his work properly and had been told off by the officer and I believe he was fined. The Landi Khotal camp is surrounded by a thick barbed-wire perimeter which is closed at night and patrolled and in the middle of the camp is the stone fort with high walls, the gates of which are also locked at night. Only troops and personnel connected with the camp, all having passes, are permitted to be within the perimeter after the gates are closed.

The two murderers had either secreted themselves within the fort or during the darkness had got to the wire perimeter and over the wall of the fort and there they waited at Lt Hawks' quarters. They appear to have woken him up by throwing mud pellets at the window of his room and then he must have got up, switched on the lights, unlocked the door and walked out onto the veranda, where he was clubbed and stabbed. He had apparently put up a fight and a short blood trail was found leading out of the garden. The murderers were never brought to book.

Chapter 10

Belzona

Edna was due to return at the end of November and I took 10 days' leave to go to Bombay to meet her after which we would go to Belzona, 350 miles south of Bombay, where I had to do a course at the chemical warfare school.

Edna duly arrived and after a few days in Bombay, where I saw my first talking picture, we proceeded to Belzona. Belzona is a small cantonment in the Western Ghats and for thousands of square miles in all directions are the pine forests of Kangra and Una, containing every variety of big game and many elephants. Fortunately the weekends were available for students who wished to go out shooting and some of the shooting blocks were reserved for the use of the Belzona garrison.

On my arrival I obtained an introduction to the conservator of the forest and was given a shooting block 35 miles away for the next weekend, with permission to shoot two elephants. A friend of ours Captain Steve Price, the Indian Army tennis champion, who had not been out shooting before, came with us and we arrived at the forest bungalow at the block the following Friday evening at about 6:30pm.

I was delighted to hear from the ranger officer that they had nine elephants, with a fine tusker amongst them. They had been feeding during the day nearby and had only moved off about half an hour previously.

Leaving Edna at the bungalow with the bearer to get a meal ready, Price and I, with a local shikari and a few coolies, drove down the forest road for about five miles where we left the car and went into the jungle, hoping soon to come up on the elephants. We guessed that they would probably make for a nearby river. The light was beginning to fade and the undergrowth was very dense. We had only moved 30 yards along the forest road when there was a large snort and a big bison crashed away in the undergrowth, with no chance of a shot.

It was then almost dark and we decided to return to the bungalow. We'd gone perhaps two miles when after a small descent, the headlights of the car came down onto a level road and there a short distance ahead, in the middle of the track was a fine panther. I signalled the driver to stop but before I could take aim the panther leapt into the forest.

As we drove into the bungalow compound we saw Edna standing on the veranda with a shotgun in her hand. "Thank heaven you've come!" she exclaimed. We learned that after dark one of the coolies had seen a panther in the jungle come right up to the bungalow compound. The forest guard, who lived in the servants' quarters, had hastily pulled out an old single barrel gun which he gave to Edna to use and a few minutes later a horrible growling in the darkness came from the jungle as the panther prowled about and on this, the forest guard and the coolie rushed inside the bungalow and locked the door.

The panther kept snarling and growling but could not be seen, so Edna could only wait and pray fervently that we would soon return. The miscreants inside the bungalow had only just opened the doors as we arrived and having heard what had happened and being extremely angry, I roundly abused them and chastised them in the severest terms, so that they realised that they had very much upset the officer sahib. Afterwards we soon completed cooking of the interrupted meal, which was a tasty curry of bully beef hash and we spent the rest of the evening on long chairs on the veranda, looking down the dark, steep hillsides below, watching the fireflies playing amongst the branches and talking about plans for tomorrow.

The following day Price and I drove some miles down the forest road and then the shikari led us off into the jungle once again on the trail of the elephants. The going was very hard and on one occasion we had to crawl through the thickets on our hands and knees. While doing this, I gazed down and saw that I had lost the gold watch that Edna had given to me as a birthday present, which upset me considerably.

We slowly made our laborious way through the jungle for several hours more and at last heard the sound of breaking bamboo made by the elephants while feeding. We could even hear their stomachs rumbling but could not see them in the dense jungle. We now had to approach very carefully, testing the wind when quite suddenly the noise stopped and the shikari said disappointedly, "Vo chale gae", (They have gone). So it turned out to be. The great creatures, having smelt us on the wind, moved away in the dense jungle, without a sound, across the Kabani River, where they were out of my area.

There was nothing more to do than make our way back to the car, which would take us several hours to do. On the way back when I was once more crawling through the thicket, I saw my watch lying amongst dead leaves and could hardly believe my eyes. The area could have been searched by hundreds of men for years and the watch would probably never have been found.

The next day we spent roaming the jungle on the hillside above the bungalow and saw several herds of bison in the distance. We enjoyed the shoot, such as it was, as an eventful interlude in the beautiful forest.

Chapter 11

Peshawar and the Loot of Kabul

My brother Leslie came to spend Christmas 1929 with us in Peshawar where seasonal festivities were in full swing. Dances at the club, cocktail parties in the regimental messes, polo matches, golf tournaments and meets of the Peshawar Vale Hunt all made up part of the vivacious life on this fascinating city of the frontier.

In those days tourists, including ladies, were permitted to visit the Khyber Pass and go as far as Landi Kotal, a piquet which overlooked the Afghan post of Landi Khana on the international boundary.

One day we went for a drive up the Khyber, the trip eagerly looked forward to by Edna and Leslie, neither of whom had been there before. At the battleship – like fort at Jamrud we passed through the barrier guarded by Afridi khasadars. These tribal levies were employed by the political department for road protection and escort duties. The tribe was paid for these duties, to assist them in meeting their economic difficulties, and also acted as a measure of control, designed to ensure their good behaviour.

The road and the railway lines run close together throughout the length of the Khyber and wind in and out of the bare stony valleys along the grim hillsides. On two great dominating crags are the forts of Shahgai and Ali Masjid. Halfway up the pass where the valley widens there are several groups of stone towers of the Afridi and Shinwari tribes. Occasionally movement on the road was interrupted by local battles going on between the opposing tribes or perhaps by the progress of a blood feud. If this happened when a party of tourists was moving along the road, the tribesmen were informed, they stopped their fight, allowed the tourists to go through and then resumed their fight again.

An army brigade was located in Landi Kotal and all was military activity. Here the visitor realised that there was a constant state of preparedness for war. The relentless savage mountain warfare of the tribes meant a trifling incident might cause conflict to blaze forth at any moment.

Our drive through the Khyber was without incident and on arrival at Michni Piquet we climbed up to the lookout post and spent some time gazing over at the Afghan hills.

The next day a dreadful tragedy was to occur at Michni Piquet. Two English bank managers, who were proceeding into retirement after a lifetime of service in India, decided they would like to see the Khyber Pass before they went home to England.

On arrival at the Khyber they were given an escort of a havildar, i.e. an Indian sergeant, and a sepoy from the Frontier Constabulary, both Pathans, to escort them through the Pass. The car was halted along the road below the piquet and the two Englishmen started climbing up to the piquet, followed by the havildar and sepoy. Suddenly the havildar raised his rifle and shot both of them dead. Instantly the havildar was shot dead by the sepoy. Probably this dreadful incident is now just part of the bloody history of the frontier but it was a tragic ending for the two, who were then a matter of hours from their embarkation on one of the homeward-bound liners from Bombay, hoping to enjoy the remainder of their lives in comfort and a well-earned retirement rest. It was said at Peshawar that the havildar had had a brainstorm as a result of a previous attack of meningitis, but many of us believed that he had gone 'ghazi' (or a 'fighter for the faith'), that is he believed that by killing an unbeliever [of Islam] that he would immediately enter paradise.

Leslie returned to Moradabad early in the new year and shortly afterwards had to go to Lucknow to have his appendix removed. On the journey down, the train he was travelling in was involved in one of the worst rail accidents to occur on the Indian railways. It was a head-on collision between two trains at night at Clutterbuckganj, a junction near Bareilly. Both trains were completely wrecked and caught fire. Leslie was hurled through the window of his compartment and when he got to his feet the night was hideous with screams of the injured some of whom were trapped in the burning wreckage.

There were several British troops on the train, who had escaped injury, and they organised a party to extricate the injured from the wreckage and release others who were trapped. In half an hour a relief train was on the scene to take over medical and rescue work. Leslie was by then feeling the effects of his exertions but was able to get to Bareilly, from where he continued to Lucknow and underwent a successful operation. There were 50 killed and nearly 200 injured in the train crash and it was certainly not the best preparation for a serious surgical operation.

We must now return to Peshawar where beyond the jagged Khyber hills Bachai Sakao's star was setting. He had only a loose hold on the Afghan tribesmen and that was only achieved by the giving of presents and favours, reinforcing the influence of the more powerful tribal leaders, so that when Nadir Khan, an Afghan general who had fought against Britain in the Afghan War in 1919-20, raised a tribal army at Shegal, Bachai Sakao was soon fighting for his life.

Trouble in Afghanistan was a wonderful opportunity for Waziri and Mahsud tribesmen from our side of the frontier to join in the fun. Bachai Sakao's forces were defeated, and he and his henchmen captured by some Waziris from British territory. Knowing what his fate would be, Bachai Sakao sent a request to Nadir Khan saying that if he was to die, could he be permitted to cut [mutilate] his wife, so that his soul might rest in peace. His wife was reputed to be a beautiful Circassian blonde and it was fortunate for her that the request was ignored by Nadir Khan. Any civilised person would be appalled by such savagery and callousness. Distressingly, this behaviour is not untypical of these fanatical Mohammedan tribesmen, whose womenfolk occupy a very lowly place in their scheme of existence.

When the Waziris were taking Bachai Sakao and his henchmen to court for trial they decided to anticipate the verdict and there and then on the maidan outside the court they erected a long gallows of bamboo poles and put ropes round the captives' necks, pulled them up by the neck and left them to die of strangulation. After they were dead their bodies were taken down and mutilated in the horrible bestial fashion which is well known on the frontier. Photographs of this dreadful scene were on sale in Peshawar some weeks later. Nadir Khan was proclaimed King of Afghanistan with the title of Nadir Shah and he soon set about establishing more peaceful conditions. Soon the first 'Kafila', or camel caravan, passed through the Khyber, after the absence of a year. It was a huge caravan of about 15,000 camels and in their loads were hidden an enormous amount of loot from Kabul obtained during the fighting, over the previous year. The looted goods included thousands of beautiful Persian carpets and rugs, piles of furs, lovely jewellery and precious and semi-precious stones.

Buyers quickly gathered from all parts of India at Peshawar and many good bargains were obtained. An army officer friend of mine, who was an expert on Persian carpets, saw a tribesman carrying one on his shoulder and stopped him to examine the carpet. After a brief glance at it he offered the tribesman 250 rupees, which is about £19, the tribesman accepted with a grunt and went on his way. It was an immensely valuable carpet and within a week the buyer had resold it for 20,000 rupees.

There were other events stirring in India at this time whose consequences we could not then have guessed.

Mahatma Gandhi had launched his civil disobedience campaign, the object of which was to eventually force the withdrawal of British power from India. The campaign was intended to be non-violent and it was to gain its end by means of the vast Indian masses being persuaded to refuse to cooperate in the administration of the government of the country and to boycott British goods by the supplanting of British controlled enterprises by village industries. Gandhi supported the Indian Congress Party, the only political body of any consequence in India, which was used by the wealthy Indian industrialists and the Brahmin hierarchy of the Hindus to further their own ends.

The Mahatma's intentions may have been good but human nature being what it is, the 'non-violent' campaign quickly led to numerous communal riots and police and troops often had to use force to restore order. Because the Mahatma was of the Vaishya, the trading caste, his saintly characteristics and acumen caused a lot of Brahmins to revere him and this fact led to a very serious situation in Peshawar.

The little Hindu's creed of non-violence found surprising support from Abdul Ghaffār Khān, an enormous Pathan, who became known as the Sarhadi Gandhi, or 'frontier Gandhi', who formed a party of followers, the Khudāyī Khidmatgār, or 'Servants of God'.

Eventually when the provincial governments were brought into being, a fantastic situation arose. The trade and commerce of the frontier province was largely carried out by a very small minority of Hindus, who were better educated than the tribesman and the first government was a Congress government of Hindus, in a province in which 90% of inhabitants were Pathan tribesmen who had a bitter hatred of the Hindus.

In March 1930 serious rioting broke out one day in Peshawar city and the 2nd battalion, the King's Own Yorkshire Light Infantry (KOYLI), with a section of armoured cars was sent to the city to restore order. The narrow streets were packed with armed and angry tribesmen and eventually the leading armoured car had to halt, at which point kerosene oil was thrown over the vehicle and it was set alight. Two crew members were killed, as they tried to leave the burning vehicle and the supporting infantry was also attacked, leading to fire being opened on the crowd.

With the seriousness of the situation becoming apparent, an Indian regiment, the first 18th Gwalior Rifles, was ordered to stand by in readiness to move on Peshawar city. There were a number of Brahmins in this unit and one of the companies had several Viceroy commissioned Indian officers who were also Brahmin. Platoons of this company refused to march into Peshawar city. The implications of the situation were serious. The KOYLI were required for the defence of the cantonment and the protection of several hundred European men, women and children. With the Gwalior Rifles unavailable, only one regiment was immediately at hand to deal with further trouble in Peshawar city that might, if left unchecked, start general hostilities by all the tribes in the Peshawar area. Quick action was essential.

The Essex Regiment was stationed at Nowshera, 27 miles from Peshawar. This regiment was moved in hurriedly by rail to Peshawar and, from Ahmadabad, 100 miles away, a Gurkha battalion was also dispatched. Once at Peshawar, the Gurkha battalion escorted the Gwalior Rifles back to Ahmadabad where they were confined in a wired camp.

The activities of Abdul Ghaffār Khān and his Khudāyī Khidmatgār, also popularly known as 'Red Shirts', in the troubled Peshawar city had caused the Afridis to become restless and by April, Laskhars (or the 'Army of the Good'), were reported to be gathering. Attacking of piquets became frequent, and a number of raids were carried out on peaceful villages near Peshawar.

The Mail [train] from Bombay was attacked between Nowshera and Peshawar and an escort of troops had to be provided for it. Small activities, such as riding and shooting outside the wire ceased, and Peshawar was virtually beleaguered. In order to remove this threat to Peshawar, two additional brigades were concentrated there and operations commenced to build a line of forts and a barbed-wire blockade fence on the far edge of the Khajuri Plain and into the hills, from which the Afridis were bound to attack.

On the opening of operations, I was commanding a section of no 15 MT Company, RIASC but a week or two later I was transferred to a detachment of the company at Rawalpindi and was occupied, during the hot weather, with moving troops to and from the Murree Hill station.

One of a line of forts and barbed wire blockade
fences erected on the on the Khajuri Plain to
protect Peshawar from Afridi attacks, 1930

Artillery in readiness for action on
the Khajuri Plain, 1929/30

The Author in the Khyber Pass, 1929

A Khasadar or tribal levy paid to provide road protection in the Khyber Pass, 1929

Chapter 12

Kashmir 1930

*"Pale hands, pink tipped, like Lotus buds that float
On those cool waters where we used to dwell"*

Kashmiri Song or Pale Hands I Loved,

Laurence Hope (Adela Florence Cory Nicolson)
(1865-1904)

In June 1930 I had a month's leave and Edna and I took the opportunity of visiting Kashmir, surely one of the loveliest places on the earth's surface. Much has been written about this truly beautiful country by far abler pens than mine but perhaps Kashmir cannot be written about too often, as seen from different perspectives by those who are lucky enough to visit it.

The Rawalpindi to Srinagar mountain road is 296 miles in length, traversing for the greater part of the way the valley of the Jhelum River. The altitude of the road rises to 7,000 feet and then it descends for some miles to Kahala where at an altitude of nearly 2,500 feet a bridge crosses the Jhelum River. For the remainder of the journey the road follows the valley of the Jhelum, gradually climbing again to a height of 5,000 feet and enters the Vale of Kashmir at Baramulla

The route from Baramulla to Srinagar is bordered on either side for 35 miles with an avenue of giant poplar trees, which were planted in the days of the Moghul emperor Shah Jahan. As the road was originally constructed for the passage of elephants

121

with howdahs, it is wide enough to take two-way motor traffic.

The whole journey usually takes two days, and every 12-15 miles there are comfortable dak bungalows where a traveller can stay for the night. It can be done in one day by starting at dawn from Rawalpindi and driving very fast if there are no undue delays such as landslides.

The drive along the mountain road is in itself quite an experience. The mountain sides drop away thousands of feet to the river valley below and in other places vertical sheer cliffs tower up thousands of feet above one.

At times the road approaches close to the river and in the great roaring torrent, enormous tree trunks can be seen being thrown about like matchsticks, on their way down to the plains of India and the sawmills. As the road climbs higher the mountainsides are covered with great pine forests and the cool mountain air and sweet scent of the pines give a tremendous feeling of exhilaration.

At the customs post on the Kashmir state border the contents of one's baggage and car are declared and officials are particularly concerned to see that no beef of any sort, even tinned beef is taken into the state. The reason for this is that the maharajah is a Hindu and the eating of the flesh of the cow is strictly forbidden, so amongst the bounteous plenty of Kashmir, European meals have to be beefless and it has become legendary that the first meal on leaving Kashmir state is a prime beef steak.

The extent to which the sacredness of the cow is regarded by Hindus was shown in an incident in the 1930s, when the maharajah Sir Hari Singh, while driving along the great poplar avenue between Baramulla and Srinagar, struck a cow which suddenly ran out behind the screen of trees and was killed. The poplars were so close together and the road so straight that the country on either side was completely hidden from view. To prevent a recurrence of such an accident, the maharajah ordered half the trees on either side of the road to be felled. The great avenue which had reached its soaring perfection in a span of 350 years had much of its majesty removed but in spite of this it is still most impressive.

Srinagar city is built on either side of the Jhelum River and several bridges cross it, including a picturesque wooden-pile bridge [now called the 'Zero Bridge']. On the left bank stand the great white Rajbagh palace and the bazaars and on the right bank the club of the British residency, banks, hotels, etc. To the north and west are the lovely lakes: the Dal Lake, the Nigeen Lake and the Khusal. Nearby are the famous Moghul gardens, the Shalimar and the Nishat Bagh, above which the pine-clad, snow-capped mountains, rise another 3,000 feet. Wherever one looks there is a picture of breath-taking loveliness, vast expanses of pure sunlit waters with stands of tall poplar trees and surrounding all in a vast circle, the mighty Himalayan Mountains.

On arrival at Srinagar we engaged a houseboat called the 'New Moon' which was lying on the Dal Lake. Houseboats in Kashmir range from large elaborate three-bedroomed boats down to simple ones that have grass matted roofs and sides and can be hired at very cheap rates. A boat is tied up behind the houseboat on which the boat owner, his family and servants live. The boat owners usually do the cooking and most of them are excellent cooks. The delicious meals and plentiful supplies of every variety of fruit, both English and tropical, adds to the pleasure of a holiday in Kashmir.

A shikara is provided with each houseboat to give a means of travelling about the lake. This is a craft of the punt type with narrow sides and a canopy over the top. Other varieties of shikara ply as taxis and are provided with well-sprung cushions, often rejoicing in names such as 'Jolly Roger', 'Hot Stuff' etc.

They are in great demand on moonlit nights by amorous couples who are lazily paddled about the lake, lowering their hands in the cool waters and enjoying the cool of the lovely romantic setting of their dalliance. Unless one had planned to go out fishing or shooting or on a trek in one of the valleys, the days and night provided their own enjoyment without effort. Before breakfast one would paddle in the shikara out to a moored bathing platform in the middle of the Dal Lake where everybody gathered to bathe, after which we returned to the houseboat to eat.

After breakfast we would go ashore to Srinagar and do some shopping, then have drinks at the club on the riverbank or at the Lalit hotel before returning for lunch. The rest after lunch followed by another bathe would occupy us until dinner time and after dinner we could either go to a cinema or to a dance at the club or Lalit hotel or visit friends.

Shops selling wood carving and papier-mâché goods were a source of great interest and one never got tired of looking at them. The craftsmanship and art were superb but they were the result of sweated labour. A poor, sickly-looking man produced these lovely works of art, working all day and half the night in a small crowded room for a pittance.

One afternoon shortly after we arrived, we went by shikara to the romantic Shalimar gardens, immortalised in the Indian love poems. It was the first of many visits to the gardens and all were a very pleasant experience. We also visited the even lovelier Nishat Bagh gardens to appreciate their design and beauty.

From the lake's edge one approaches the garden by a flight of steps, under an archway formed by an oriental pavilion. Then before one is the whole vista of the garden, rising terrace above terrace in the distance and behind it, great towering mountainsides.

At the centre of these terraces running the length of the garden, is a reach of water in which fountains play on either side of a very well-kept lawn, beautiful beds of flowers tastefully arranged amongst them. Terraces connect to each other by means of a series of tessellated stone walls, down which runs the water from the terrace above, so that one appears to be looking at a fine lace curtain.

Walks on either side are bordered by giant chinar [sycamore] trees, whose large, deep brown leaves throw a cool shade below and on the topmost reach in the middle of water is a large black stone slab, on which the emperor used to sit on in the cool shade.

In the evenings when we had no arrangements for after dinner, we would call the servants and paddle downstream or to the houseboats of friends or they would visit us, and have drinks, after which we would all go over to the diving boards and bathe for several hours. In Srinagar bathing platforms were moored on all the lakes. There were dressing cabins, water chutes and diving boards on the platforms, in addition to cooking facilities, so that parties could go on most of the night. For bathing we would lie on the top of the platform, listening to the gramophone, until we felt it was time to bathe again. Later the houseboat owner, or the ladies of the party, would make some sausages and mashed potatoes or fried eggs and in the early hours we would paddle back to our own houseboats completely content after a perfect evening.

It was *de rigueur* for all officers, officers' wives and civil officials of similar status to sign the Maharajah's and the Resident's visitors book on arriving in Kashmir and in due course we were bidden to a garden party at the Residency or to a dance at the palace, which was set in lovely spacious grounds on the Jhelum river. The Residency's vast lawns and shady trees meant it made a perfect setting for such events. Tables were set out on the lawns under the cover of umbrellas and guests were waited on by the uniformed Indian bearers of the Residency staff. The Resident and his wife moved round talking to the guests and the function concluded with the serving of cocktails.

Kashmir is a fisherman's paradise. The lovely mountain rivers and streams have been stocked with brown and rainbow trout and the Wular Lake and Jhelum River are full of Mahseer [Indian Salmon], a fine Indian sporting fish which can attain the size of 100lbs or more. Many other varieties of smaller fish are found and also a coarse fish known as Rohu, which can attain a weight of 50lbs.

Our houseboat owner was a very keen and expert fisherman and so we had the houseboat moved to a lovely place called Ganderbal, on the Sind River 15 miles from Srinagar, where it emerges from the

Sind valley into an open area of green parkland. The river is very broad and swift and is icy cold, as it comes from the glaciers in the high mountains.

An effective method of fishing in this water was to spin a spoon [a concave lure] up to four inches in length and a large triangular hook. The line had to be well-weighted to keep it low in the swift current. On the first day after about an hour's spinning, I caught a large fish and after half an hour's play I landed him. He weighed 25 lbs. The fishing was really magnificent and by 5pm I had caught six fish between 15 and 25lbs and a number of smaller ones from four to ten pounds in weight. I also caught several more fish on a light rod, the biggest, being a nine pound chirra.

We had marvellous fishing for the next four days and then returned to Srinagar, well satisfied with the excellent sport we had had at Ganderbal.

Those who were keen on hill-shooting could trek into the high nullas of Ladakh, Gilgit-Baltistan, and Leh, there to pit their stalking skill and climbing powers against the great mountain sheep and goats. The Ovis Ammon Polii [Marco Polo sheep] has tremendous curled horns and the horns of the Markhor and the Ibex are also equally impressive. These marvellous animals graze at tremendous height, often up to 16 or 18,000 feet and days of stalking and climbing with immense care, patience, courage and endurance are necessary to obtain the chance of a shot.

We returned to Rawalpindi from Kashmir and in October 1930 I was given six months furlough in England. At the end of my leave, as we were expecting our first-born, Edna remained at home and on July 22nd, 1931 Brian, our son, was born at the home of his grandparents at Broughton near Preston. I went home on two months privilege leave in August and on completion of it we returned to Rawalpindi with Brian and rapidly became aware of the inherent responsibilities of parenthood in India.

Houseboat, 'New Moon', at Chinar Bagh, Kashmir, 1930

Edna with Friend, Dal Lake, Kashmir, 1936

Edna with Valerie and Brian, Kashmir, 1936

Chapter 13

Mountain Interlude

In November 1931 I was posted from Rawalpindi to Abbottabad in the North West Frontier Province, which is also on the western road to Kashmir. It was the regimental centre of the 5th and 6th Gurkha rifles and 13th Frontier Force regiment. There was also a battery of mountain artillery located near there.

The pretty little cantonment at a height of 4,500 feet above sea-level was only a few miles from the Black Mountain tribal border, against whom several punitive expeditions had been mounted in the past but comparative peace had reigned since the end of World War I. There was a plain between Abbottabad and the tribal territory in which three villages named Oghi, Bapa and Khaki were located. It was the name of the last village from which the Indian khaki uniform got its name.

Sir Sam Browne VC, the originator of the Sam Browne belt, who raised Sam Browne's cavalry regiment of the Indian Army, had experimented with drill cloth dyed a neutral colour, similar to the brownish nature of the terrain on the North West Frontier and equipped his troops with khaki-coloured uniforms for better camouflage when in action against the enemy. In operations against the village of Khaki, the troops engaged wore the new uniform for the first time and thereafter it was known as 'khaki'.

[Other sources attribute the development of khaki-coloured uniform cloth to Harry Lumsden (1821–1896), agent to the Governor-General for the North-West Frontier, stationed in Lahore and first worn by the Corps of Guides, raised in 1846, the name, 'khaki' being derived from an Urdu word meaning 'soil-coloured'. These differing explanations are not incompatible, as Sam Browne was a close contemporary of Harry Lumsden and, based upon their practical experience of field operations; they may have independently introduced khaki uniforms to their units.]

I had not been in Abbottabad long however when an incident occurred to break the normal routine of the station. Twenty miles from Abbottabad, on the road to Rawalpindi, was the Haripur jail, an enormous fort-like prison, in which were confined the outlaws and criminals of the frontier province. At the time the inmates numbered several thousand, as a result of the fighting and outlawry around Peshawar the previous year.

On Christmas morning 1932 information was received in Abbottabad that a number of prisoners had attacked some of the frontier constabulary guard and seized their rifles and a battle was in progress inside the jail. The rest of the jail guard who had not been killed or captured by the prisoners had managed to prevent any of them breaking out. A most serious situation would have arisen if the prisoners managed to escape, as the majority of them were hardened criminals and multiple murderers, and they were only a few miles from tribal territories.

A constant state of readiness of all units on the North West Frontier enabled such situations to be dealt with promptly, and within two hours a battalion of Gurkhas from Abbottabad were on their way to Haripur and the jail was cordoned off. By the evening, a battalion of the Shropshire Light Infantry had arrived and within 48 hours the rising had been completely quelled.

In February 1932 the 1st Rawalpindi division had gone into camp in the Haripur area to carry out divisional manoeuvres, during which some Pathan rifle thieves had congregated in the area. One night the thieves managed to get into camp and stole four rifles from one of the battalions. This caused a terrific uproar, as it is a most serious offence to lose a rifle or ammunition on the frontier. A modern rifle is the most valuable possession a tribesman can have and rifle thieves are ever on the alert to make away with them.

These thieves developed incredible skill and cunning and constant vigilance and care had to be exercised both by units and individual troops to prevent the theft of their weapons. In the barracks all rifles not in use are kept locked in rifle-racks in the strong room and they are under the constant supervision of the sentries. They are checked several times a day in camp. The rifles are secured by chains running through the trigger guards, which are secured by locks. Despite these precautions and having to get through a wire perimeter, avoid detection by patrols and sentries and saw through the chains, rifle thieves were often successful. At night the strictest vigilance was observed by the regiment concerned and it was surrounded by two Gurkha battalions but rifle thieves, with typical audacity, made another attempt and one was actually seized by a soldier inside a tent. The practically naked and oiled thief struggled out of the soldier's grasp and in the darkness made his escape but without the rifle.

At Abbottabad we were fortunate enough to see the Gurkha brigade Khud Race. A 'khud' means mountainside and this is possibly a unique sporting event and certainly one of the toughest in the world. Ten battalions of the Gurkha brigade took part on this occasion, with Abbottabad serving as the venue for the event.

A course is laid out on a mountainside and from the starting point teams run and scramble up the mountainside to the first point, which may be 1000 to 1500 feet above the start. They then descend at breakneck speed to the second point, which is near the level of the start and up again to the third point and so on to the fifth, the last high point and down to the finishing point. Each team consists of four men and each team has different-coloured attire, to enable them to be distinguished. It was also a very social occasion as the Gurkha officers mess placed a large shamiana [tent or marquee] at the starting point, the Gurkha band played and refreshments and drinks were served. It was a most enjoyable event in every way.

From the start the competitors tear up the mountain-side, jumping and scrambling, pulling themselves upward. The khud selected for the 1932 race was very steep, almost vertical in places, with outcrops of boulders, patches of short, thick scrub and small ravines to be negotiated. Without a pause and with the expert eye of the born hillmen that they are, the sturdy little Gurkhas chose the best course, streamed up the mountain to the first flag and then began the breakneck descent. They came bounding down the khud, leaping from rock to rock as sure-footed as the wild sheep and goats of their own mountains. Down they came, almost hurtling through the air towards us, a wrongly placed foot or a chance tumble would have resulted in serious injury, or perhaps even death.

No mistakes were made however, and the race was still neck and neck as the second ascent began. By the time the second high point had been reached, the competitors were further along the mountain-side and on the final ascent to the last high flag, binoculars were needed to watch the race properly. The pace of the course was slower by that time but it ended with an exhilarating final run down the mountain-side to the finishing point in front the shamiana. The leaders finished amidst the cheers of their comrades in arms 5/6th Gurkha rifles and the assembled guests.

There was also another unique and amusing scene to be enjoyed in the Gurkha station. Small Gurkha boys, like their fathers, live for soldiering and as toddlers form squads and attired in uniforms consisting of little black jackets, white shorts and black stockings and the little black Gurkha pillbox hat, march about all round the station. The object seems to be to bag officers to enable them to give a salute, particularly British officers. They send scouts out round the cantonment and whenever an officer is spotted, a message is passed hurriedly back and the squad is diverted to a route which enables them to give the officer a smart 'eyes right'. It is quite a delight to see their round cherub little faces and the terrific pride which they take in playing at soldiers.

Dog fighting was a popular sport amongst the tribal villages and one day a bull terrier belonging to an officer of the 13th Mountain Force disappeared. Despite a reward of 100 rupees nothing further was heard of the dog, until about a year later rumours came of a dog that was the king of Hazra, the local name of the area. The country constabulary got on the trail, they tracked this dog down and it turned out to be the bull terrier belonging to the aforesaid officer. The dog had killed all of the local champions and established itself as the king dog. In order to avoid it being identified by the authorities, a tribesman had burned a black patch over one eye with acid, but otherwise it seemed, apart from the scars and scratches it had from its fights, in good health.

Abbottabad, 1932, watching the Gurkha 'Khud Race'

The Author and his wife, Edna, are sitting in the centre of the second row (behind two empty chairs)

Chapter 14

Back to Tiger Land

"When sunset lights are burning low,
While tents are pitched and camp-fires glow,
Steals o'er us, ere the stars appear,
The furtive sense of Jungle Fear."

Laurence Hope (Adela Florence Cory Nicholson)
(1865-1904). The Jungle Fear, from
'Stars of the Desert'

In March 1932 I was transferred from Abbottabad to an MT company at Bareilly in the United Provinces. Edna and my infant son, Brian, went there by train, a two-day journey, and I drove down in my car, along the Grand Trunk road to Delhi and then via Moradabad to Bareilly. Such moves, sometimes over great distances, are of course part of one's life in the armed forces and we were quite pleased with this one, as the lovely hill station of Nainital was only 90 miles away, to which Edna and Brian could go in the hot weather. Only a few miles away were the magnificent Turi forests, at the foot of the Himalayas, where I knew I had once more an excellent opportunity to hunt for tigers.

At the beginning of the hot weather, Edna took Brian up to Nainital and I arranged to have two weeks shooting in the Tugari block at the foot of the Nainital range, after which I was to spend the balance of my two months' leave in Nainital.

In the south-east corner of the Tugari Block there was a small jungle township called Tanakpur on the banks of the Sarda River and a few miles away the border of the kingdom of Nepal. The river issued out at this point from a beautiful valley in the mountains and it fed the magnificent Sarda canal system which irrigated thousands of square miles of the United Provinces. To get to Tanakpur I had to proceed to Pilibhit, 50 miles by road, and from that point I went along the Sarda canal bank road, for which one had to get permission to cover the ten miles to Tanakpur.

The forest was magnificent one either side of the canal, immense trees in full leaf. In the early morning there was a mist about and it was comparatively cool and I came across herd after herd of sambar, chital and nilgai, drinking on the canal edge, numerous jungle fowl and peafowl and packs of the great grey langur monkeys.

Five miles north-west along the forest road to Tanakpur was the forest rest house of Sonapani which was on a small hillock overlooking the Turi forest and the Himalayan foothills.

Donald Stewart was the divisional forest officer of the Hildwani division, in which the block was situated. I had arranged for the local shikari and four bhens (i.e. buffalos) for tying up purposes, to be awaiting my arrival at Sonapani. The shikari, an old Kumaoni tribal hill man, turned out to be a very good man indeed. I discovered he had been shikari to Mr. Wyndham, a great big game hunter, who was commissioner of the Kumaon, and who had shot at least 250 tigers back in the late 19th century.

The old shikari told me there were a number of tiger and panther in the block, in addition to nearly every form of Indian big game and also a herd of wild elephant. Elephants were however strictly preserved and were an unmitigated nuisance. On a number of occasions I found fallen trees, pushed down by the elephants, blocking the forest road and to continue on the road required that they had to be lifted out of the way. Included within the block's limits was a section of the Turi forest, to a depth of 10 miles, at the foot of the hills and then several miles of Kumaon foothills leading into the Himalayas.

The block's length was about 12 miles and started from Tanakpur in a north-west direction towards Nainital. It was adjacent to an old road that ran through the Turi forest for hundreds of miles at the foot of the hills, leading to the Himalayas and constructed originally by the Moghuls.

Most nullahs from the valleys ran through the forest towards the plains and the points where the forest road crossed the nullahs were ideal places for tying up the buffalos. These were tied up the first night and in the morning I found one had been taken in a valley in the foothills where the forest road crossed the nullah, about two miles from the bungalow. There were trees and plenty of cover in the area and the tiger had not bothered to drag the kill.

I decided to sit up to await the return of the tiger. The usual procedure for putting the machan in place was carried out and I got into it at 4pm. In the United Provinces no shooting is permitted from one hour after sunset to one hour before sunrise and in addition, torches are not permitted to be used for shooting. For the purpose of shooting game this means that if the tiger or panther does not come before nightfall the sportsman has to spend the night in the machan, very uncomfortable and sometimes very cold if a wind blows down the valleys.

The tiger did not come before nightfall and as there was no moon the darkness was intense. It was impossible to see anything. However, at about 8pm I suddenly heard the sound of meat being torn off the kill, so I pointed my torch, to see what the animal was. In the light of the torch was a large hyena which after a curious glance up the tree continued to feed unconcernedly. I threw a few branches down at it and it shortly went away.

Later I went off to sleep but woke up to the sound of heavy breathing and rumbling directly beneath me. It was a little lighter by then and I thought I could see a dark shadow beneath the machan. A few seconds later there was a terrific exhalation of air and an elephant walked from underneath the machan and was lost in the darkness. It was a great relief the elephant had not detected my presence, as it could have easily had me out of the machan which was not more than five feet above its back.

In the morning, when returning to the bungalow, I found the footprints of several elephants on the nullah bed and on the forest track, across which lay several uprooted trees. Back at the bungalow Sher Singh, the shikari, reported that none of the other buffalos had been taken but the pugs of an enormous tiger, well known in the area, had been found in a nullah three miles to the north-west of the bungalow. This tiger had taken a number of buffalos on a number of occasions but never returned to the kills and seemed to sense the presence of or to detect any shikari who sat up over a live bullock.

As this big tiger was a cattle killer, I decided not to tie up anywhere in the nullah or immediate area for three days and I sent out the shikari and coolies to warn the few forest villagers to take particular care of their grazing herds and have them locked up securely at night. I also offered a reward for any information of a fresh kill of cattle or game. The plan was meant to as far as possible prevent the tiger from getting any meat for a few days and make him hungry and then careless, if he did manage to make a kill.

This appeared to go well and on the fourth evening following this I sat up over a buffalo at the junction of a nullah. The sun was just dropping below the treetops when the buffalo snorted and pulled hard at the rope tethering him firmly to a sapling, and from the bushes and small trees on the corner of the fire line an enormous tiger leapt onto his prey.

The tiger bit the buffalo on the top of the neck, placed his right paw on its withers and its left on the buffalo's snout and then gave a terrific wrench which broke the buffalo's neck. Both animals fell to the ground, the tiger still retaining the buffalo in his mouth.

I was practically hypnotised by this swift and dreadful jungle drama but I realised I must act very quickly and with great care. The tiger had of course killed its prey quickly and cleanly as the tiger normally does. Only a few seconds had elapsed between the buffalo detecting the presence of the tiger and its death. The tiger lay facing me his jaws still closed over the buffalo's neck. Its eyes seemed to be fixed at a spot on the ground just in front of it. Carefully without making a sound I brought my rifle up to my shoulder protruding the barrel a few inches through the small hole made for the purpose in the machan.

At this moment the tiger released his grip on the kill's neck and peered intently straight across the nullah. A great round head hid most of his body from view and I had to take the head shot. Pointing between the eyes I pulled the trigger and as the loud report reverberated through the jungle the tiger's head dropped and the body half turned on its side. I had loaded quickly in order to place an 'anchoring shot' [a shot designed to drop the animal in its tracks] if necessary, but the tiger was quite dead and a further bullet was not needed.

I could see it was an enormous tiger and I waited impatiently for the interminable hours of the night to pass so that I could examine the beast at close quarters. The shikari and a number of coolies arrived at dawn. They had heard the shot and were wondering what had happened. There were sounds of admiration and awe as they saw the great beast lying next to the kill and I felt very elated at bagging this magnificent trophy. I had left my car the previous night at the forest ranger's house three miles away, so I walked back and drove the car back along the forest road to the place where the tiger was lying.

It took the combined effort of all of us to get the tiger across the back of the car and its enormous weight pressed the mudguards right onto the tyres, but by careful driving we managed to get back to the ranger's house safely.

The tiger measured ten feet between pegs, but his tail was only 29 inches long as opposed to the average length of 36. His entire muscular development was colossal, his forearms being 22 inches in circumference.

The following morning I was driving along the forest road towards the valley where the first kill had taken place when after about half a mile on the forest road I saw two beautiful peacocks in the middle of the road, with their tails full spread performing their dance. Going round and round, occasionally making quick little side steps, they took no notice of the approaching car. They continued until I was within a few yards of them and then ran off into the jungle.

On arriving, I found that the bait had been killed and was lying half-eaten in the patch of grass on the edge of the nulla bed. I entered the machan at 4pm and as usual while daylight lasted my vigil was entrancing. Green parrots, green pigeon, mynah birds and many others were flitting about in between the trees. A barking deer made its way across the nullah and disappeared in the forest. Langur monkeys made their way among the treetops and then disappeared into the forest.

By nightfall the tiger had not come. A few hours later, however, the roar of a tiger ran down the valley and it roared several more times as it came nearer. There were several more distant roars from the Turi forest near dawn and if it was the same tiger, I expected it would remain in the area. It was quite cold during night in the valley and a cold wind blew down from the high mountains. When dawn broke the grass below was covered in dew.

I looked in the direction of the kill and then from behind a thick bush out stepped a tiger, looking directly up at me, like a great tomcat, I quickly aimed and fired, again taking the head shot. The tiger fell on his side. I put in another bullet to make sure it would not move and the tiger lay still. As the noise of the shot died down, I heard an excited chattering and saw Shere Singh and the coolies coming up the nullah about 100 yards away from me. I called to them to say the tiger was dead and descended from the machan.

They excitedly gathered around and began the usual performance of admiring the tiger, stroking his whiskers and fur. The tiger measured 9 foot 6 inches between pegs but did not have the same terrific muscular development as the previous one. It was later carried to the Sonapani forest bungalow and skinned. I was very satisfied at having got two tigers within a matter of ten days and decided to leave the next morning for Nainital to rejoin Edna and Brian.

It was 45 miles along the southern mountain forest road at Hildwani, where the motor road climbed up to Nainital 27 miles away. I knew the forest road would be bad but in parts it was perhaps worse than the appalling track to Kanger. The road crossed many nullahs issuing from the hills and in many cases the crude wooden bridges had collapsed into the nullah beds and I had to get passers-by to help me to build up causeways of boulders and logs and brushwood.

The nullahs were several hundred yards wide, with their hard stone and boulders all over the tracks and I very often had to get these obstacles moved out of the way before I could proceed.

By nightfall I reached the lovely forest rest house at Rani Bagh. From there one could see the lights of Nainital burning bright 5,000 feet above. Rani Bagh was the headquarters of the Mechanical Transport Company in which I was serving at Bareilly and a few of my brother officers were there when I arrived.

I had to get the tiger skins out of the car and show them to my friends, who were very envious of my good fortune. After dinner we sat in long chairs on the lawn, looking up at the mysterious mountains looming above us and talked far into the night of tigers and jungles. As it happened, tigers had actually been reported in the vicinity of the forest rest house on two or three occasions, in the recent past.

The next morning I motored up to Nainital to the guest house where Edna and Brian were staying. One of the guests there was a Mr. Garston, a retired officer of the Indian Police, who was very interested in my shoot and especially my big tiger skin. He said a friend of his would be calling to see him that evening. The friend duly arrived, and I was introduced to non-other than the great Jim Corbett, India's most famous hunter of man-eating tigers.

Corbett's fame had spread throughout most of India by then. In later years many people around the world would know of his exploits through his marvelous books including, the 'Man-eaters of Kumaon', 'The Rudraprayag Man-eater', 'The Temple Tiger' and many others.

Jim Corbett was a tall, loose-limbed and powerful man, slow of speech and possessing great natural charm. He had spent all his life, since boyhood, on the family estate in a little forest township in the jungles below Nainital and about eight miles west of Hildwani. Over the years his knowledge of the enormous forests of Manali, the Turi and Bardiya and the Garhwal and Kumaon mountains of the Himalayas had become unequalled.

The ever-present limitless jungle, its beauty, mystery and excitement and something underlying, almost a sense of fear, had moulded the pattern of his childhood days and he had learned to love and admire the splendid wild creatures that lived there. Now at the height of his fame and powers, Jim had practically given up shooting and was making films of the animals and the jungle.

We chatted on and on about tigers and the spell of the magnificent forest. A friendship began which was to last until we parted company in 1947, at the handover of power in India. Jim went to East Africa and settled there in Nyerere, Tanzania. His vast experience of the jungles and success as a shikari were later put to good use, during the Second World War, when he was given a staff appointment at the HQ of Eastern Army India, as lecturer in jungle lore and of course was connected with the jungle training of the Chindits.

There was a Mr. Shepherd who had owned a saw mill at a forest depot between Hildwani and Bareilly and he also had a taxidermist business at Bhowali, a pretty little hill station five miles from Nainital. I took the two skins to Mr. Shepherd in Bhowali and asked him to mount them and set them up. This took six months but two very fine trophies resulted from it.

In addition to the very pleasant social life of Nainital, the yacht club dances, the regattas etc, there were also very many pretty rides which could be undertaken to Bhowali, Sattal, a place which really means 'Seven Lakes', and other lovely picnic spots. On days when the 20,000 foot snows were visible from Cheena Peak, a white flag was hoisted on the flagstaff on a mountain ridge east of the lake and parties would make their way to Cheena to picnic and see the snows before returning.

When my leave was over I returned to Bareilly but in July Edna phoned me one evening to say that Brian, who had had gastro-enteritis, had also been attacked by pneumonia. His condition became worse and two days later Edna telephoned to say that he was very, very ill and that the doctors wanted me to go up to Nainital immediately.

Brigade HQ granted me leave and I drove like one possessed the 90 miles up to Nainital. I left my car at the motor stand above the lake I hurried up the hillside to the hospital where Brian was being treated. Seeing him, my heart sank. He had lost seven pounds in weight and his cheeks were sunken but he raised a smile when he saw me. In despair, nothing I thought could save him, as he was only a year old. At that moment into the room walked Father Amadeus, a wonderful old Jesuit priest, well-known in the Kumaon hills and he prayed by the bedside. We were not Roman Catholics but the innate goodness of the venerable priest did help raise our spirits and miraculously Brian began to recover after only a day or two.

Immediately afterwards, Edna herself was taken ill and had to be sent to the military hospital at Rhanikhet 60 miles away in the hills for x-rays, where the cause of the illness was diagnosed. However, a little later I was posted to the detachment at Rani Bagh and at weekends, and sometimes during the week, had to opportunity to go to Nainital to see them, when Edna eventually returned from Rhanikhet.

The Rani Bagh detachment was for me a nearly perfect appointment, the camp being set as it was the entrance of the valley above which Nainital lay and surrounded by thousands of square miles of the Turi jungle.

My section, being employed on the movement of troops in the hills, would proceed from camp down to the railheads at Rhanikhet and Bhowalikhet, then to the military hill stations, 100 miles into the Himalayas and return to Rani Bagh the following day. The whole route was through lovely mountain scenery, the air was cool and the work could not have been in more pleasant conditions.

Returning from convoy one day, I found great excitement in the camp. The previous afternoon the men had been playing basketball on a piece of ground just behind the camp, where about 20 yards away was a buffalo grazing. Without any warning, a tiger galloped out from some bushes and scrub and attacked and killed the buffalo. The men who were at the time withdrawing towards their tents had then shouted at the tiger, which started drag the kill to the edge of the nulla, down the bank into a dry area of nullah bed, where it began to feed. After a short time it left the kill and went up the nullah into the jungle on the far side.

The tiger had fed on the kill during the night and just before my convoy had got back into camp, had been seen crossing the nullah. It had been lost to sight in a dense patch of jungle just in front of the forest bungalow and between the nullah and the motor road.

I knew there was a good chance that the tiger would still be in the patch of jungle so calling for a motorcycle, I strapped my rifle-case on the carrier, put Tom my spaniel on the tank in front of me and rode up the bridle-path for about a mile to a point where the patch of jungle ended. I thought that if the tiger could be moved from the dense patch of cover it was in, it would probably re-cross the nullah to the hill forest on the far side rather than attempt to cross the motor road, on which there was still a fair amount of traffic both vehicle and pedestrian.

Once stopped, I assembled my rifle and moving into the nullah commenced walking down towards the bungalow. I sent Tom into the jungle and, busily wagging his tail and sniffing hard in all directions, he was soon lost from view. I moved slowly down the nullah and had only gone about 20 yards when there was a loud yelp from Tom who came galloping out the jungle, his tail between his legs. He rushed to my feet and stood against me trembling, looking back into the jungle. Poor Tom was badly frightened. There was no other sound to indicate what had frightened the dog but it may have been the tiger.

The light was fading by then, and nothing more could be done, so I returned to the Rani Bagh bungalow. My attempt to flush the tiger with a cocker spaniel may seem unorthodox and perhaps a little unfeeling but it was not so. Normally a tiger would move into other cover if disturbed or if not would not do anything to disclose his position.

I proceed to Ranikhet again the next day and in the evening some villagers saw a tiger drinking at a pool in the nullah and warned the Indian officers in the camp. They came out and had a shot from a safe distance with a shotgun, which elicited an enormous roar from the tiger that then disappeared, as did my hopes of getting it on that occasion.

On another morning, as I started for Ranikhet in my staff car, I came upon an enormous hamadryad stretched right across the road. The hamadryad, or king cobra, is the largest poisonous snake in the world and its venom the deadliest of all. It is also a vicious snake and will, more often than not, attack human beings on sight. They can move as quickly as a galloping horse and are a terrifying creature to meet if one has not a shotgun or a rifle. I ran right over the hamadryad and it rolled off into the undergrowth like a big cartwheel. When I came down the hill the following day I took a party of troops and searched the jungle but did not find the snake. It must have been fatally injured and probably hid into a hole to die.

At the end of September, Edna and Brian came down to stay at Rani Bagh but soon orders arrived transferring me to Agra city. We moved at the end of October. I was rather sad at leaving Rani Bagh and the lovely valleys, and forest and Kumaon Himalayas.

Chapter 15

The Phantom Mughals

"If there is a paradise on earth it is here,
it is here, it is here."

(Attributed to Emperor Jehangir,
4th Mughal Emperor, 1605 to 1627)

We stood at the great archway of the entrance gate, looked down at the dark avenue of cypress trees bordering the water and saw it before us in all its exquisite beauty. The great white marble building was shimmering in the bright afternoon sun and the perfect dome appeared to be floating in the clear blue sky.

Tall slender minarets, at the four corners of the great marble courtyard in which the building stood, completed the loveliness of the whole scene. This was the Taj Mahal, one of the wonders of the world, perhaps the most perfect building ever created by man, and its beauty completely fulfilling the expectations that we had held in anticipation of that moment.

I have visited the Taj Mahal on very many occasions since then, by day and night, in the glaring afternoon sun of the hot weather, in the light of the full moon, at dawn and sunset and never have I not been thrilled by its perfect beauty. This poem in marble marking the immortal love of a man and a woman draws one to it again and again, and its loveliness will only cease to give contentment to the soul of man when it crumbles into dust.

As one walks down the Approach Avenue and then climbs the staircase onto the great white marble courtyard, the grandeur of the Taj becomes apparent. There is a great arch over the entrance to the building, soaring over 100 feet high. The external walls are completely covered in a tracery of precious and semi-precious stones in delicate flower patterns, inlaid in the white marble walls, all with inscriptions from the Koran and endless repetitions of the hundred wonderful names of God.

Past the main hall under the gigantic dome, any noise created echoes round and round. At the centre is a circular screen carved out of pure white marble with such superb artistry that it appears to be to be a lovely lace curtain. Inside this screen are the facsimile tombs of Shah Jahan and his empress Mumtaz Begum, for whom he built this glory of love. A short distance away, some steps lead down to the tomb chamber proper in which are other sarcophagi containing the illustrious remains but even in that sacred place the avarice and greed of human nature are present. The guides of the tomb place coins and notes on the sarcophagi with the object of inducing visitors to do the same. During the 1939-45 war, when thousands of American troops visited Agra, a golden harvest was reaped by these guides.

North of the Taj Mahal runs the river Jamuna [now Yamuna] and from the courtyard can be seen on the opposite bank of the river the foundations for another building which was to have been identical to the Taj but in black marble. However, this was not to be. Before his great design had begun to materialise, Shah Jahan had been driven from this throne. He was imprisoned in Agra fort by his son, Aurangzeb.

From there, in a small balcony room, he could look down the river at the marble glory that he had caused to be erected to the memory of his beloved wife.

There are many beautiful and interesting buildings in and around Agra. The great fort is still in a state of perfect preservation, with a lovely little pearl mosque in which the Moghul emperors worshipped and the tomb of I'timad-ud-Daula [the grandfather of Mumtaz Begum] in a delightful garden on the banks of the Jamuna.

Seven miles away at Sikandra is the tomb of the emperor Akbar, a building in the oriental style of domes and minarets that are to be found all over India. In the gardens surrounding the tomb is a pack of tame langur monkeys and they are fed well by visitors. On one occasion I offered some grain on the palm of my hand to the head of the pack and it looked over and squatted down in front of me. The langur held my wrist with one hand and then started stuffing the grain into its pouches. When the grain had nearly all gone I attempted to withdraw my hand but the langur held it in an incredibly strong grip. I was, at that time, a powerful man and I exerted a lot of force to withdraw my hand but the vice-like grip of the langur held me quite firmly. It showed its large white razor-sharp teeth several times, so I let it finish the grain without further demand.

Perhaps the most famous and important historical monument, after the Taj, is the deserted city of Fatehpur Sikri, 26 miles from Agra. It is a magnificent red sandstone city of victory, built by the emperor Akbar to celebrate his conquest of Gujarat and the gift of a son to one of his wives. The birth of a son had been predicted by the Mohammadan saint, Shaikh

Salim Chishti, whose tomb is in the courtyard of Fatehpur Sikri.

Akbar moved the whole of his court there from Agra but within 25 years his magnificent courtyards and buildings were deserted, as the city had to be abandoned because of a lack of water. The walls and many buildings are all perfectly preserved and contain many interesting traces of the Panch Mahal, a pagoda-like building where Akbar's queens lived.

In a lower courtyard is an enormous stone chessboard laid out in five feet squares, on which living chessmen moved according to the instructions of the emperor who sat on a black stone throne in the centre. I think, however, the most impressive site is the Buland Darwaza (i.e. the gate of victory) by which one enters the great courtyard. The city is built on a low hill and the Panch Mahal approached by a very wide staircase, at the top of which is the enormous arch of the gate of victory towering more than 120 feet high.

It was a boiling hot day when I first visited Fatehpur Sikri and as I climbed the stairway there were many lizards lying in the sun and immediately came to my mind Omar Khayyam's quote, "They say the lion, the lizard keep the courts where Jamshyd [the fourth Shah of the mythological Pishdadian dynasty of Iran] gloried and drank deep".

Of course, it was included in the itinerary of every round the world cruise liner which visited India. Tourists left Bombay on special tourist coaches and on arrival at Agra were accommodated in Lauries Hotel, in which we were living, and the Hotel Cecil.

In the evenings, as the visitors sat on the hotel veranda after a strenuous day sightseeing, a conjuror and a birdman would entertain them. The conjuror would perform the mango tree trick, but he had a small tent and various props to assist him and his trick did not compare with the performance that I had I seen at Ahmednagar in 1927. The birdman had a cage-full of sparrows dyed in various colours and he had trained them to perform some incredible tricks.

He told one bird to fly up the tree and bring back a leaf which it promptly did, tearing a leaf off with his beak and flying back to the bird man. The other bird would pick out small cardboard discs with a number written on them, collecting the correct disk as the number was called. The nalli, the bird man, put a charge of gunpowder into a small brass saluting cannon about 10 inches long. One bird hopped on to the barrel of the cannon and a smouldering match was given to the other bird, which took it in its beak and placed it in the hole in the priming chamber of the cannon, which went off with a terrific report. The birds were completely unconcerned.

One morning in January 1933 one of the spaniels belonging to Captain and Mrs Osmond, who were in a suite next to ours in the hotel, seemed to be behaving queerly, and on being taken to the vet it was found to have rabies. This necessitated the Osmond's two spaniels and Tom being put down and both of our families had to undergo the anti-rabies treatment immediately, in addition to all the servants and any friends who may have visited us in the past few days. The total number of persons involved was 26

We all had to have 14 injections of the serum in the stomach. The first two injections were quite unpleasant and somewhat painful because our stomachs became very sore. It was particularly trying for the ladies as they were both expecting babies in the spring and also to listen to the anguished cries of the children at the thrust of the needle. Brian was only then just over 18 months and the Osmond's small daughter was about the same age. This experience and the sadness that I felt as poor Tom was led away to his fate made me vow that I would not again keep a dog while in India.

Agra was however a very pleasant station. The British regiment was the First Battalion of the King's Own Yorkshire Light Infantry (KOYLI) which had been in Peshawar in 1930 when I was there. With the Civil Service, police officials and the small European business community, a pleasant social life centred on the club. On occasions the dances at the club were attended by visitors from the cruising lines coming from Bombay.

There was a carpet factory in Agra. It was possible for us to go down at intervals and watch the carpet we had ordered being made on the looms. The small boys sitting at large wooden frames threaded the colours in and out of the string warp, on orders shouted by a man who had a coloured diagram of the carpet. Artists were at work in the drawing room and we had selected the design, from which our carpet was made. The carpet which was 14 feet by 12 and with a nice deep pile, was 100 rupees, which in those days was the equivalent of £7/10/-. [£7.50]

There were two brothers living in Agra at the time, Anthony and Lord John, one in his sixties and the other in his seventies. They had an enormous bungalow in a large garden and threw terrific parties. They were Armenian in origin. The family had arrived in India about the same time as the first Europeans and, known as the 'John Company', had established themselves as traders in Agra. When the East India Company's expansion reached the area, they were regarded as part of the old trading establishment. In the early part of this century the John Company built some cotton mills in Agra which are, as far as I know, in operation to this day. [1974]

In the 1930s the company was in financial difficulties and a court case was proceeding, which had been going on, when we arrived, for about two years. Despite this, the brothers continued their lavish hospitality and it was rumoured that the cost of their entertaining was all put down to legal expenses.

In February Edna went home to England to await the arrival of our second child and I went to live in a bungalow in the civil lines with Hubert Evans, the City Magistrate and Mr. Wingfield, an assistant superintendent of police, two friends who were of course in touch with every facet of life in Agra and it was fascinating for me to hear something of their work.

One day Hubert Evans said that communal trouble was brewing between the Hindus and Mohammedans and the police were taking precautionary measures. Each party was ready to fly at each other's throats on any pretext, and on this occasion, a Mohammedan funeral procession taking the corpse for interment in their own burial ground had chosen a route across which was a wall owned by Hindus. The Mohammedans said that their religion forbade them lifting the body over the wall and demanded the wall should be broken down. The Hindu appealed to the police to protect his property and eventually the funeral party was persuaded to take another route.

However, the next day another Mohammedan funeral procession appeared and again crossed the wall, which by then had been broken down. This time a large crowd of Mohammedans had gathered and the police had difficulty dispersing the mob. Several days after that, the Mohammedans managed to provide yet another corpse and repeat the attacks but eventually order was maintained and after a few cases of this sort in the city, the trouble subsided.

One night a terrible murder occurred. A man who suspected his young wife, only 25, of having an affair with his own brother, had murdered her in a most brutal fashion, cutting her throat and mutilating her although she was pregnant. It came out later that having committed the murder in daylight, he went into the bazaar to a tea shop and sat waiting, drinking tea, until he was arrested by the police. In due course he was tried, sentenced to death and hanged.

At the handover of power in India in 1947 Hubert was offered an appointment in the British diplomatic service and in due course became our ambassador in [South] Korea and later ambassador in Nicaragua.

Chapter 16

The Tiger that got away

In April 1933, having obtained a shooting permit again for the Togari block and made the necessary arrangements, I took ten days' leave and once more found myself in the Sonapani forest rest house, where Shere Singh, the old shikari, greeted me with a broad grin and told me there were lots of tigers in the block.

Buffaloes were tied up that night, and although none were taken, I saw the pugs of a very big tiger in a nullah leading up to the spot where I had shot the big tiger the previous year, and I decided to sit up that evening over a live buffalo in the same place as before. I came to the machan at about 4pm and from it I looked directly down the broad fire line cut through the forest. At about 5.30pm I was looking up the valley when I heard an animal galloping over the leaves and a snort from the buffalo. I turned my head and caught a fleeting glimpse of a tigress disappearing out of sight below the machan. Silence for a few minutes, then I heard the tigress start to run and she came into view leaping over the buffalo's back, striking at his neck with her claws as she did so.

The buffalo dropped its head and brought his sharp horns forward causing the tigress to jink in mid-air but no sooner than she had alighted on the ground, she leapt back over the buffalo's head, striking at him again and the buffalo, using his horns again, prevented her from doing him any serious damage. At the second attempt, the tigress ran into a patch of grass at the edge of the nullah, about 40 yards from the machan and sat up in the grass looking at the buffalo.

I had been fascinated by this jungle encounter but realised I might lose the tigress unless I acted quickly. It was impossible to get a shot at her sitting down in the machan, so I decided to risk standing up, taking a shot over the top of the machan. I managed to stand up and come into the aim without attracting the tigress's attention. I shot at her head and she dropped and did not move.

The buffalo had one or two scratches on its neck but otherwise seemed unharmed and it was soon placidly eating his grass again. I resigned myself to an uncomfortable night in the machan. Twenty minutes later the quiet of the jungle evening was broken by the loud distinctive sound of the sambar as it delved some distance down the fire line.

There was immediately the low grumble of a tiger, coming from the point where the fire line turned out of view round the hillside and I saw a large tiger move quickly across the fire line and disappear into the jungle. The tiger would most likely make its way down to the junction of the fire line and the nullah where I was sitting up. It must have been one of its favourite routes and I arranged my position so I could take aim and fire the moment the tiger arrived.

A few moments later, there was a noise in the undergrowth in front of me and the tiger came galloping into view. With a bound it hurled itself onto the buffalo and biting it over the back of the neck, promptly appeared to break the neck with a wrench of its paw. The tiger dropped to the ground with the buffalo in its mouth directly in front of the machan. I was forced to take the head shot and I aimed and fired.

On the shot the tiger released the buffalo, jumped up and bounded across the fire line into the jungle on the hillside. As it reached the edge of the fire line, it hit a tree but picked itself up and was gone. While watching this, I heard the buffalo take a deep breath and when I looked down he was standing up breathing heavily and eventually settled down to feed again.

I was disappointed and annoyed over this turn of events, as I was certain I had hit the tiger or it would not have struck the tree. At the same time I now had to resign myself to waiting the whole night in the machan and I was unable to sleep.

At about 10pm a cold breeze began blowing down the valley from the mountains and soon mutterings of thunder and flashes of lightning in the hills showed a storm was approaching. Eventually it started to rain and developed into a torrential downpour. Enormous flashes of zigzag lightning scarred the heavens and the roaring wind became very cold. Fortunately, I was partly protected from the rain by the thick foliage of the tree but my clothes were soaked.

The thunder and lightning became more intense and shortly there was a blinding flash and a crashing sound in the jungle some 60 yards away, as a tree was struck down by lightning. Eventually the storm died down and at long last the dawn came.

I got out of the machan went over to the tigress, not of great length but with a nicely marked skin. On the arrival of Shere Singh and the coolies, I quickly organised the follow-up of the second tiger and we began to move forward in bounds. The look-out in the tree would give us the all-clear signal. The storm had obliterated all signs of the tiger and as the jungle was very dense, we were only able to advance slowly.

We had gone perhaps 200 yards when, from an area of bushes and grasses ahead, there was a thunderous roar. My rifle was at the ready in an instant. I peered hard into the undergrowth but could see nothing. Shere Singh had slipped into a crouching attitude and was looking into the scrub just above ground level. The complete silence after the earth-shaking roar was nerve-wracking, as there was no indication as to where the tiger was, while at any moment there might be a charge.

Suddenly Shere Singh said, "Vah ja raha hai", i.e. "He is going away". Bending down, I could just see an animal in the bush about 50 yards away, the limit of visibility at the time. We moved on for another hour but as there was no sign at all of the tiger, I returned to my sitting-up place and arranged for the tigress to be taking to Sonapani for skinning.

The buffalo had a swollen throat from the scratches and teeth wounds from the big tiger. There was no mark on its horns or any sign of the bullet hitting the ground in the vicinity and there was no blood trail. I think the high velocity bullet must have been deflected by touching the buffalo's horn which was in front of the tiger's head and given the tiger a nasty whack on the frontal bone between the eyes. This would have caused it to momentarily lose control and explain why it had hit the tree. The deflected bullet wound would probably have given the tiger a terrific headache as well, but there would not be much blood.

I made several more attempts in the next few days to track this tiger down but there were no reports of anything unusual in the area, such as an attack on human beings. It had been a most unusual experience, as very few hunters have seen a tiger actually attack its prey and I had had two examples in the space of an hour, each mode of attack being different because of the different sizes of the tigers involved. In the end the poor buffalo eventually recovered from its wounds.

One day a telegram forwarded to me from Agra arrived at the forest rest house, informing me that Edna and I were now the proud parents of a baby daughter whom we had decided to name Valerie. I could hardly fail to remember Valerie's birthday as it was that night I had spent in the machan during the dreadful tropical storm.

A few days later I was back in the searing heat of Agra and late one afternoon, as Hubert and Winfield and I were waiting for the sun to drop low enough to enable us to go and play tennis, a dust storm began to blow up. It became stronger and soon the sound was a roar. The sky was hidden with a red cloud of dust and it began to get dark. A violent wind was now tearing branches off the trees, many of which were blown down and within minutes it became pitch black. It was literally impossible to see one's hand in front of one's eyes, and ears and nose were clogged with dust and sand. To shelter from the storm we got into the bungalow and closed all doors, windows and shutters but it was of little use. The storm passed and the light returned. Everything was covered with a layer of fine dust and it took many days to get things clean again. I couldn't sleep at all that night and drank glass after glass of cold lemon squash. At 2.30 am the thermometer registered a temperature of 103 degrees Fahrenheit [39 degrees C.] inside the bungalow.

In May I received news from my brother Leslie, who was then superintendent of police at Shahjehanpur and who was not at all well. I obtained three days leave to go and see him. I made it over to Shahjehanpur, making the crossing of the Ganges at Fatehgarh, where my experiences of the long road journey of 1929 stood me in good stead, enabling me to cross without difficulty.

Fortunately, Leslie soon recovered from his indisposition and I was able to go round with him and get to know a little of how law and order were maintained in an Indian district. On these outings in the forest area about 30 miles from Shahjehanpur, the local notables, landowners and magistrates suggested we should have a beat for game. The beat was to be in a strip of jungle about a mile wide which ran from the main forest along the side of a large irrigation canal for two or three miles.

A set of twelve machans was put up near the end of the strip of jungle and one dozen coolies assembled from nearby villages. When all were in the machans the beat started, at a distance of about one and a half miles to the north of the guns. Very soon birds and animals began to appear in the jungle ahead and the odd barking deer and hog deer, pea fowl and jungle fowl. The beating continued and as the beat got closer yet more animals began to come out. We saw several small herds of chital and sambar; at the conclusion of the beat it was found that our party had shot 19 deer, which meant a welcome supply of meat to the local villagers.

In August 1933 I went home to England on two month's leave, to escort Edna and the children back to India and Agra. On our return in October, we occupied bungalow, number 1 Taj Road. It was about one mile from the Taj Mahal.

One day as we were having lunch, I felt an earth tremor and saw the electric lampshade swaying from side to side. I shouted to Edna, "Earthquake, get the children!" We dashed into the nursery where the children were resting, picked them up and ran outside into the open garden away from the bungalow, followed by the bearer and ayah.

The tremors were now very violent and the iron electric lamp standards on the roadside were shaking furiously. The tremors continued for about two minutes and then subsided. Afterwards, I inspected the bungalow and as there appeared to be no sign of serious damage at all we went inside again.

This was part of the the great earthquake that devastated the provinces of Bihar and Orissa, killing hundreds of people and destroying thousands of buildings. Enormous cracks appeared in the ground and the level of stretches of country for miles on end was altered. In one place the great Ganges River disappeared into the ground.

Practically everybody's thoughts in Agra flew to the Taj Mahal, but very fortunately, only slight damage occurred to one of the minarets and the glorious building was itself unharmed, partly due, perhaps, to its firm foundations and the excellence of its structure. The vast tomb at Sikandrabad was damaged rather badly and a number of houses in Agra city were damaged or destroyed but without loss of life.

We were due to go on one year's furlough in April 1934 and one evening when sitting in the club on the lawn having chota pegs with several officers, I said,

"I'd like to get another tiger before I go home on leave, I think I'll pop up to Haldwani and get one". They were amused at this, especially a Captain MacLachlan, who had done a lot of shooting in East Africa, but had not bagged a tiger.

I wrote to Donald Stewart the divisional forest office of the Hildwani division and got a permit for the Chakrata block which was at the foot of Nainital hill and ran approximately south-east for seven or eight miles from the motor road. I made all the necessary arrangements to be put into operation for when I arrived at the block. The forest rest house in the Chakrata block was called, the 'Eseldion' forest bungalow. I had only a week before I would have to return to Agra to catch the homeward bound P&O mail ship.

At the block a buffalo had been taken the previous night and the half-eaten remains dragged up a very steep hillside for about two hundred feet. The kill had been left on a small ledge and I was forced to put the machan in a small tree jutting out at an angle from the hillside. While I was in the machan, the tree quivered with the slightest movement and the hill rose so steeply above me it was possible for the tiger to look straight down into my position.

Nightfall came and as the tiger had not arrived, I decided to try and sleep. At 9pm a tiger moaned several times from the hillside above me and later I heard an animal making its way down towards the machan. I was absolutely immobile for about half an hour but nothing further happened and then I heard the tiger again moving on the hillside above me. No other tiger came to the remains of the kill that night.

It is my belief that the tiger did come down the hill to feed on the kill but saw the machan and went away. The next morning on returning to the bungalow, I found that another buffalo had been killed by a tiger at another nullah. The buffalo, which had been securely fastened to a tree, had not been dragged and very little of it had been eaten, indicating that the kill had only probably been made a few hours before and that the tiger might return.

Walking down the forest road to the bungalow with the shikari and coolies, I looked up the nullah and there about 75 yards on a large granite boulder was a beautiful panther. Not wanting to disturb the jungle, with a shot that might miss from that distance, I hurried towards the animal but he immediately bounded off the boulder and disappeared on the hillside.

Later that day the machan was erected over the second kill and I was inside at 4pm. The shikari and coolies had hardly left the kill, when above me a deer started calling in the nullah behind. It kept on barking so I craned my neck round to look up the nullah and soon I saw a magnificent tiger come into view about 100 yards away. It came closer and when about 50 yards off, it stopped behind a clump of bamboos. At that moment a convoy of several bullock carts came down the road from the direction of the bungalow and having crossed the nullah, halted close by and began to cook a meal aboard their bullock carts, making quite a lot of noise. They were completely unaware of my presence or that of the tiger. I was very frustrated about this situation because I was sure their presence that would drive the tiger away from the kill. At the same time the deer had stopped barking and I could see no sign of it.

After an hour the bullock carts moved on again and very shortly after that the deer began barking again. I looked round and to my amazement saw the tiger coming right down in line with the machan only about 15 yards away. I could still hear the bullock cart drivers talking. I held my breath and kept my eyes fixed on the kill. A few seconds later the tiger appeared to be right under me and with easy lovely grace softly padded towards the kill. Once at the kill it stopped and gazed intently down the nullah for perhaps five seconds and then looked slowly to the left and right.

I had in the meantime aligned my rifle on the tiger and was ready to take my shot. The tiger then lowered his head. He bit into the buffalo's shoulder and as he did so I aimed at the tiger's neck, immediately behind the ear and fired. The tiger dropped in his tracks and lay on his left side without the slightest movement. It had been killed instantly by the first shot.

It was a magnificent sight as the tiger lay there in the mellow evening light. Its striped skin had the deep golden of a tiger in its prime and would add one more marvellous trophy to my bag. While I admired the tiger, I thought of the undoubted envy that would be felt by many of Agra's sportsman and was rather pleased that I was able to do what I had said I would do.

The light then quickly faded and darkness descended with tropic suddenness. I was nearly five miles from the forest bungalow and though it would probably have been quite safe to walk back there, except for a possible chance encounter with a bear or hamadryad which would have been very unpleasant in the dark, I decided to stay in the machan overnight.

At dawn, Shere Singh and the coolies arrived and once I had called them forward to the machan the usual procedure of admiring the great beast began. I set them to work quickly to make a stretcher to carry it back to the forest rest house and sent off a man to collect some more coolies at a woodcutter's camp about a mile away, as the heavy tiger's carcass was too much for my own men.

I sent a messenger to Haldwani telegraph office five miles away to dispatch a telegram to Mr. Shepherd at Blalpur, to meet the train the following evening, and take the skin for curing and setting up. Skinning was completed the following day. The next morning I boarded the Agra mail, and Mr. Shepherd was standing on the platform at Lalitpur when the train arrived. I handed over the skin to him and told him I was going on a year's leave immediately, after arriving at Agra and would take delivery of the skin on my return.

That evening I was back in Agra and we departed for Bombay on Friday, sailing from there on the P&O liner, RMS *Maloja*, for home. From Edna's point of view it was not a good voyage. The sea was very rough all the way from Aden and the Red Sea was very hot indeed. From Port Said to Gibraltar we had a very rough passage in the Mediterranean. Unsurprisingly, Edna was confined to her cabin for most of the voyage and the cares and duties of a father were thick and fast upon me. Brian was nearly three years old and Valerie almost a year which resulted in me having to make five bottles a day and feed the baby, take Brian to the saloon for his meals, visit Edna frequently to see if she required any attention, have my own meals, pushing the perambulator up and down the deck most of the day and change nappies as required.

We were in Gibraltar on April 18th, Valerie's birthday, and went ashore to look round the town. Edna returned on a tender to the boat about half an hour before the last one, which I intended to go on, sailed. I arrived at the ship, to find a friend of ours standing at the head of the ship's gangway, who said, "Something awful has happened. Go to the ship's surgery immediately".

I went down to the surgery and found the ship's sister holding Valerie in her arms, a great wound on the left side of her head. The baby was not unconscious, but she was whimpering. Edna was in a dreadful state and I really felt awful myself. The surgeon said that the only hope was to get ashore immediately for an operation and he signalled the British military hospital near the top of the Rock.

While waiting for the ambulance to arrive, Edna related what had happened. She had put Valerie on the bunk while she changed her frock and the baby had over-balanced and fallen forward, catching her head against the sharp iron corner of a life-jacket cage, which was situated between the dressing table in the cabin and the bunk, causing a deep fracture of the skull above the left ear.

Having collected nursery items and clothing for ourselves and the children, we packed two suitcases and went down the ship's gangway where a launch had been made ready for us and we left for the shore. When we arrived there, a military ambulance was waiting and we were taken to the British military hospital immediately. After examining Valerie the surgical specialist told us he would operate the following day, and although it was very serious he told us that he had every hope, a baby's skull being so soft and pliant, that an operation would be successful. The operation lasted three hours, which seemed like an eternity but at last a nurse appeared carrying a small white bundle in her arms and as she went by, told us all was well.

In a day or two Valerie was remarkable lively and the plaster of paris wound round her head did not seem to worry her at all. We had to wait a month before we could continue the journey and when we knew that Valerie would make a complete return to normal health, enjoyed the remainder of our stay in Gibraltar very much. It was of course a godsend that we were actually in harbour. If it had happened at sea, the result might have been very different.

The hotel where we stayed was a first-class place in every way and we were able to go on many interesting picnics and trips into southern Spain. The re-organisation of the defence of Gibraltar had just been completed by the Royal Engineers, which included the installation of the latest 9.2-inch heavy artillery to all of the bastions and gun emplacements. We were taken round the rock defences by a Lieutenant Colonel of the Royal Engineers, and we climbed right to the top of a ridge, where we saw a great gun which had just been installed.

The living quarters of the crew, electric powerhouse, magazines etc were all cut out of the rock below the gun emplacement. I was also taken to the tunnel, which had been driven right through the width of the rock from side to side and gave access to the great water reservoirs that had been excavated there, some of them having a capacity of over one million gallons.

While we were there, on one day, gun practice was being held at towed targets in the Straits. One of the reports sounded rather strange to me and I said to Edna, "I think that was a premature", and so it proved to be. A great 9.2 shell had gone off in the breach, completely wrecking the gun and killing or wounding all of the crew. It was a very rare occurrence with such a type of weapon.

Our journey home was completed on RMS *Strathnaver*, which was boarded by a large contingent of high-spirited boys and girls returning to school in England. Their escapades kept the crew on tenterhooks, and one caused a great deal of amusement. A couple who had been married just before the ship sailed, were going to England on their honeymoon and it happened that their cabin was next to one occupied by some school children. The children knew about this and bored a hole in the wooden partitions between the cabins. The unsuspecting couple returned to the cabin for a night of love and passion and at the appropriate moment, the miscreants in the adjoining cabin squirted ink all over them from a syringe. On another occasion they set all the fire alarms onboard ringing, which was of course a most dangerous thing to do.

By the time we arrived in London, Valerie was in great form and bubbling over with good health. She was then put in the charge of a charming and most competent northern nurse, and we looked forward to a pleasant leave.

As I was to leave tiger land for several years, it may be of interest here to refer to the question of the conservation of the tiger by wildlife authorities which is now being undertaken [at the time of recording in 1974]. They estimate the tiger population in India is approximately 1,800 [now c. 3,000 in the early 2020s]. In the 1920s or 1930s the tiger population had been 75,000 to 80,000. As I have already noted in most parts of India, except in the United Provinces, there was no limit on the number of tigers that could be shot but nevertheless there were always tigers in most of the jungle blocks, and sportsmen continued to obtain good bags.

In Hyderabad State and Rewa State in the Central Provinces, only the rulers and most eminent personages likes the Viceroy and governors of provinces were permitted to shoot, however, tigers had become so numerous they were a real burden on the peasant farmers. In Hyderabad, the Nizam was asked in 1928 to carry out improvements in the organisation and administration of the state, one of which was to open the reserve tiger forest, which had been hitherto kept for his use, to the general public.

European hunters in the Christmas camp of 1928 shot 80 tigers in the ten days. One of them was 'Panther Smith', who bagged 14 alone. In the mid-1930s the Maharajah of Rewa had shot over 1000 tigers and the Maharajah of Cooch Behar about 800 tigers. It should be realised that each full-grown tiger kills the equivalent of 100 cattle or game in a year and it is essential that the cultivator's and farmer's livelihoods should be protected.

Despite this heavy shooting, the tiger maintained its numbers and there were still around 40,000 when British rule ended in India in 1947. Some sources in India have stated that shooting under British rule, was kept for the British officials, army officers etc.

This is entirely wrong. Anybody of a certain status (with appropriate experience and proficiency) could apply to the divisional forest officers for shooting permits and they were issued in strict order of priority of receipt. The number of permits issued was only limited by the number of shooting blocks available, with special regulations for dealing with cases when a man-eater was in a particular area or where forest work was being carried out. The present situation [in 1974] is due entirely to the lack of control and the lack of proper regulations for the preservation and the shooting of game, since British rule ended in India in 1947. It cannot be blamed on the administration of the British Raj.

In 1942-44 my younger brother, Leslie, was seconded to the Indian Political Service and was assistant resident in central India. The state was Rewa, the home of the white tiger and of the Maharajah, with his 1,000 tigers shooting record.

On the other hand it is essential the balance of nature be preserved. If tigers are shot out, then pigs and herds of deer increase and will also, in their turn, do immense damage to the cultivators' crops. Wildlife and conservation needs constant and active supervision, like any well-managed activity.

Chapter 17

Return to India

In November 1934, I was notified that at the end of my leave I would be posted to a mechanical transport company at Mir Ali in Waziristan. As it was likely that I would carry out a two-year tour of duty on the frontier, we decided that Edna and the children should remain in England until the time was opportune for them to return to India.

At the time, my mother and father were living in Heliopolis near Cairo and my brother was superintendent of police at Lalitpur in the United Provinces. I left England six weeks before my leave was due to end, to spend some time with my parents at Heliopolis and then with my brother, perhaps on a tiger shoot, at Lalitpur.

I arrived at Heliopolis in February in 1935 and decided to see as much of Cairo and Egypt as I could during my stay. In the company of my parents or their friends, I visited the Pyramids and Sphinx on several occasions and was able to examine them and gain quite a useful knowledge of their construction, architecture and history.

The attractive Mina House Hotel, quite close to the Great Pyramid, with its lovely gardens and cool swimming pool was a very pleasant place to spend an afternoon and evening, when not sightseeing. While staying there, we had the opportunity to go to several very enjoyable dances.

A village called Matariya, not far from Heliopolis, had a splendid obelisk and an ancient well and tree under which the holy family were supposed to have halted during their flight into Egypt. There was a lovely little church nearby and I was vividly aware of the sacredness of that holy place.

In Cairo there was the Citadel and the great mosque to visit. Contemporary attractions were the Shepheard's Hotel and Roofie's restaurant together with other places of rendezvous for Europeans; in fact all nationalities. Monday night was English night at Roofie's, just as Wednesday night might be French night or German night.

Drinking coffee on the veranda at the Shepheard's Hotel, (here I refer to the old Shepheard's Hotel, burned down during riots in 1952) was very pleasant. On any day, on walking down the steps into the street one was immediately besieged by Egyptian dragomen [interpreter, translator and guide] offering to show you the sights of the bazaar and also with 'French photographs' for sale.

I spent many hours in the museum of antiquities and was enthralled by the wonderful exhibits from the tomb of Tutankhamen, which occupied one whole wing of the museum and had been completed only a short time before, for opening to the public. The coffin of gold, massively embellished with precious jewels and wonderful carvings and hieroglyphs is breathtaking in its perfection of craftsmanship. The other thousands of exhibits from the tomb are also most impressive and wonderful work has been done with cleaning, preservation and reconstruction, so that one can actually see and wonder at the magnificence and the culture of this oldest of civilisations.

The Great Sphinx [at Giza] came fully up to my expectations and this, one of the mightiest of monuments ever erected by man, gave a tremendous impression of what it is possible for people to achieve in an organised society.

One afternoon two shipboard friends, on the journey to Port Said, and I went to the bazaar area of Cairo, known as the Mushqi, [now the Khan el-Khalili bazaar] to see the native shops and wares they had for sale. Eventually we arrived at the shop of a carpet and perfume merchant that had been recommended to us. The entrance was through the wall on a very narrow street and then we found ourselves in a spacious courtyard which led into a large room furnished with low divans, many cushions etc. and the whole floor was covered with rich oriental carpets. We were received by the proprietor and a relative and while we supped strong black coffee and smoked some excellent Egyptian cigarettes, we were offered carpets for display and also some oriental silk ware. This was very interesting and then, after a while, the proprietor enquired if we were interested in purchasing what he called 'umber' which was produced in a tiny porcelain pot. It turned out that, according to our host's description, it was a very strong aphrodisiac. The price quoted was outrageous and in any event we said we were not interested. In a final effort to make a sale he produced his order book and there showed us an order for an appreciable quantity of 'umber' from a well-known personage in England who was entertaining a large party of guests in his 'dahabiah', or houseboat, on the Nile at the time.

At a race meeting at the attractive Heliopolis racecourse there was a horse running called Sergeant Major, which I could not resist putting a bet on and Sergeant Major duly won at a nice price, which added to the enjoyment of the occasion.

At the end of my pleasant stay in Cairo, I boarded the *Strathnaver* at Port Said. Among the other passengers there was a conducted party of American world tourists. The party consisted of the conductor and guide, who handled all travel arrangements and planned the trip, an elderly gentleman, a youth of about 18 and seven ladies. As soon as I and several other men entered the bar they called us over to have drinks and we quickly got to know our fellow passengers.

We were, I think, a decided acquisition and helped to liven up the voyage for the party. There were only about 80 first class passengers on the *Strathnaver* and several of us, including myself, had our own staterooms on the top deck, which enabled us to have parties late at night without disturbing any other passengers. The three youngest women were a Miss Marjorie Snively, from Cairo, Illinois, a girl called Kathleen and a young widow of 23, who was popularly known as 'Texas Bess'. They were lovely and charming and I am sure broke quite a few hearts on the trip to Bombay.

Every evening there was a dance or a treasure hunt and invariably we finished up in a party in one of the staterooms. At one of these in the early hours, there was a knock on our stateroom door and a person in a white drill uniform entered. I assumed him to be the steward and said, 'Steward, we did not ring for you". The person drawing himself up to his full height said, "I am the ship's surgeon and you people have been disturbing the ship every night and disturbing some of my sick patients".

We apologised to the surgeon but we did not think we had caused any serious inconvenience because the nearest passengers were several decks down. However, being in the army and a person who could be subject to discipline by the ship's captain, I was arraigned in front of the mast the next morning and was dually reprimanded.

One of the English passengers, a young man called Carslake, had fallen very heavily for Kathleen and it was understood that they were to be engaged when the ship reached Bombay.

As the American party were going on to Agra and Delhi in a special tourist saloon attached to the train, I travelled with them as far as Lalitpur, which we reached the following afternoon. The train drew into Lalitpur station, Leslie was on the platform and there was a guard of honour of police, consisting of a havildar, (i.e. an Indian sergeant), and 12 police constables, very smart and lined up at the very place where the tourist saloon halted. My American friends were very impressed by this and we had a drinks party with them in the saloon before the train drew out on its long journey to the north.

About a month later, I received a letter from Miss Snively on her arrival at Honolulu. She said that their journey around the world had been a wonderful experience and all members of the party were agreed to do it again. They also agreed that the most pleasant part of it was the time they spent on *Strathnaver* between Port Said and Bombay.

At the time, my brother was the only European in Lalitpur. Superintendents of Police in India are very busy and at certain times of the year, often throughout the 24 hours of the day. Were it not for this, life would be very trying in such lonely and remote places. Leslie, on his previous leave, purchased a short wave radio set which worked most efficiently and was a blessing.

The Author (2nd right) visiting the Sphinx
with his father, Frederick (1st left) and
mother, Kate, (2nd left), February 1935

Chapter 18

The Wild Borderlands

"In this belt of country there live the Wazirs and Mahsuds, tribesmen who from time immemorial have lived by brigandage and thus form a menace to the plain of the Indus."

[Rousseau (1926), Waziristan Circular Road, R.U.S.I. Journal, vol. 71, issue 483, p.569]

The narrow gauge railway line to the west of the Indus was an important strategic communication link. On the eastern side of the Indus River, where the single line diverged into two, heading north and south, was a little junction called Lakki Marwat consisting of a few mud huts, one of which was a refreshment room, well-known to generations of officers who had served on the frontier. The proprietor, who ran the refreshment room in those days, was a very old man who invariably produced wonderful meals, in that really grim and desolate spot.

The visitors' book contained many names that are now famous in history and I think that Lord Roberts' [Field Marshall Frederick Roberts, 1st Earl Roberts, VC] name was among them.

On arrival at Mir Ali I took over my mechanical transport section and was soon busy with the alternative daily columns to Razmak, the largest and strongest military post on the frontier, or to Bannu.

The Waziristan circular road ran from Bannu through the Frontier Hills to Mir Ali and on to Kurram and the Tochi Scouts garrison and thence on through to Razmak which was 75 miles from Bannu.

From Razmak the road continued south through three Waziristan Scout posts, Sararogha, Jandola and thence to Mansai to the south. The latter place is nearly 1000 feet below sea level and in the hot weather must be one of the most unpleasant places on earth.

Movement on the road was only permitted by day and the whole route was piqueted by khasadars, that is the irregular tribal levies paid by the government but who provided their own rifles. Before nightfall all traffic had to be clear of the road and inside the forts or posts.

At that time no actual punitive operations were being carried out against any of the tribes so cars and lorries were permitted to proceed independently between Bannu and Razmak and most of the other sections of the military road in North Waziristan, during road open hours. But outrages occurred regularly; some of them being committed by the khasadars, who were supposed to afford protection to the travelers.

British officers stationed in Razmak and Mir Ali, Wana and other posts were permitted, if they wished, and if there was accommodation available, to live in Bannu or Dera Ismail Khan the only two family stations in Waziristan.

Married officers had an opportunity of visiting their families about once a month, if the columns were not out, but each time the journey was made the risk of murder had to be accepted. This state of affairs was nerve-wracking for the wives but it was something they had to accept and with quiet courage, as their husbands played their part in the business of policing the wildest and most dangerous portion of the earth's surface.

Many books have been written about the North-West Frontier Province [NWFP] of India, both fact and fiction, but for the purpose of continuity of my story and for the benefit of those who know little of this savage and turbulent borderland of the now lost Indian empire, I shall very briefly describe it and the towns to be found there.

The North-West Frontier is a tangled mass of mountainous country which has borders with Afghanistan and Iran in the west and the north-west and with China to the north. [Much of this territory is now in Pakistan's North West Frontier Province.] In the extreme north the territories of Pakistan, Afghanistan, the [then] USSR, and the former state of Kashmir meet in the region known as the Pamirs, [known as] 'the roof of the world'. This mountain range, known as the Hindu Kush rises to about 6,000 feet in height, but some of its peaks exceed 10,000 feet.

For the most part the mountains are bare rock, but some are covered with low dense scrub and in a few places such as the Kurram Valley there are pine forests.

The climate runs to extremes. In the lower valleys during the hot weather the temperature may exceed 120 degrees F. [49 degrees C.]. In the cold weather the temperature falls well below freezing point and the roads in the higher areas are often covered with five feet of snow, and communications are blocked.

This terrain is traversed by five passes which have been the historic avenues by which the conquests of India have been carried out in the past. They are the

Broghol, Gumal, Tochi, Khurram and Khyber Passes. The general appellation of the inhabitants who live in this inhospitable area is Pathan. They are fanatical Mohammadans who are divided into many large tribal groups and the tribes themselves are further divided into many sub-tribes. The most powerful of the groups in Waziristan are the Waziris and the Mashuds and their villages are frequently inextricably mixed; thus one can find a Mashud village right next to a Waziri village in the middle of a area of Waziri territory and vice versa, from north to south of the country.

The country has never afforded sufficient grazing for domestic animals or arable land for crops to support the Pathan. From time immemorial they have raided their weaker neighbours or the villages in the Indus valley and Vale of Peshawar. The objective of these raids is to obtain food, cattle, women, rifles and ammunition. Tensions also often exist between families in the same village, so that various families, utterly and inextricably mixed, may often be at war with each other.

The [blood] feud is the inheritance of every male Pathan child born, and is known as the 'Tabadala', (i.e. an exchange of a life for a life). Tabadalas are continued for years and only end by the complete extermination of one of the parties (or even a whole family). Tabadalas can, by arrangement, be held in abeyance during inter-tribal wars or when fighting intervenes with external enemies such as the Indian Army under British rule or, today, Pakistan forces.

Individual and tribal conduct is governed by the law of Islam as laid down in the Koran [Quran] and the tribal mullahs or priests exercise supreme authority in these matters. These essentially internal disputes could also be a constant source of trouble more widely, outside the tribe. Cases of offences against tribal or Islamic law are tried by a jurga, (i.e. a tribal gathering) where a council of Maliks or headmen hear the evidence and award punishment.

For the Pathan life is very definitely a matter of 'survival of the fittest' and these circumstances have produced a breed of men of great hardihood, tough, cruel, relentless, treacherous and cunning. They are probably the finest hill fighters in the world and any carelessness in conducting military operations against them can incur swift and sudden disaster.

A visitor can claim asylum in the name of the Prophet and he will be given protection and food and, if need be, defended from enemies when under his host's roof. The next morning after the visitor has gone on his way the former host could, quite willingly, shoot the traveler dead, for no other reason than to gain possession of the visitor's rifle, or for the fact that visitor was a stranger in that territory.

The Pathan tribes, combined, could put over a million men in the field mostly armed with modern rifles, but because of the way the tribes and sub-tribes are scattered and the never-ceasing inter-tribal quarrels and blood feuds, they have never been able to combine to fight against the forces of the British Raj, and it has been possible to deal with each incident separately.

The 'Tribal Territory' is that country lying between administrative India, which is generally at the foot of the hills and on the southern side of the Hindu Kush mountain range, and the Durand line that marks the political boundary between Afghanistan and modern-day Pakistan. The territory varies in width from 30 to 120 miles.

In the tribal areas the tribes had complete freedom to do as they wished amongst themselves, including making war on each other. But if military posts or communications were attacked, or raids made into the administered territory of the government of India, punitive action was taken against the tribe.

Tribal territory presented two problems. First the five passes had to be defended adequately to prevent an invasion by Russia through Afghanistan, and secondly, the tribal areas had to be kept quiet so they would not interfere with our communications in the event of a major war.

In order to deal with this situation the Indian Army established strong military garrisons within tribal territory, strategically located to defend the passes and linked to each other and British India with good motor roads. This policy provided work and income for the tribes in the form of road-making and building, and the provision of khasadars, for road protection duty.

This policy known as the 'Forward Policy' took a number of years to implement.

Up to World War One, the majority of posts in tribal territory were garrisoned by frontier scouts or militia, but a mutiny by the South Waziristan militia in 1916, during which nearly all the British officers were murdered, necessitated a military campaign being fought and thereafter permanent garrisons of the Indian Army were established in the tribal areas.

The Afghan War of 1919-20 resulted in further military posts being established in North Waziristan and in the Khurram Pass. In 1930 there occurred operations against the Afridi tribe, after which a line of forts on the Khajuri plain was established. There were also operations against the Memon Tribe, to the northeast of Peshawar that took place in 1932 and 1933. During which more [defensive] posts were built and roads constructed.

Occasional sniping of the forts or column camps occurred throughout the year and was regarded as a form of sport by the tribesmen, but if it became serious a column of troops would proceed into the tribal area concerned and subject to direction by the political department of the Government of India would take hostages, secure a fine of a fixed number of rifles, or in the most serious of cases destroy one or more tribal towns.

The political department of the government, who were nearly all officers seconded from regiments of the Indian Army, who spoke Pashto fluently and were located in the various areas, and known as 'political agents'. These officers were the expert advisers to the central government and the local military commanders on tribal matters. They paid out the Malaki, to the maliks, as a chief's allowance, and the kassadari, i.e. payment to the khasadars, on road protection duties.

At times they would investigate complaints against the military or police forces, and always accompanied columns if punitive operations were taking place against the tribesmen. It was essential in all dealings with the tribes to respect their religious beliefs and customs, and not to offend them in any way in these matters.

Where operations necessitated aerial bombardment, 48 hours warning of this was invariably given to the tribes to enable them to move their women and children to safety. At the same time of course they moved their cattle, sheep, camels, gathered-in crops and anything else of value; which was a considerable handicap to the government in carrying out operations designed to punish the tribe.

Mosques and graveyards were scrupulously respected and if any copies of the Koran, the holy book of Islam, were found they were handed over immediately to the Political Agent for safe-keeping and eventual return to the tribe.

Troop formations on the northwest frontier consisted of 12 brigades, or approximately 70,000 men; always held in a continual state of operational readiness and some portion of them were always on active service against one or other of the tribes. As I have already said, a modern rifle was the tribesmen's most valuable possession and in the Kohat Pass the Afridi had a tribal factory which made copies of the .303 Lee Enfield rifle. Rifles were also smuggled into the tribal areas in very large quantities from Afghanistan and the rifle thieves never gave up their efforts to increase their arms haul still further.

It was on the north-west frontier, at any hour of the day or night, that murder, other violent outrages and utmost savagery might be loosed without warning. In one instance, a few miles from Mir Ali a blood feud was in progress between two very powerful Waziri families. One of the families managed to obtain a homemade cannon from Afghanistan and used this in an attack on their enemy's fort. Eventually they managed to break into the tribal town, where the occupants, numbering, 29 men, women (including some pregnant women) and children were all slaughtered. In other words, the family was completely exterminated for all time.

A few weeks after arriving at Mir Ali I was transferred to Wana in South Waziristan and in the tribal area of the Mahsuds. It was the next largest frontier post to Razmak and claimed, that in relation to population it was the second largest place in the world without a single woman in it, but it had the largest drinks bill in the world, head for head.

Fortunately, things were reasonably quiet. The occasional sniping of a camp picket and the fight between two villages near the camp were the only violent incidents that occurred in May. But one morning our signal detachment received news that there had been a terrible earthquake at Quetta, only 200 miles from Wana as the crow flies, and that the city had been completely destroyed with the loss of over 30,000 lives. Lord Carslake, the general officer commanding and the father of my friend Carslake on the voyage on the *Strathnaver*, quickly mobilised all military resources to assist in rescue work, evacuation of casualties, feeding the homeless etc. All available military transport was moved to Quetta and for a few days Wana was an important organisational and news centre, via wireless communication, to the outside world.

This appalling earthquake had unfortunately occurred at about 2 am in the early morning when the whole populous were inside their houses and asleep, resulting in an immense loss of life, in a matter of just a few seconds.

In June we celebrated King George V's 25th Jubilee with sports, entertainments, mess parties etc and a firework display at night. Major Beedham who commanded the Punjab Regiment was the officer in charge of organising the celebrations and he vowed to have a bonfire on the Gibraltar Piquet outside the camp, large enough to be seen in Afghanistan. The piquet was located on a pinnacle of rock, rising about 600 feet out of the Wana plain, where the bonfire was constructed on a ledge below the piquet. Well-soaked with kerosene, the bonfire duly went up in a wonderful blaze. It was so terrific, however, that the troops in the piquet had to leave it and move down the slopes of the hill away from the fire. The whole area was illuminated by the fire and it was most fortunate that the Mahsud did not attempt to interfere with the piquet or the celebrations might have ended in tragedy.

Our only relaxation in the camp after dark was a game of cards and there were many marathon poker parties lasting until the dawn, sniping permitting. Radio sets had not yet reached such a remote area and portable gramophones were really the only form of musical entertainment. New records could only be obtained on rare visits to major westernised urban centres.

The telegraph lines down to Mansai and Bannu were often cut by the tribesmen, so our only source of information on happenings in the great world outside was from our signals wireless set, which however was so busy they had not time to do more than issue a brief typed bulletin.

The South Waziristan Scouts, and other Frontier Corps units, were led by British officers, seconded from regiments of the Indian Army. They all had to speak Pashto of course. Their conditions of life were so dangerous they had to be bachelors and were given three months' leave every year, in addition to 300 rupees a month, i.e. about £22, extra duty pay.

When they left the fort on a 'gazma', (i.e. patrol), with their men they had to be dressed exactly the same so as not to be too obvious a target. It is true to say that their lives were at risk every moment they spent outside the gates of the fort.

In July 1935 an incident occurred that went against all logic and circumstances that existed on the frontier. Two Scots friends of mine, one in the RAMC [Royal Army Medical Corps] and the other also in the medical service, went off on ten days leave to Rawalpindi and the Murree Hills. They had a very hectic leave and in due course arrived on the return journey at Mansai, the rail head, and made their way to Jandola, the headquarters of the South Waziristan Scouts. After a meal and a convivial drinks party they left Jandola and made their way to Chagmalai, another South Waziristan post, on the road to Wana, commanded by a magnificent man called Sajeer Garrow, of the Baloch Regiment.

Travelling in a hired a car, driven by a Pathan driver, they duly arrived at Chagmalai safely. Of course, this was against the stringent regulations about travelling on the road at night and I do not yet understand why the Scouts permitted them to leave Jandola after dark. However, they had another drinks party with Garrow at Chagmalai. Afterwards, now really very merry, they continued their journey to Tanaie, a fort about 14 miles from Wana, and where the Waziristan South Road branches one to Fort Sambaza and on to Quetta, and the other to Wana and the Afghan border. This time they were in a very merry mood and singing bawdy songs and there was no doubt that by then the whole of the area had been alerted. They made their way towards Tanaie Fort but were greeted by a fusillade of shots, on which they returned in their car to the khasadar post, two miles from Wana.

This was a very dangerous section of the road and every so often the car would come to a halt and the Pathan would shriek, "Dushman, sahib" which means 'enemy'. They eventually arrived at the khasadar post that contained about 50 men and they were taken inside by the subahdar in charge. Who then phoned Wana brigade headquarters and the brigade major being very angry at being pulled out of bed at about 4 am in the morning decided that they must be brought back to the fort as if the tribesmen knew they were in the khasadar post there might be an attempt to get them.

Men from an Indian battalion were turned out and made their way to the khasadar post where the two men were taken into custody and brought back safely to Wana. The culprits were duly reprimanded by the brigadier the next day and each lost a year's seniority to chasten them. It really was a miracle they were not murdered en route.

In 1935 an unusual event took place for the North West Frontier, when I was in Wana. We had no cinemas and it was announced that a mobile cinema would come to Wana. This was the very first time that any entertainment of such a nature had been provided in that part of the world. The cinema duly arrived and a large screen was erected on tubular poles and the loudspeaker was a six foot square box placed to one side of the screen. Attached to it was an electric generator, which was in a small fortified installation, located outside the barbed wire perimeter, which provided the required electricity. All lights in the camp had to be turned off to enable it to produce enough power for its operation.

4,000 troops sat on their haunches, in an open area in front of the screen, and the officers sat on benches behind. The film was a musical drama, 'Blossom Time', starring Richard Tauber and it was really most enjoyable. The sound production was quite good and of course it was completely intriguing experience to enjoy such things on the wild Afghan border.

The film had been going about half an hour when several cracks alerted us that snipers were shooting up the camp. It was a wild dash for cover and of course the lights went out and the performance ended temporarily. About half an hour later it was decided to try and show the film again; it started up quite merrily and continued for another period, before the 'crack' 'crack' of bullets again sent us to cover. This continued but we stuck to it and after about four and a half hours we had seen the film through, fortunately without incurring any casualties.

This area of the frontier became quite disturbed in July and August and military columns were frequently sent out to calm tribal tensions and all leave stopped. However, in early September I was given leave to go home to bring my family back, as I had been posted to 25 Animal Transport Company at Bannu, which was a family station. The reunion and journey back with Edna and children, after a break of nearly nine months was lovely and we had an enjoyable leave before returning to India.

The Italian attack on Abyssinia [Ethiopia] was in progress at that time [1935] and when we passed through the [Suez] canal we saw several Italian troop ships which were given a very frigid reception by the

British ships with catcalls, raspberries etc. Arriving at Bombay we transferred to a British India Steam Navigation Persian Gulf ship for the voyage up to Karachi of about 36 hours and during the whole of the day we passed through school after school of whales varying in number from 20 to 50 or 60. We must have seen 500 whales during the day, some very close to the ship.

Between Karachi and Bannu the journey on the Punjab mail was through the blistering heat of the Sindh desert, along the banks of the river Indus, and finally to Bannu. These long train journeys make arrangements for young children very difficult and worrying. All water has to be boiled and scrupulous hygiene observed in every way. This means one has to have a primus stove in the compartment, boil all water and handle all the meals personally.

At Bannu I had been allotted a large bungalow with a nice garden but it was right on the edge of the barbed wire perimeter and on the banks of the Khurram River, which was tribal territory. Bannu was located at the entrance of the Tochi Pass and the frontier militia was known as the Tochi Scouts. The officer commanding the Bannu brigade or the 'Tocol' (Tochi Column) was a Brigadier Maynard, a Canadian, who had been at the Royal Military College, Kingston, Canada. He was a splendid soldier and his charming wife and twin daughters, Di and Trish, at that time aged 18, were a great asset to the station.

This wonderful old warrior still attends the Indian Army reunions at Hurlingham and was present there in June of this year. [1974]

The wives of officers at Razmak, Mir Ali and Wana lived in what was known as the family camp, which consisted of a square compound with huts built round the compound and a bungalow mess building in which meals were taken and space was provided for a writing room, and ante room etc.

Winter passed very pleasantly in Bannu with plenty of golf, tennis and riding to fill in our leisure hours and the usual enjoyable Saturday night dances at the club.

Military units from Bannu went out twice during the winter and though on one occasion we marched into tribal territory where troops had not been before the tribes remained quiet and we returned to Bannu without incident. At the end of each day, as the column marched into the camp, the group brigadier halted at the perimeter and watched the whole brigade including the transport column of 1,000 mules march into camp. This enabled him to see the condition of men and animals. Whilst marching from Mir Ali to Bannu, a distance of 25 miles, the brigadier completed the whole march on foot; a gesture to increase, still further, the devotion and respect of his troops.

On New Year's Eve in 1935 the Guide Infantry arrived in Bannu on route to join the Razmak brigade. That night there was a traditional fancy-dress dance held at the club. It was a gay [jolly] affair, thoroughly enjoyed by all. Perhaps our appreciation of those few carefree hours was heightened by the circumstances in which we and our womenfolk lived. Unknown to us, however, events were about to take place that led to the fiercest of all the campaigns on the frontier, to be fought during our time in India.

A Hindu girl was kidnapped in Bannu by some local Banuchi tribesmen and forcibly converted to the creed of Islam. The girl was later recovered from them but legal action followed. The party who carried out the kidnapping of the girl claiming she was a Mohammadan and that they should have custody over her. The magistrate finally ordered that the girl should remain with her Hindu relatives. This decision caused great excitement amongst the Pathans in Bannu district and the tribes of the adjoining tribal territory, the most important of which were the Turi Khel, the Turis and the Dir tribes.

The instigator of this unrest was the Faqir of Ipi, a Muslim Haji [a Muslim who has made the pilgrimage to Mecca], who lived in the collection of tribal towers called Ipi about five miles from the Mir Ali post. Tension grew and in April a Lashkar, that is a small tribal army, of about 2,000 assembled on the border about 12 miles from Bannu.

Warnings were dropped on the Lashkar by aircraft from Kohat issuing an ultimatum to the Lashkar to disperse or aerial bombardment would be carried out. The Lashkar dispersed and the Faqir of Ipi then moved into the Khaisora Valley in the Turi Khel tribal territory and started inciting the tribes to take action against the government of India.

The hot weather was now upon us and our thoughts turned towards the lovely cool valleys and pine clad mountains of Kashmir and so at the end of April we loaded up our Chrysler car and with our luggage and an orderly for the children we headed for Srinagar.

Chapter 19

Kashmir 1936

A journey of about 185 miles took us through the blistering heat of the foothills of the frontier to Kohat and then over the Indus at Kushalgarh. We continued on to join the Kashmir road. The northern branch of this road goes to Srinagar via Abbottabad. The road climbs higher and higher, the cool fresh air wafting the clear sweet scent of the pines to us.

Just before dusk, when the jagged frontier hills and blistering heat were a long way behind us, we arrived at Nigeen Lake where the owner of the 'New Moon' houseboat, we were to stay on, was waiting to greet us. The car was parked under huge poplar trees on the edge of the lake and the contents quickly unloaded. Then we were paddled in a shikara to our houseboat. Once settled in, we were able to bathe, trek up into the mountains, fish for trout and mahseer. In addition we could enjoy a wonderful round of parties on other houseboats, dances at the clubs in Srinagar, garden parties at the residency and a dance at the Maharaja's palace. We were lucky to picnic in many world famous beauty spots and above all we were able to experience the complete relaxation and peace of mind that the remote region of Kashmir gives.

On the morning after our arrival, Arndu, the houseboat owner, brought us a dish of chochwor [soft round bread], a cup of tea and some fruit, after which we got into the shikara and were paddled over to the bathing platforms in the middle of the bagh. These were amusingly named 'Piccadilly Circus' and 'Leicester Square'. The bright warm sun was above the mountain tops, the air was cool, and the waters clear and warm.

Wherever one looked there was a vista of breath-taking beauty; stretches of clear water, clumps of tall graceful poplars, forest-clad mountains and, at the end of the lake, the Hari Parbat Fort on the hill overlooking Srinagar. Depending upon the number of people gathered at the bathing boats a happy, laughing hour could be spent bathing or aquaplaning [water skiing], before returning to our houseboats with appetites ready to do justice to the excellent breakfast that the manjhi [raftsman] would provide.

One day Edna and I went for a day's trout fishing in the Sindh River about four miles above Ganderbal and approximately 16 miles from Nigeen Bagh. We had Aashu Khan, the children's orderly with us. Some years later Aashu Khan was to die heroically on the beaches of Dunkirk.

As the car approached the small wooden bridge over the stream, lined with willow trees, there was a commotion amongst several Kashmiri girls who appeared to be washing themselves in the stream. They had been hidden behind bushes and ran under the bridge and then peeped out at us. We stopped the car and sent Aashu Khan to find out what was happening. He went down the bank and there were shrieks and peals of laughter from the girls. Aashu Khan came rushing back up to the car as if all the devils from hell were after him. We asked him what was the matter, and he smiled in a very embarrassed fashion, shook his head and giggled.

Edna told me to go and see what all the fuss was about so I went down the bank and looked under the bridge. There were more feminine squeals of laughter, and no wonder. There I saw three comely young ladies dressed only in blushes. They were squatting in the shallow stream with their shapely backs turned toward me and were peeking coyly over their shoulders. We had surprised them having a bath and they had rushed under the bridge to hide. We withdrew and soon we were driving away from the source of Aashu Khan's embarrassment.

We fished all day but the conditions were bad and I did not catch a single fish, though Edna did get two small trout. When we returned to the houseboat in the evening we were greeted by our three year old son, Brian, who was holding up a fish a foot long, that he had caught from the houseboat. We could not part him from the fish, but it went missing the following evening. The next day there was a very unpleasant odour in the houseboat which eventually became so bad that we were forced to search, high and low, to try and locate it but were unsuccessful. By mid-day the following day it looked like we would have to vacate the boat as the smell was appalling. At last Arndu unearthed the decomposing, maggoty remains of Brian's fish from inside the upholstery of the settee in the lounge where he had hidden it.

As on our previous visits we would, several mornings of the week, take a shikara and paddle into Srinagar, a one and a half hour's journey from Nigeen Bagh. A lovely tree-shaded stretches of water and the pleasant, easy motion of the shikara more than compensated for the odorous stretches where dwelling houses were on the water's edge.

After an hour's shopping and collecting the mail, we would meet most of the other European visitors at the club and have drinks on the veranda, overlooking the river. In June there was a garden party at the residency at which Peter Fleming and Ella Maillart, who were the social lions of the moment were present, having reached Srinagar after their great journey from Peking [Beijing] across the whole width of China and Turkestan. This wonderful feat was described in Peter Fleming's very fine book, 'News from Tartary', which was a pleasure to read.

On 3 July 1936 the Maharaja gave an evening party at the Raj Garden Palace on the banks of the Jhelum River in honour of the birthday of His Highness the Maharaja of Jodhpur to which Edna and I received and invitation. It was a very hot night and by 9.30pm when the Maharaja made his entrance to the ballroom most of us were bathed in perspiration and dying of thirst. The Maharani of Cooch Behar, by then the Dowager Maharani, looking as attractive as ever, was there and appeared to enjoy the dancing very much. I had known the Maharani and her family for many years, as a relation of hers was at Sandhurst with me and they had a palace in Calcutta.

Cooch Behar ladies of the palace were of course in purdah and watched the proceedings from a box overlooking the ballroom floor. For some reason soft drinks only were available in the various ante-rooms until 11pm, at which hour the long bar opened and was soon crowded with hot, perspiring dancers. Unlimited supplies of excellent iced champagne were then available and the party became really enjoyable and lively. Dancing went on almost until dawn.

The drive back to our houseboat on Nigeen Bagh was six miles and the road the whole distance was on a raised causeway winding across the lake, with water on either side. In the six miles it had 22 right-angle turns to the left and 23 right-angle turns to the right and if the car went off the road it went into the lake. To make matters worse that early morning there was a heavy fall of rain which made the road surface very treacherous as it was only partially metalled. In view of our very convivial evening I had to drive with the greatest care I could summon. Though there were one or two anxious moments we, in due course, reached the 'New Moon' houseboat safely.

In Srinagar at that time one of the establishments was called Skinner's Agency in the charge of a Colonel Skinner. He was the grandson of the famous Skinner who raised Skinner's Horse, nicknamed the 'Yellow Boys' [because of the colour of their uniform].

One of the shops on the far banks of the Jhelum was known as the 'Suffering Moses'. At this, one could see wonderful Kashmir wood carving, papier mâché work, etc. I journeyed back to Bannu at the end of our leave but returned again in October, to take Edna and the children back to Bannu where they were to live in the family camp. I was transferred to Razmak to command 25 AT Company and to be the Brigade transport officer.

The bungalow opposite Edna's was occupied by Mrs Tindal the wife of Major Tindal of the 4/7th Rajput regiment and her next door neighbour was Mrs Pollard wife of Captain Ronnie Pollard of the Guides, a friend of mine when in Razmak.

Chapter 20

The Faqir of Ipi [Haji Mirzali Khan]

"The extent of the opposition offered to the columns was a surprise which exceeded all estimates."

[N.W. Frontier of India 1936-37,
Official History of Operations, p.15]

In November 1936 the government of India decided to test the agreement with the Tori Khel tribe regarding troops training in the Khaisora valley lying in the tribe's territory. The Razmak brigade was to move down the Khaisora and meet the Tochi brigade at place called Biche Kashkai. When the government intention was made known to the Tori Khel, the young bloods of the tribe immediately threatened to oppose any move that the troops might make. The Faqir of Ipi used all his influence to form a lashkar [tribal army] to further this purpose.

As no punitive action was intended the Resident in Waziristan, Colonel Parsons and Major General Robertson, General Officer Commanding (GOC) the Waziristan district, decided to accompany the Razmak brigade. The brigade moved out on November 24th 1936 and on the 25th went into camp at a place called Damdil near the point of entry to the Khaisora Valley. That night I and several other officers in conversation with the magnificent old Subahdar of the khassadars asked him if there would be any trouble when the columns marched down the Khaisora valley the following day. His reply was interesting, "If the general sahib takes the column back to Razmak the Tori Khel will forget all about it and go back to their villages. If you march down the Khaisora tomorrow you will have your bellies filled with fighting".

Before dawn on the 26ᵗʰ the advanced guard piqueting troops moved into the Khaisora valley, which ran practically due east and west for the whole of the march to Biche Kashkai, and began the slow and laborious task of piqueting the mountain ridges on either side of the riverbed to give protection to the main body moving out. The ridges were 1000-2000 feet above the valley level and were covered with very thick scrub and a few small trees. The piquets had not gone more than a mile when they were fired on by tribesmen hidden on the ridges above them.

Later as the piquets above the camp were being brought down they were also fired on and by the time the column had got into the valley the piqueting troops on the other side were also heavily engaged along the entire length of the column.

As transport officer I had under my command three and a half companies of animal transport carrying the ammunition, machine guns, equipment and clothing for the brigade. The transport column, or 'train' as it was called, was a vital factor in operations on the frontier. The train had to be protected because the brigade's effectiveness as a fighting force depended on the equipment, ammunition and supplies it carried. As it was thus imperative for the supply column to be inside the camp perimeter and securely protected by nightfall. It was necessary that the train moved at maximum speed, to enable the commander to complete his march by nightfall.

Spare mules could be taken but when these were used up in the replacement of casualties, the loads from further casualties had to be left behind. As we were well aware, the transport column was invariably one of the main targets for snipers, as also was the camel corps which among their duties carried the Khenchnay (stretchers to carry the wounded and dead). Men wounded or killed on the mountainside needed from two to four men to carry them and so the effect on fighting strength was rapidly reduced by relatively few casualties. The wounded and dead had to be recovered as the tribesmen were liable to carry out terrible mutilations.

The sun was right in the eyes of the piqueting troops and the greatest gallantry and determination was required to push the advance steadily against the hidden enemy who were rarely seen but whose accurate and murderous rifle fire was very much in evidence. Along the column it was also discovered that some of the khasadars who had been brought along as guides had slipped away into some of the tribal towns in the vicinity and were also shooting up the column. We moved steadily on but progress was slow. I and my Indian officers were continually on the move, often at the gallop, reconnoitering routes for the mules. Every path or route that could be negotiated by mule had to be used to march as quickly as possible and to shorten the length of the train and reduce the task of the piqueting troops.

As the valley broadened out the strings of mules were closed up at the double and in bottlenecks where nothing much could be done it was often possible to string the mules out in four or five different lines, one below the other on the hillside.

About 10:30 am there was a definite hold up and the advance guard did not really get moving again until about midday. The Tochi Scouts, under Major Felix Williams, were acting as a screen in front of the brigade had been involved in fierce fighting from the outset and had suffered fairly serious casualties. This had also been steadily occurring in the transport column and I had three men and about 15 animals wounded. Before the advance continued there was very heavy firing from the front, especially from the 3.7 Howitzers of the mountain battery, so I rode forward to see what was happening.

The 1st battalion of the Northamptonshire regiment, the British battalion of the Razmak brigade had taken over piqueting duties. At that point the piquets were being sent up a very steep and bare hillside rising 1,200 feet sheer above the nullah bed. The howitzers were bombarding the ridge right above the advancing troops and the platoon of the Northamptons in extended order were moving calmly and steadily up the hillside. Rifle fire was fairly heavy and a man dropped here and there but there was no pause in the steady upward movement of the Northamptons who finally cleared the ridge and the advance proceeded.

The column continued the slow advance during the afternoon but the heat in the nullah made it very hard work. On several occasions deadly incidents occurred as tribesmen, who had hidden themselves and allowed the piqueting troops to pass by them, opened fire at point blank range. One old grey beard was spotted in a cave right over the river bed and when some 4th Gurkhas brought him out they found dozens of empty cartridge cases round him. A group of tribesmen suddenly opened fire on the mountain battery, which was just going into action, their fire striking some of the guns, as they were being assembled, clanging and winding away from the gun shield. The big Sikh gunners assembling the guns were leaping about like cats on hot bricks, and I'm afraid I started to laugh until a menacing 'phut' [sound of a bullet near miss] passed my ear, causing me to dash for cover.

Operations in mountain warfare are of course normally limited in extent and because of this wherever one is in the column it is usually possible to get close to the scene of any action. Hard going had caused the transport column to extend over about two and a half miles and in order to get quick and accurate information on its progress the Brigadier sent a pack wallah back to me and I was then able to radio map references showing the exact extent of progress of the column.

A curious situation developed during the day as a result of the limitations of wireless communications in those days. Early in the day wireless contact with the Tochi brigade was lost because of a high mountain ridge lying between the two brigades. As the action developed both brigades tried to communicate with each other and situation reports of the progress of the battle were sent out. Although they were separated by only a few miles both brigades knew little of the other's progress. Reports were however being received at HQ northern command in Rawalpindi and other stations. The authorities receiving the messages had a most dramatic account of the battle being fought by the brigades and they also realised that 'Razcol' and 'Tocol' knew little of what was happening to each other.

The fighting continued during the afternoon. In one attack on the hillside Major Secombe, the second in command of the 6/13th Frontier Force Rifles, was killed and it was not possible to bring his body down the hillside. A long halt ensued and it was dusk before the main part of the column started moving forward again. The advance guard, however, had managed to reach the selected camping site at Biche Kashkai before nightfall and had commenced putting up the camp piquets and building a low perimeter wall.

It was pitch black and there was no moonlight. As we hurried along the rock and boulder strewn bit of the nullah, tripping up every few paces, the tribesmen came lower down the hillside through the piquets and started shooting into the column at short range. Several knife attacks were made without warning and the situation was most unpleasant.

The field ambulance, already burdened to capacity with the dead and wounded, had to attend to casualties in the dark as best they could. At the point where a small nullah entered the main Khaisora Valley several tribesmen hidden in the small nullah fired into the vanguard of the transport train as it travelled through the darkness. A big Punjabi gunner of the mountain battery was hit in the thigh. Captain Johnson of the field ambulance stopped with the detachment to attend to the wounded man. It was however most difficult for Johnny to do his job as mules and men were trampling over him and the wounded man. Seeing what was happening I called to my Risaldar-major [senior Indian cavalry officer], my magnificent senior Indian officer, to stand with me and we diverted the mules and troops away from Johnny and his patient. This was fairly effective and although both of us received blows and kicks and were knocked down on several occasions, Johnny was able to bandage up the wounded gunner and put him on a stretcher.

Before we were able to move forward however the tribesmen in the small nullah re-opened fire which added to the hazards of the mêlée of mules and men passing in the darkness. With rifle fire and the 'phut' of near misses; I was very relieved when Johnny had done his job so we could get away from that unpleasant spot.

The affair must have been very frightening for the badly wounded gunner and later he related what had happened to Major Fiskin, his CO. Fiskin, appreciating what had been done for one of his men reported the matter to higher authorities and later Johnny, the Risaldar-major and I were decorated. The main thing was that the Punjabi gunner's life had been saved.

In my way forward in the darkness sometimes accompanied with an occasional mule or horse running past me we came across several wounded animals and shot them, to end the poor creatures' misery. Eventually I heard noises away to my left and realised with a start that I had gone past the track leading to the plateau above the nullah where the brigade was forming camp. I hurriedly retraced my steps keeping close to the high ground on the left. To my relief I came upon a track that enabled me to get to the top of the plateau where I found the mountain batteries forming a rear guard and with them entered the camp at 10pm.

There were some 4000 men and over 2000 animals inside the perimeter which was around 600 yards square. It was pitch black and heavy sniping from the tribesmen was in progress. The efficiency and experience of the frontier soldier however enabled order to be sorted out of chaos. In a reasonably short space of time each unit had occupied its bivouac area, dug its foxholes and then taken over their sector of the perimeter. Outside in the lonely darkness on the hills surrounding the camp the piquets were facing the nerve-wracking strain of the threat of sudden murderous attack which would only cease at dawn.

Once I had found my units I went round to check my casualties as best I could in the darkness. In some miraculous manner each troop had arranged to get its 90 odd animals in orderly lines and given them their feed. Fortunately water had been available during the day in the Khaisora River.

I found brigade headquarters where all units submitted their casualty reports. They were found to be, killed: Major Tindal, 3/7th Rajput regiment, Major Secombe, 6th battalion Frontier Force Rifles, one British other rank, Northamptons, nine Indian other ranks and five other ranks of the Tochi Scouts. The wounded were: Captain Boyd 1/7th Rajput regiment, Captain Phillips 3/7th Rajput regiment, nine British other ranks, Northamptons, 52 Indian other ranks and 14 other ranks of the Tochi Scouts.

Throughout the night, lying in my foxhole in the stony ground, I heard the rattle of musketry and automatic fire as the camp piquets fought off repeated attacks by the tribesman. In addition to periodic assaults the piquets were also subjected to heavy rifle fire and throughout the night constant attention and first aid had to be given to them.

During the day the Tochi brigade had left Mir Ali and were moving due south to link up with the 'Razcol' at Biche Kashkai. They however met opposition and finally had to go to camp four miles short of our position. On the 27th they moved forward and linked up with the Razmak Brigade at about midday. They had faced strong opposition but suffered no casualties and had inflicted fairly heavy casualties on the tribesmen. On the 28th November both brigades marched north to Mir Ali, again meeting considerable opposition. At one part of the route the valley was fairly wide and I had stretched the train cut on a broad front. We came to a patch of scrub and some foot high rushes and as we were moving through it I came across the bodies of half a dozen sappers and miners. I eventually ascertained that their position had been noted for recovery.

At this point a small officer on a large horse galloped up and said, "Who are you?" and when I told him he said, "You mustn't lag behind, keep moving, keep moving". It was Major Reed, the brigade major of the Bannu Brigade, later to be a famous commander of a division in Burma. I gathered that he had galloped into the close area to obey the call of nature and a few tribal bullets had hurried him on his way.

We reached Mir Ali at nightfall and were safe for the moment.

Re-equipping and re-organising began in Mir Ali and a few days later we learned that the government of India were determined to make the Tori Khel carry out their agreement and were going to assemble a force consisting of the 1st Rawalpindi Division and the Waziristan division to carry out operations. After a meeting one day with General Robertson, the GOC, he said, "Well I hope we will have an exciting and successful time and I think I can guarantee that you will all be able to go on your Christmas shoots".

The Fakir of Ipi and his followers were still waging war against the Pakistan army in 1955.

The end of the Tori Khel 'War' was reported in 'Statesman' [an influential English language daily newspaper, published in Calcutta, committed to liberal values and British owned until the 1960s] by their New Delhi special representative, dated January 22nd 1937 and is of interest.

<u>Quote</u>

"Including the first action fought on November 25th 1936 the casualties among government forces in the Tori Khel operations have been 30 killed and 127 wounded. The dead are three British officers, one Indian officer, 25 Indian regular other ranks, one British other rank and seven men of the north Waziristan Tochi Scouts. The tribesmen's verified casualties, the names of nearly all the men among them are known, were a 119 killed and 186 wounded, and three taken prisoner in an ambush. It is not certain of course that this is the total of the enemy's losses.

"The [tribal] *jirga* held on January 15th brought so great an improvement to the situation that the Razmak brigade has now returned to its peace station at Razmak. The 2nd Infantry brigade from Rawalpindi and the Tochi Brigade from the Bannu area remain at Jaler camp in the Khaisora country. It is hoped that the former will be able to withdraw at the beginning of next month. The Faqir of Ipi is still sojourning in the caves of Shaktu Valley several miles further south, but his recruiting campaign is so unsuccessful that it has been found possible to allow villagers of the disaffected Khaisora country to go back to their homes and to promise no further hostilities if they continue to behave well. About 120 Tori Khel *khassadars* have been dismissed because of misconduct or untrustworthiness and the tribe's hostages and deposit rifles will be retained for the time being as security against further naughtiness.

"The new fair weather motorable road is likely to be completed along its length in a few weeks' time when it will be about 31 miles long altogether.

"It was hoped to carry it westward from Biche Kashkai up the Khaisora valley to Asad Khel on the frontier road between Razmak and Damdil. It was found however that in this direction the engineering difficulties and costs would be too great and that road would also pass through some very debatable ground covering the trade and shepherd route annually used by the sensitive Masuds [sic]. The Masuds have been such good boys during recent trouble and their feelings must not be hurt.

"Harassing tactics then reduced the tribesmen to a shortage of food and shelter and they began to find the game wasn't worth the candle. Having established this advantage the troops had no wish to stay there longer at the risk of prejudicing the Masud's good behaviour and they therefore moved out to call the second Tori Khel *jirga*...

There is now every reason to hope that the sober majority of the Tori Khels will be able to control their hotheads.

"The affair may now be said to have ended and no further *communiques* or official accounts are expected."

Unquote

As soon as news was received in Bannu, on the 27th November, that heavy fighting with the tribes had broken out both the wives in the family camp, as well as all other wives with husbands who were with units engaged in the operation, became very worried and anxiously waited for news. Later in the day Mrs Tindal was informed that her husband had been killed and all of the wives rallied around to give her as much comfort and assistance as they could.

The bodies of all ranks that had been killed were taken to Bannu the next day in an ambulance convoy, every yard of the route being protected by troops. There they were buried according to their respective prescribed religious rituals. This was the beginning of anxious months and in some cases of years of mental distress and anxiety for the wives and families involved.

This was a quite large-scale war scarcely known about in England and it was just one facet of 'peacetime' soldiering in India.

The situation was fairly quiet during the Christmas period and most of us in Razmak were given a few days' leave to spend with our families in Bannu. At home a pony had been bought for Brian and a small donkey for Valerie and the children had orderlies [servants] to look after the animals and keep them in perfect condition. The orderlies took Brian and Valerie for rides morning and evening. Both of the orderlies and the children's ayah [nanny] looked after them with great affection, not to say love. Christmas was gay and enjoyable in Bannu inside the thick belt of barbed wire, though armed guards were placed on all accommodation containing ladies or children. In addition, if playing golf, ladies had to have a male escort with them.

These happy days passed all too quickly and operations by all the brigades commenced early in January 1937.

The Author as commanding officer (on horseback)
of the 'Razcol' supply train in the Khaisora Valley
Operation, 1936

Ambulance column transporting the killed
and wounded from the Khaisora Valley Operation, 1936

The Author leading (on first horse) an AT supply
column in Waziristan, 1936/38

Chapter 21

War in the Mountains

The re-equipping of all units that had taken part in the Khaisora operations and reinforcements to bring them up to strength was completed by mid-December and 'Razcol' (Razmak Column) marched back to Razmak before Christmas. The 1st division from Rawalpindi had been concentrated in the Mir Ali area and a full building programme consisting of construction of new motorable all-weather roads in the Tori Khel and the Turi Territory had been planned to commence in January.

The building plan was designed to build roads from north to south, linking the northern sector of the Waziristan circular road with the southern sector via the Tori Khel and the Turi Tribal territory, hitherto inaccessible by wheeled transport, and an east-west road passing through the Tori Khel territory along the line of the Khaisora valley.

Road Building Under Fire

The meeting point of the new roadway system was an area known as the Sham Plain. The brigade based in Miramshah, the headquarters of the Tochi scouts in the northern sector, operated southwards constructing its mileage of road each day to eventually establish a camp at Ghariom. Up to this point road construction from Razmak advanced in an easterly direction and in the early stages over an 8,000-foot ridge, only a couple of miles from Razmak.

A perimeter camp was established on the top of the ridge and from there operations moved further eastward to Ghariom. In the first few days we returned to Razmak for the night while the distance was within the radius of operations of the column. It so happened that in one of the stoniest areas in the world there were hardly any large stones on the top of the ridge, but there were enough stones, of 12 inch in length or more, to build a perimeter wall and to form barriers to protect our canvas water tanks holding about 10,000 gallons each. The day that we were due to remain on the ridge and use it as a base for further movement forward every man on road building duties had to carry a sufficiently large stone into the camp area which provided enough stones to erect a perimeter wall and protect the water supply.

Fortunately sniping by the tribesmen was not heavy but the hillside was covered with quite thick scrub and the utmost vigilance had to be exercised to prevent surprise attacks or an ambush. On one day, as we started to withdraw towards Razmak the tribesmen made their way in the thick cover close to a piquet of a Punjab regiment and as it commenced to descend they opened fire and Second Lt Lloyd was hit by a bullet just grazing his neck. In the scrum I saw some of his men gather round him and start moving him down the hill.

In the meantime covering fire from other piquets held the tribesmen back. After some weeks in hospital in Razmak several attempts were made to move him to Bannu but every movement caused him such pain that he had to stay in Razmak until an ambulance was constructed with special springing and a mattress. Then he was successfully moved down to Bannu and eventually sent home to England.

Road-making work continued and every day we had a brush with the tribesmen but we completed our sector to Ghariom and then returned to Razmak to resume road protection duties.

Damdil

On the 20th March Razcol had marched to a camp called Damdil about 20 miles away. One of the camp piquets comprised an inner sangar i.e. a circular stone breastwork containing another breastwork within it, situated on a low knoll about 100 yards away from the perimeter and occupied by units of the 2nd battalion of the 5th Royal Gurkha Rifles Frontier Force. Firing started during the night and eventually very heavy fire from the Gurkha piquet made us aware it was being attacked. In mountain warfare all piquets must hold their own position after nightfall and though a terrific fight was in progress, within our hearing, we were not able to help them.

A band of 50 Wazirs was attacking the piquet and the heroic Gurkhas fought off attack after attack. The tribesmen withdrew just before dawn taking their dead and wounded with them before a strong fighting patrol from the camp arrived. Of the heroic garrison of eight men, two were dead and the remainder had all been wounded several times.

Later, Captain Springhall, the staff captain of the Razmak Brigade, and I returned to Razmak from Bannu with a convoy of troop reinforcements. As we approached Damdil, we heard firing. On arrival there the convoy was halted, and we were instructed to report to Lt Col MacDonald, commanding the mountain artillery brigade. We were told that road piqueting troops moving towards Razmak had been attacked and that fighting was spreading on the hills all round the camp. The reinforcements were to be brought into camp and formed into company and platoon strength units and act as the camp reserve, under my command.

When I walked into the camp I met a company of 5ᵗʰ Royal Gurkhas marching out onto the road led by Oscar Bethune, a fellow cadet in my term at Sandhurst, whom I had met before, in Abbottabad in 1931. He was a very nice person indeed; quiet and rather hard of hearing but a dedicated and efficient soldier. I said, "Hello Oscar, where are you going?" He smiled and said, "Just for a walk up the road, we'll have a few tonight".

I never had that drink with Oscar. He was killed a few hours later and I saw his body brought back into the camp.

One of his subalterns, Peter Nicholson, had also been hit by dumdum bullets and his foot smashed to bits, necessitating its immediate removal, on arrival at the field ambulance. We lost about 60 men, killed and wounded, by the late afternoon. A battalion of Gurkhas was holding a ridge several miles in length about 2000 yards north of Damdil and had been heavily engaged all day. To help the Gurkhas carry out the crucial withdrawal to camp the 1ˢᵗ Battalion South Wales Borderers, of Rorke's Drift fame, was pushed forward to take over the ridge from the Gurkhas who then withdrew with the utmost speed to Damdil, as the light was fading. The South Wales Borderers now also had to be within the perimeter before nightfall.

The Borderers began their withdrawal steadily and with tactical perfection. First one flank retired, platoon by platoon, in open order to a fixed layback and then the other flank in the same manner. The reserve company kept moving steadily to the rear without pause. During this procedure covering fire from the mountain artillery guns and machine guns in the camp was put down on the ridge and the reverse slopes. Tribesmen kept up a moderate fire but the South Wales Borderers finally withdrew into camp just at nightfall. It was a splendid operation by an efficient, highly disciplined regiment.

What may be regarded as a sequel to this incident occurred, over 25 years later, in 1963. At that time I was living in Herefordshire and was President of the local branch of the Burma Star Association. To raise funds for the Association I organised a military tattoo. Fortunately, I was successful in securing the attendance of the band of the South Wales Borderers, who were stationed at Worcester only 27 miles from Hereford, to perform in the tattoo. Writing to the Colonel, of the Borderers, I related the incident at Damdil. Suffice to say my letter had been of the greatest interest to them and had been published in their regimental journal. There was just one man left in the regiment who had been in the action at Damdil that day.

The day the casualties and dead were taken to Bannu the road was opened specially for this purpose and it was decided that our reinforcements and equipment should also proceed to Razmak. The southern sector of the circular road ran through Bhittanis tribal country to Manzai. There, a convoy would be formed to proceed to Wana and Razmak.

At the western sector of the circular road, Jandola, the headquarters of the South Waziristan Scouts, the convoy was to divide into two parts with one part proceeding south-west to Wana and the other northwards to Razmak.

Shahur Tangi Ambush

The road from Janadola to Wana passes through a terrific ravine known as the Shahur Tangi where sheer cliffs rise 2,000 feet from the nullah bed. In some cases the width between the walls is only two or three hundred yards. The road is cut into the hillside throughout the length of the Tangi. The defile is about 1,000 feet above the riverbed and the cliffs tower another 1,000 feet straight up on the other side.

The road was so narrow that vehicles could not be turned. A convoy with two armoured cars; a sub-section at the head and a sub-section at the rear and one company of infantry as escort left Manzai early one morning and later arrived in Janadola. There, the Wana section went on its ill-fated journey and I, fortunately, was with the section moving to Razmak.

The Waziristan Scouts piqueted the road to Razmak for us and as we arrived at one of their big posts, called Sararogha, we heard that some fighting had started in the Shahur Tangi. Our column fortunately arrived at Razmak without incident and there we got a full account of the terrible events affecting the other convoy. The head of the Wana convoy had reached approximately the middle of the forbidding gorge when heavy fire opened from the sides of the gorge above the convoy. The leading lorry drivers were killed and the lorry petrol tanks set alight. This completely blocked the progress of the convoy. The armoured cars could not use their mobility or their fire power so all that could be done was for the troops to get out of the lorries, take cover under them and engage the enemy as best they could.

Heavy fire was kept up by the tribesmen from their position of advantage but at some points they were able to get in close enough to launch murderous attacks with their knives. The deadly struggle continued throughout the day but the Mahsuds were not able to overrun the position. The convoy had no wireless set and as the scene of the action was some miles from the nearest scout post it was to be several hours before Wana and Janadola became aware of the battle.

Once alerted the South Waziristan Scouts moved quickly into action and launched attacks from the east and west, while army units from Wana and Manzai moved to support them. During the evening and the next day the convoy moved on to Wana and the wounded and the dead were escorted back to Manzai. The casualties were 72 killed and wounded. There were 14 British officers travelling with the convoy of which 10 were killed and the others all wounded. Among them was a 2nd Lieutenant, who had joined his regiment in India straight from Sandhurst. His father was a major in an Indian regiment also then in Waziristan. The Lieutenant was killed while lying under a lorry but a tribesman had managed to get under the lorry and behaved in the barbaric manner that is normal to them. This shocking and tragic event upset us very much, especially as the young officer's father was a very well liked and respected soldier.

It must be remembered that while events such as this were happening, the army wives, particularly those in Bannu, had no information at all about their husbands' welfare. There were no radio services in those days and the telephones lines were cut by tribesmen every day, including the military signal lines following the brigade. Signal Corps wireless sets were fully employed in operations. The only news made public in Bannu and other frontier stations was in a small type written bulletin which, for security reasons, only gave the most meagre information. It was dreadful for the wives to have to wait, fearfully, month after month in such circumstances but they bore themselves bravely.

At the end of March, after the action at Damdil, Razcol returned to Razmak.

Kaniguram and the Gurkha Piquet

About a week later Razcol marched out again into the Mahsud country, via a South Waziristan Scout post at Ladha and established a camp, on a high plateau, overlooking the largest Mahsud village, Kaniguram that contained about 500 tribal tithes. The plateau sides were almost sheer for 500 feet and as the nearest hills were about 2,000 yards away it was practically impossible for it to be the subject of serious sniping.

It was approached from lower ground by a long spur on which a sangar was located approximately 200 yards outside the camp perimeter. At night heavy firing in the direction of the piquet, occupied by the 1st /9th Gurkhas, commenced followed by two grenade explosions and the shouts of men engaged in mortal combat. It was over in a few minutes and then there was silence. About half an hour later a slight noise in the darkness on the 9th Gurkha sector of the perimeter alerted the piquet and they trained their rifles, ready to shoot, when a voice called from out of the darkness, "Do not shoot, I am a Gurkha." After being called forward, to the perimeter wall, the man was identified as a wounded soldier from the piquet, which had been attacked. He was taken to the adjutant and given medical treatment and was also placed under arrest for leaving the piquet. It was learnt the piquet had been attacked and all were killed after a short struggle. Feigning death himself the wounded Gurkha waited until the tribesmen had withdrawn and then made his way to the camp. At dawn stand-to a Gurkha patrol advanced to the piquet and found all its defenders dead except for the Gurkha corporal, commanding the detachment, and he had over a dozen bullet and knife wounds and expired just after the patrol arrived.

From the wounded Gurkha it was ascertained that noises in the darkness, from the barbed wire fence, that surrounded the sangar and that had empty tin cans attached with stones in them, had alerted the piquet. Fire was opened on the piquet and a grenade exploded between the inner and outer sangar walls. This was followed by another grenade which fell inside the inner wall. At the same time firing increased. Tribesmen then rushed into the piquet in the darkness. The second grenade killed or wounded most of the garrison. All who were still able to fight continued to fight on in the darkness but were overwhelmed by sheer numbers.

Later at stand-to in the camp the brigadier made his rounds inspecting the perimeter piquets on each regiment's sector. At the time I was with Captain Peacock, adjutant of the 6th/13th Frontier Force Rifles and the subahdar-major of the regiment (i.e. the senior Viceroy commissioned officer), who was himself a Mahsud of the Abdul Rahman Khel. When talking about the Gurkha piquet the subahdar-major said,

"About 35 years ago, exactly the same thing happened at the same piquet, at that time occupied by the Wana Militia. The tribesmen made their way up the hill, towards the piquet, in the darkness and then a small boy crawled close to the barbed wire around the sangar and tied a length of string to it; he took cover behind a boulder and then caused a noise by pulling the string. In the meantime the tribesmen got into position on the opposite side of the sangar and rushed in and killed the defenders."

The brigadier said, "That is a very interesting story Subahdar-major."

The grim Mahsud said, "Yes, it is. I was the small boy who pulled the string."

This is typical of the Pathan, having taken the government's salt he would serve faithfully and loyally, not hesitating to kill his tribal brothers in any action for the government. Once having left the government service he would use all of his knowledge and experience and take the greatest delight in attacking any government forces that came his way.

One Gun Hooper

Shortly after this the Abdul Rahman Khel attacked the khasadar post on the Ladha to Wana road and had been fined 50 rifles and a sum of money by the political agent, as punishment. They were very slow at handing in the rifles and tried to get rid of some the most antique and bizarre weaponry, such as Jezails [hand-made smooth bore musket type firearms], blunderbusses etc. It was therefore decided to take more stringent action about the slow payment of the fine.

The tribesman's practice in the winter, when the snow could be 5ft deep on the ground, was to return to their towers at night, to keep warm and cook meals. They knew that we never moved at night and they also knew the range of our mountain artillery guns [3.7 inch howitzers] and only occupied towers that were out of range. There were, however, in Razmak two 6 inch howitzers for camp defence. One of these guns was brought over to Usman Hunza by Lt. Hooper of the Royal Artillery. A group of towers, about five miles from the camp where we knew that tribesman resorted to at night was selected as the target and in daylight a flight of bombers from Kohat flew over and dropped a few bombs around the area, which enabled Lt. Hooper to fire some ranging shots from his gun and lay it on night firing lines. The tribesmen were thus unaware that the 6 inch howitzer had been firing. About 10pm there was a terrific bang and the Howitzer fired several rounds and some more were fired at intervals before dawn.

The next morning the headmen of the Abdul Rahman Khel requested a meeting with the Brigadier and the political agent. They were very angry and said, 'It was not cricket.' using big guns with a longer range and that we were a lot of bounders. The 6 inch howitzer had done a substantial amount of damage and there were also a few casualties. Eventually, after a considerable amount of argument, they agreed to hand in the full quota of serviceable rifles by a specific date. Thereafter our gunner officer was known as, 'One gun Hooper'.

Risaldar-major, Dewan Shah Bahadur, my senior Viceroy commissioned officer in 25 AT Company, and the most senior Viceroy commissioned officer in the Indian Army, had been selected to attend the coronation of His Majesty King George VI in London. He left Usman Hunza in a convoy, towards the end of March and together with his orderly eventually arrived in Delhi to be fitted out with a full dress uniform and to proceed to England. Having played his part on this great occasion he duly returned to India three months later and one day when the road was open for a convoy to come in from Razmak, there sitting on one of the lorries was the Risaldar – sahib with a broad grin on his face. He had wonderful tales to relate to the men about the Coronation, London and the numerous agricultural establishments that they took the Indian officers to visit. It must have been with mixed feelings that he found that he had to return to Usman Hunza and to the Mahsuds and their playful habits.

Fate seemed to play a large part on the Indian frontier. All units had to be kept up to strength and because of that the Northamptons had to hold back some of their 'time expired' men. That is men who had completed six years with the colours and were due to be sent to Bombay to be repatriated to England. As far as we knew in Razmak, the column into the Khaisora was to be just an ordinary operation and we expected to return to Razmak in a couple of weeks.

In the operations of 26th November one man from the Northamptons was killed and 14 wounded. The man who was killed was one of the 'time expired' men; a very cruel quirk of fate.

In another instance, when inspecting my company on the morning after the battle in the Khaisora at Biche Kashkai, I felt a bullet pass close to my head and the sepoy who was standing directly in front of me fell to the ground with a bullet in his throat. He was rushed off in a field ambulance and I am glad to say that he eventually recovered. Lying nearby were the bodies of the men killed in the action the previous day, including that of Major Secombe, his body only recovered early that morning.

On another occasion when riding down a nullah, accompanied by a mounted orderly riding alongside me, I felt the wicked 'phut' of a passing bullet again and the orderly was shot through the head.

The Revenge of the Gurkhas

After the Gurkha piquet incident at Usman Hunza a tribal outlaw, Sher Ali, who later in our situation reports was given the sobriquet of, 'bloody bill' appeared with a lashkar of about 250 men and began depredations in an area between Kaniguram and Wana. He was eventually located on a 6,000 ft ridge, covered with dense scrub and patches of small trees. In addition to the Wana brigade and the Razmak brigade there was also a brigade from Fort Sandeman, in Baluchistan, operating towards the Mashud country from the south. Relying on the strength of the troops available a plan was made for the three brigades to surround the ridge, under the cover of darkness and to attack at dawn.

A large scale action was fought and at the conclusion 40 tribal bodies, with their hands missing, were recovered. There had been a number of mutilations by the tribesman in the previous weeks and troops were warned not to retaliate. However, after the action that day a Gurkha battalion had to turn out its packs and the missing hands came to light. Gurkhas believe that they cannot enter paradise unless they are whole men, so tribal mutilations of their comrades were regarded as very serious. The Gurkhas were berated by their commanding officer but they were quite happy at being able to get their own back, as they saw it.

Tauda China and the Escape of the Transport Train

We marched back to Razmak at the end of July 1937. There was no opposition as far as Ladha and we were due to reach Razmak the following day after a march of about 12 miles. At the camping ground called Tauda China, about 6 miles from Razmak, the road runs above a nullah bed with an almost perpendicular hill of about 1,500 ft above the road. On the western side there is a plain of about two miles in width and then the foothills towards the Afghan border six miles away. It was a Mahsud enclave, with its group of towers known as Makeen [Makin]. The Guides infantry were the advance guard piqueting troops at this point and had not gone far up the hillside before shooting started from the top of the ridge. The rest of the brigade took cover as far as possible and I was able to conceal most of the transport train in the nullah bed. The Guides could only make slow progress on the difficult hillside and were suffering casualties. The machine guns of three battalions, numbering 24 in all, were then brigaded and put down a terrific barrage on the ridge. The tribesmen could, however, not be dislodged and by the afternoon the brigade had only advanced a mile. A message came for me to attend brigade headquarters.

On my arrival there, Captain Springhall, the staff captain, said, "The brigadier has decided that the transport train should push on to Razmak without delay using the bed of the nullah as far as possible. We will give you a field company of sappers and miners, a platoon of 1st Northamptons and a platoon of 4th/8th Punjab as escort. You will be in command and act as a flank guard for us and on no account get involved with the Mahsuds. Good luck, you will need it."

On the far side of the nullah, on the nearest ridge, there were hundreds of Mahsuds, all behind cover with their rifles trained on us. At this place the nullah banks were eight feet above the nullah bed and the transport was in dead ground to the enemy on the ridge to the east, except when the bank height dropped and then the transport column became visible in certain places. Using the Northamptons as an advanced guard, the field company of sappers and miners as a reserve, moving at the centre of the train and parallel to it, and the 4th/8th Rajput as the rear guard, I put the Rajputs on the high ground east of the nullah, to maintain liaison with the brigade and to ensure that they did not get mixed with the Mahsuds, as they would have done had I placed them between the Mahsuds and the train. On the high banks above the nullah the Rajputs were better placed to repel an attack if the Mahsuds got nasty. I hurried the train on as fast as possible, keeping a very wary eye on the Mahsuds. In places where the train came into open ground the ridge snipers switched their fire and some casualties occurred.

We kept moving on while a terrific battle on our right continued as the brigade made slow progress. Finally about an hour before nightfall we were within one and a half miles of Razmak. On my left flank was a low knoll, about a mile away. If the Mahsuds intended trouble this was the most likely point for an attack to be made. I ordered the subaltern, in command of the Northamptons, to occupy the knoll and then withdraw, entirely at his own discretion, after the rear of the train had passed. If he met opposition he was to hold it off and protect our flank until we reached camp. We arrived in Razmak without interference and I heaved a sigh of relief because had fighting broken out with the Mahsuds the whole frontier would have been ablaze. The brigade finally arrived in Razmak at nightfall.

Later in the club that night Captain Springhall said to me, "It was a really serious business when we decided to send you off with the train. We did not know if we would have to make camp for the night and prayed that you would not get involved with the Mahsuds and would reach camp safely." The Brigadier referred to this operation and the action in the Khaisora also, in his report and congratulated my units on their conduct.

Later the political agent told us that about a dozen tribesmen were involved in this fighting, which shows that with the right type of country what trouble a small force can cause.

The Evacuation of Families from Bannu

Sniping by tribesmen from outside the perimeter at Bannu occurred almost nightly from January 1937 onwards. By the time the action at Damdil occurred

233

in March it was decided that all families should be evacuated to stations in India, the Murree Hills and Kashmir etc. The camp had been caught up in sniping fire on many occasions but fortunately no women or children had been injured. A special train to Rawalpindi was arranged and with the two companies of infantry as escort and protection over the whole journey the women and children were conveyed to safety. They would normally have gone up to the hills, anyway, as the hot weather set in. At that time my son, Brian, was six years old and my daughter, Valerie, was four years old. Brian had made five voyages between England and India and been under fire and Valerie had made three voyages from England to India and been under fire.

It was also decided that units that had served a long time in Waziristan should be relieved at the end of the year, whenever there was a lull in operations that would make it possible. I was very glad about this as my devoted troops had been in Waziristan for three and a half years and prior to that in the Khyber for two years. Later, during the hot weather, I had a few days leave to escort my family back to Kohat from the Murree Hills. We were allotted a bungalow near the brigade headquarters and the club, pending my move from Razmak. However, Kohat was still a frontier station with a barbed wire perimeter, so the troops' families would still not be permitted to join them there. This was rather bad luck on the company. The company's move was to be made in two parts; headquarters and two troops just before Christmas and the remaining troops between Christmas and New Year.

A Road Accident and Rescue under Fire

A few days before Christmas, my convoy set out for Bannu and passed by the khasadar post at Asad Khel. Here the road follows a fairly wide valley area, where it is possible for three ton lorries to increase their speed. I was shepherding the convoy from the rear and on seeing there was a hold-up I made my way forward in my command car. I found that a lorry had turned over on its side, its contents spread all over the place. The column had thus been held up. The driver was pinned under the lorry with a broken thigh, was very badly contused and covered with blood. At this moment tribesmen started sniping from the hills.

Having summoned aid from a field ambulance detachment I proceeded to see what could be done for the injured man. At the same time I ordered the convoy to continue on to Mir Ali without delay and to request a breakdown vehicle and assistance.

The poor driver was in agony and I lit a cigarette for him which seemed to give him a little comfort. With only a few light jacks available it did not seem possible to lift the lorry high enough to free the driver. But, when we tried, it was possible to lift the lorry sufficiently to apply a tourniquet. With some further effort we were able to get the driver from under the lorry, just as a field ambulance arrived to take the injured driver away for medical assistance.

We continued to Mir Ali and met the breakdown vehicle and an MT sergeant with fitters en route, proceeding to the scene of the accident. It was fortunate that during this period a more serious attack, by the tribesmen, did not develop. Once in Kohat I returned to Razmak to bring the rear party down and we arrived safely at Kohat the same evening.

A Little Local Difficulty and a Long Hard March

The 1st January Proclamation Parade was due to be held, as customary, but the frontier produced yet another of its surprises. The Froz Khel tribe in the Kurram Pass was of the Shea sect of Muslims. To the north and south their neighbours were the Afridis and Waziris who were of the Sunni sect, and were bitter enemies of the Froz. The Froz Khel rarely gave any trouble, wishing to be on friendly terms with the government of India. However, a few young hot heads had become bored and started shooting up most of the forts and posts in the Kurram including, Tirah, Saragarhi and Fort Lockhart.

An immediate decision was taken to prevent the Waziristan troubles spreading and the Kohat brigade marched up the Kurram Valley on 1st January 1938. The column operations continued for six weeks. The tribesman had taken note of the attitude of the Government and we had no severe opposition. Some elements of the brigade were railed back to Kohat but the 20th Lancers and 25 AT Company had to march the 75 miles back in two days. It poured with rain and when we arrived back in Kohat at 7.30pm on the second day all our equipment, harness, saddlery and clothing were soaked and the men were deadbeat.

Posted to the Burma Army

In Kohat a telegram had was waiting, informing me that I had been appointed the embarkation staff officer at Rangoon and seconded to the Burma Army. I was to leave for Calcutta on the 12th February. We had 48 hours to pack all our belongings, dispatch about 14 cases and trunks by train to Calcutta, return our furniture and sell that which was not hired.

My colonel in Kohat said that he would carry out an early inspection of my unit before I left for Burma. The day appointed happened to be, *Eid al-Fitr*, a very holy Muslim celebration, and my men were all Punjabis. In the circumstances it was a disgraceful thing to do. Risaldar Dewan Shah was very angry and said, "Sahib this has never been done before." However, a senior officer heard of this and the parade was cancelled and my colonel was ticked off by the brigadier.

'Will Ye No Come Back Again'

On the 12th February, with our car loaded up, we drove down to the lines to bid the officers and men farewell. I had raised a pipe band in Razmak, when I took over the unit, which was very smart and played well. The band played and speeches were made by me and by Captain Wainright, who was taking over command of my unit. Then it was time to leave and we were garlanded. The children's ayah or nanny was crying unashamedly at the departure of her charges.

We then drove away on our journey towards Rawalpindi on the grand trunk road on our long journey of 1,500 miles to Calcutta and then 800 miles sea voyage to Rangoon. The mournful sweet music of, "Will Ye No Come Back Again", was my last memory of the gallant band of men with which I had shared much adversity.

"The next morning the headmen of the Abdul Rahman Khel requested a meeting with the Brigadier and the political agent. They were very angry and said 'It was not cricket.' using big guns with a longer range and that we were a lot of bounders."

Waziristan, 1937

Chapter 22

On the Road to Mandalay

The whole length of the Grand Trunk Road from the Frontier to Calcutta lay ahead of us, one of the great roads of the world, renowned in history and song. A road down which, over centuries, invading armies had marched to victory and empire and had, at other times, withdrawn in defeat.

The old Mughal road had been improved, widened and made into a strategic highway by the British Raj. It was the chief instrument through which Britain established and administered the Indian empire, which was the jewel in the imperial crown. Previously I had traversed it in parts but my journey to Burma would take us the whole length of it; from Rawalpindi, in the Punjab, through Delhi, the United Provinces, Bihar, Orissa and Bengal to Calcutta.

The first section was from Kohat, via the Khushal Garh Bridge over the River Indus to Rawalpindi, a distance of 101 miles. The Punjab wet weather had not yet got into its stride, so after taking a meal in Rawalpindi we drove on to Jhelum, 65 miles ahead and stayed for the night in the Dak bungalow there.

The next stage was a long one; I had to break the journey for five days at Kasauli in the Shimla Hills, where I was given certain information and instructions concerning the work in Burma and the Burma Army. It was 350 miles from Jhelum to Kisauli. So, starting very early in the morning I drove at a fast pace the whole of the day, passing through Lahore, Amritsar,

Jalandhar and Ludhiana, the country of the Sikhs. In the afternoon at Ambala I took the road to Kalka at the foot of the Shimla Hills. The drive up the mountain road with its lovely scenery was pleasant and cool and before nightfall we arrived in Kasauli. It had changed little in the 13 years since I had last been there.

With our business over in Kasauli we continued our journey, the next stage being 177 miles to the imperial capital, Delhi. We stayed the night in the renowned and lovely Settle Hotel. It had beautiful grounds, shaded by large trees and with flower beds giving a riot of colour with a fine swimming pool and well watered green lawns that were delightful after the hot and dusty Grand Trunk Road. We were loath to leave it the next day. The next stage was through the United Provinces, via Agra and Mainpuri to Cawnpore, a distance of 279 miles.

There was little wildlife to be seen from the Grand Trunk north of Delhi but we were then to pass through country where bands of the common Bengal monkey were numerous and small herds of Black Buck, Chinkara and Nilgai were to be seen. This gave more interest to Brian and Valerie who were finding the long journey in the piled up car and the heat uncomfortable and boring. The monkeys could be seen some distance ahead, sitting in the shade by the roadside; as the car came close to them, they scampered away into the trees. They invariably ran to one side of the road thus showing better road sense than the human travellers who usually waited until the last possible moment and then ran in all directions often from one side to the other, going right in front of the car. There is a legend in India that the cunning simian can actually speak but he does not do so because men would make him work.

We arrived in Cawnpore early enough to enjoy its lovely gardens in which stands a beautiful white marble memorial for British women and children who were so foully murdered during the Indian Mutiny in 1857. It has a large circular wall of white marble that surrounds the well head over which is a plinth of a weeping angel, also of white marble. The whole monument evokes great pathos and while it is still there it will proclaim to the world the sorrow and grief that is enshrined.

We went on to Benares [Varanasi] the next day, covering 178 miles, through the well cultivated Gangetic Plain. Green parrots and troops of monkeys were numerous and pea fowl were everywhere. In the United Provinces there are a number of wealthy zamindars or landowners and there are also a number of native states and the elephants kept by them are fairly frequently seen. During the drive we came across some elephant droppings in the road and I promised Brian and Valerie that in about 15 minutes we would see an elephant. Shortly afterwards they were delighted when an enormous elephant loomed up beneath the trees ahead of us. Its great head was moving up and down to the slow rhythm of its silent majestic stride.

There were many sights to be seen in Benares of course, the holy city of the Hindus, which has stood for several thousand years on the banks of the sacred 'Mother Ganga' [River Ganges]. We visited the Golden Temple, the Gurkha Temple, fed a troop of sacred monkeys at another temple and finally drifted by boat down the stream past the burning fires where the dead were being cremated, after which their ashes were cast into the holy river. Halls and palaces crowded the cliffs above the river. Below them came the never ending precessions carrying their dead chanting, "Ram Naam Satya Hai" (Rama is the truth).

Next day we passed out of the United Provinces into the province of Bihar. The Grand Trunk Road traverses over 200 miles of jungle in this province. The aboriginal inhabitants are members of the Santhal tribe. The Santhal and other tribes were still living in the primitive state and survived by hunting game and some cultivation. They used bows and arrows and we came across several bands of them. The high spot of this day's journey was seeing two elephants owned by Sadhus [Hindu holy person], going to a religious festival at Bodh Gaya, the holiest Buddhist shrine in India. The Sadhus willingly halted their elephants and then took the children and Feroz Khan, our house bearer, for a ride on them, through the Sal jungles. We arrived at our destination of Dhanbad, 229 miles from Benares, in the evening and stayed at the traveler's bungalow.

The next day 5th March we arrived in Calcutta at one pm after a journey 154 miles passing through Burdwan and the French settlement of Chandernagor [Chandannagar]. Our journey down the Grand Trunk Road had been full of interest. The colour and glamour of Hindustan unfolded itself from day to day and with one all the time was the feeling of being surrounded by history. For the reader, who wishes to find the real essence of India, a journey down the Grand Trunk Road and the golden pages of 'Kim' await.

During our journey down the Grand Trunk Road we kept passing a cream coloured Chevrolet and quite often we would choose the same area, usually a copse of trees, to have picnic lunch. We never had any actual contact with each other. The party consisted of a husband and wife and a small boy, of five or six years of age. Immediately on arrival at Rangoon we saw this family. It turned out that he was to be my second in command and had been posted to Burma and his wife, a charming Armenian lady, was the daughter of a Mr. Minis, an 80 year old gentleman, whom I had the pleasure of meeting and who had been a page at the court of King Thibaw in Mandalay.

We sailed to Burma from Uttam Garh in Calcutta on the British India Steam Navigation's mail ship SS *Karanja* on 6th March 1938. When I went out on deck at dawn on the 8th I saw for the first time arising through a carpet of rich foliage the breath taking beauty of the great golden Shwedagon Pagoda, the holiest place for Buddhists, and surely one of the world's most beautiful sites.

The Author's children, Brian (right) and Valerie
(left) and house bearer, Feroz Khan (behind Brian), meet
members of the Santhal [aboriginal] tribe on the Grand
Trunk Road passing through jungle in Bihar State, 1938

"The Sadhus willingly halted their elephants and then
took the children and Feroz Khan, our house bearer,
for a ride on them", Bihar State, 1938

"There were many sights to be seen in Benares [Varanasi] of course, the holy city of the Hindus, which has stood for several thousand years on the banks of the sacred Mother Ganga" [River Ganges]

Chapter 23

The Land of Pagodas

"For the wind is in the palm-trees,
and the temple-bells they say:
'Come you back, you British soldier;
come you back to Mandalay!'"

Rudyard Kipling (1865–1936)
Barrack-Room Ballads, 1892

As a boy, when I first read Kipling's poems and stories, I thought that the Ballad of Mandalay was surely one of the loveliest songs in the English language. It had implanted in me a longing to see Burma, and now my first glimpse of it had more than fulfilled the romantic impressions that I had formed of that lovely land. I could not know then, that for most of my time in Burma, I was to live almost in the shadow of the Shwedagon Pagoda and that I was to witness the complete destruction of Mandalay by Japanese bombers on Good Friday 1942.

The Shwedagon is built on the last spur of the hills north of the city of Rangoon and adjacent to it is the military cantonment known as Sale Barracks. In the barrack area is an ancient pagoda known as the Signal Pagoda; because in the last Anglo-Burma war an army signal station operated from the top of it and maintained contact with the ships in the Rangoon River several miles away. House no 2, Signal Pagoda Road was used as the Officers' Mess of the British regiment quartered in Rangoon, and was a vast wooden, two-storied house with a large garden containing a grove of bamboos, several jackfruit trees, as well as many other varieties, and a dozen or more species of orchid.

The council gardens and the park containing the Rangoon zoo were only a 150 yards away round a corner of the road. Life in Burma, prior to the 1939-45 war, was idyllic. The lovely green land with its white and golden pagodas, its numerous colourful horse races (organised by the Rangoon Turf Club) and festivals were of immense interest and charm. This was the silken east, quite different from India and the Middle East. In many respects, life had continued unchanged for centuries and as I came to know more of the country and its people I had a feeling I was, yet again, living with history. There were people still living in Rangoon who had been at King Thibaw's court at Mandalay. I was to meet, and count amongst my friends, Princess Ma Lat, daughter of the Prince of Limbin, a brother of King Thibaw, and only a short distance from my house in lovely gardens outside the Shwedagon pagoda was the tomb of Queen Supayalat, Thibaw's queen.

Once again I felt the magic of Rudyard Kipling, just as I had done in 1929, when I passed through Seoni and the country of Mowgli, Shere Khan, the tiger, and the wolf pack.

The main products of Burma then were: rice, oil, teak, rubber and tin which were produced and marketed by great trading enterprises, including: The Burmah Oil Company, Steel Brothers Ltd., The Bombay Burma Trading Corporation, Macgregor & Company, McLeod & Richardson Company and MacKinnon, Mackenzie & Company etc. While the famous Irrawaddy Flotilla company operated the ship and launch services on the Irrawaddy, Salween and Chindwin rivers.

European staff of these trading enterprises comprised the majority of the European population of Rangoon and Burma. The remainder being members of the civil service, police, forest and other government departments and the British officers of the Burma Military Police, the Burma Frontier force, and the army in Burma.

Life in Rangoon centred on the Pegu Club that was the premier club in Burma; and also the Gymkhana Club, the Rangoon Boat Club, the Kokine Swimming Club, the Danyingon Golf Club and the Rangoon Turf Club, with its lovely little course at Kyaikkasan. Race meetings at Kyaikkasan were held most of the year. In Rangoon itself there were two very popular places for social meetings; the Silver Grill, managed by an Armenian General, and the Strand Hotel.

The facilities of Rangoon were further enhanced by an attractive nine-hole golf course on the Pegu Club road immediately west of the Shwedagon. It was very pleasant to play a round of golf under the shadow of the great golden pagoda. It was almost a ritual, for many people, to play a round before breakfast and another in the evening after the day's work was done.

The Lady Minto Nursing Association had a branch in Rangoon composed of a matron, Miss Ruth Briggs, and a number of nursing sisters. Their bungalow had tennis courts and they did a lot of entertaining, tennis parties, dinners and bathing picnics. The association was formed by Lady Minto, the Vice Rein and wife to the 4th Earl of Minto, Viceroy of India 1905 to 1910, to provide skilled nursing facilities for the European civil population of India and Burma. Very often their duties took them to quite lonely and remote outposts, particularly in Burma.

The different trading and professional communities did their quota of entertaining and social activity in Rangoon, very often in their own individual way. Rice trading companies' managers and staff had very fine bungalows on the banks of the creeks off the Rangoon River. When they gave lunch parties they concluded with a special rice pudding made from special high-quality rice, grown for their own use. The pudding was made delicious by a marvelous mixture of spices and was covered with a rich appealing brown skin.

The Irrawaddy flotilla parties, on their launches and the big steamers, were redolent of the finest quality of life; marvelous food and wines and spirits, beautifully served. The Burmah Oil Company had a colony of fine, modern style villas at Victoria Lake, just to the north of Rangoon. In October 1941 I was able to get a beautiful house adjacent to the Burmah Oil Company area, right at the southern end of the lake and I had a vista of several miles of water, palm groves and pagodas to enjoy.

One evening at the Gymkhana club the Burma Rifles Regiment, which had a company of Kachins serving in the unit, gave an entertainment by a choir they had formed. The choir was wearing the colourful Kachin tribal dress. We were seated outside on the lawn in the darkness when floodlights were turned on illuminating the choir which was organised in several rows, one above the other, and it began to sing a most melodious tribal song. The performance was called a Kachin Koireng. Chin Koireng (or Koireng) was the language spoken by the Kachins. Their voices were beautiful and they also had in their repertoire several English hymns including 'Jerusalem'. On other occasions regimental bands played on the club lawns and it also had a London dance band which had been brought over from India after the completion of its contract there.

The Kokine Swimming Club was also a very popular resort in the evenings and at weekends, and swimming and Tiffin parties were also very popular on the Victoria Lake. The Silver Grill restaurant provided excellent meals and cabaret runs and a dance every Saturday night which went on to the early hours. The Savoy Restaurant and Strand Hotel were also first-class establishments of their kind.

I remember one night at the Silver Grill when a friend, Keith Skelton, and I were enjoying ourselves so much that we did not notice that it was daylight and we were the only guests left. Pete Aratim, the popular proprietor, was hovering around and with a twinkle in his eye he came over to us and said, "Shall I serve breakfast gentlemen?" We replied, "No thanks Pete, we'll go home for breakfast." Which we did; and then met again, later, at Keith's bungalow at the opposite end of Victoria Lake and had a marvelous Burmese meal of curried scampi and all the side dishes, all washed down with iced beer. We then swam for the rest of the afternoon.

On the occasions when a new liner or ship called at Rangoon there were terrific parties given on board and such events were always looked forward to. A popular holiday excursion was to go up to northern Burma by rail to Bhamo, a river port on the Irrawaddy, and then return to Rangoon by launch from Bhamo to Mandalay and then by Irrawaddy mail steamers back to Rangoon. These fine steamers were 300 feet long, had superb state room accommodation and offered an excellent table.

At the time Edna and I arrived in Burma a most interesting criminal case was in progress. On one of the rubber plantations in Tenasserim, in southern Burma, a planter was living with his Australian wife. There had been domestic problems arising from the planter having had a liaison with a Burmese girl who became very possessive and decided to eliminate her rival, the planter's wife. According to the evidence the Burmese girl had persuaded a Burman boyfriend to shoot her rival. The evidence as given in the papers was of great interest to a newcomer, such as me. When asked to state the time when the incident took place, one witness replied, "at the time the pungis took their morning meal". I learned later that each morning at dawn a number of pungis [monks] from each kyaung or monastery would form up in single file, carrying large earthenware vessels to all the houses in their area. The residents would place offerings of food, chiefly rice, into the vessels then, without speaking or giving any thanks, the file of pungis moved on from house to house and finally returned to their monastery.

Another witness said the time taken to do a thing was, "one Betel Nut chew" [Areca Nut]. The Betel Nut which is used as a form of digestif throughout the East takes about five minutes to chew. In another murder case, which occurred in a lane about 100 yards from my house, a witness described a noise, "like, the scream of a baby elephant". This is a very exact description and in view of the fact that the murder took place in the zoological gardens, only a short distance from the elephant house in which there was a baby elephant, I was able to ascertain the accuracy of this statement.

The pleasant life we had begun to enjoy in Rangoon was however quickly disturbed. A Burmese Muslim man named Maung Shwe Hpi wrote a pamphlet which contained critical remarks about the Buddhist faith. Great resentment was aroused in the Burmese populace and at the end of April 1938 riot and murder burst into flame in Rangoon.

The Burmese started attacking Burmese Muslims and Indians. Many people were murdered and shops and houses looted and burned. The Indians retaliated and soon life and trade in Rangoon were seriously interfered with. Europeans and Chinese were not molested but the breakdown of normal commercial life, with the closure of shops and markets, caused a lot of inconvenience and hardship to both locals and European residents.

The situation got worse each day and spread to villages and towns as far north as Tharrawaddy, 75 miles from Rangoon. Finally the rioting became so extensive that the civil and military police were unable to deal with it and the army was called out, in aid of the civil power. At that time the army's role in Burma was very limited. In an enormous country of jungle and hills with few lines of communications, the army had no mechanical transport, other than first line vehicles. The situation called for continuous patrolling of Rangoon, and the dispatch of the lower Burma Mobile Column to the disturbed areas north of the city.

In order to meet the situation it was my responsibility to requisition a number of buses from the Rangoon Directorate Supply Company and lorries from hired transport contractors. I also had to arrange for batches of troops from the 2nd KOYLI and later the 1st Gloucesters to be trained to drive the buses. Arrangements worked smoothly and soon a fleet of 43 buses and 17 lorries were in operation. In addition, I had to take steps to ensure the maintenance of supplies for European, Anglo-Indian and Burmese population as well as to the troops.

The situation improved slowly and shops were re-opened. The nightly murder quota decreased. One morning, when going to visit Mr. Stewart, the deputy inspector general of the mobile guard at police headquarters, I noticed many of the Chinese squatting on the edge of the pavement sharpening small hatchets. I mentioned this to Mr. Stewart and he said, "A Chinaman was killed last night and I think this will be end of the rioting".

That night the Chinese hatchet men went out and dozens of Burmese Muslims, Indians and Burmese were killed. The originators of the trouble apparently saw the red light and Rangoon became peaceful, once more, and the army was able to stand down.

Rangoon had a large and vicious criminal element and many of them had taken advantage of the riots to settle old scores, loot and to rob. Another reason for the continuance of the riots was that the Pungis, that is the Buddhist priests, were inciting the Burmese populace to murder. The Pungis had a great hold over the people. Many of these monks were very anti-British and indulged in seditious activities.

A most popular form of entertainment in Burma was the Pwe or Burmese theatre. Stages could be constructed and erected anywhere from bamboo and palm leaves and so they could be held practically throughout the country in any village however small. There were also some companies who had quite ornate and colourful stage scenery and moved from township to township to give performances. They were all very popular and the people never tired of them.

The plays given depicted the legends and folk lore of the country and also its history. Plays were also invariably a part of the many religious festivals that were held throughout the year in Burma.

The two most popular festivals were the Water Festival usually held, towards the end of April, the hottest time of the year and the Festival of the Lights, very similar to Diwali, the Indian festival of lights. In Rangoon and the larger cities the Water Festival occupied the whole populace, while it lasted, which was often up to ten days. The festival was centred on every street corner, where there was hydrant, or some sort of water supply. In some places canvas tanks were erected, holding thousands of gallons. In other locations there would be 44 gallon oil drums. In fact any container that would hold water suited the purpose.

At each water point there was a band of youths and girls who had stirrup pumps [water pumps] and buckets to enable them to spray or throw the water on all who came near. In various localities of the city, organisations and institutions banded together and would sponsor a crew of youths or girls, all dressed in a similar costume, with the girls wearing bathing hats. These groups would tour around in specially decorated vehicles from point to point in the town and a water battle would commence on their arrival at each water point.

Buses and lorries were decorated to look like a Peacock, a Chinthe or [mythical] Lion or other animals, in similar fashion to those seen in the Lord Mayor of London's Show or the 'Battle of Flowers' in Jersey. Chariots carried as much water as they could to allow them to drench as many passers-by as they could.

A Peacock chariot might draw up next to a large canvas water tank and then the water battle would commence. The girls in the chariot would throw buckets of water on those below and they would reply with hosepipes, stirrup pumps etc. It was all in the greatest good humour and passers-by, European, Chinese and Indians, were not drenched unless they cared to join in themselves. As the end of April was the hottest time of the year nobody minded water being thrown at them and it was, as I say, very popular indeed.

During the Festival of Lights every house was decorated with colourful Chinese paper lanterns or had candles in earthenware dishes burning. Residents would decorate the whole of the front of their house and also their gardens. It made a very pretty sight at night.

There were no private kindergarten schools in Rangoon in those days, so Brian and Valerie went to the Army Children's School in Sale Barracks which was only 50 yards from our house, and later went to a Church of England school exactly opposite our house on the other side of Signal Pagoda Road. Two children of Princess Ma Lat also attended this school and quite often the children would have tea together in our house and Mal Lat would call to take her children home.

I was able to display my tiger and panther skins and other trophies to perfection there. There was a long central foyer, about 80 feet in length, running from end to end of the house and I had three tiger skins on each side of the room with leopards in between them and the other skins and heads in other rooms. It was eventually known, humorously, by our many European friends in Rangoon as 'Whipsnade Villa' [after Whipsnade Wild Animal Park in Bedfordshire, England].

Edna had taken an immediate liking to the marvellous Siamese cats and bred them as a hobby. They were as good as a mongoose in killing snakes which was a very good thing as there were dozens of snakes in our garden and others adjoining. There were many poisonous snakes, including cobras, as well as grass snakes. One day the cats killed three snakes and on another day I saw two cobras mating in the grass verge just outside the house. They stood upright on the tips of their tails and were entwined together; a most interesting and very rarely seen sight.

There were several snake charming families in Burma who gave their performances with the Hamadryad, the king cobra, the most poisonous of all snakes. These deadly creatures were able to rear their heads 4½ feet from the ground and they had not had their fangs extracted or poison sacs emptied. Women took part as well as men and the top spot of the act was when the snake charmer eventually bent over their snake's head which was swaying from side to side and kissed it. If one of these charmers was bitten they would die in a few minutes.

One day a picture appeared in the Rangoon Gazette of a performance given in the zoo by one of these families and there, in the front rank of the audience almost joining in with the act, were Brian and Valerie!

A variety of lizard known as the taktu was found in most households in Burma, usually occupying the ceilings and the roof. They were quite large, about eight inches long, the head two inches broad. They had a loud cry of, 'taktu, taktu' and often as not they repeated it seven times, each call being weaker than the preceding one. They were supposed to be very lucky and were not molested by the Burmese.

My young daughter Valerie was very bright and when the time came to return the children to England, in September 1938, she had picked up quite of lot of Hindustani, Burmese and Chinese in addition to English.

We were pleasantly surprised in Rangoon to see Captain John Colt, a great friend of mine from the North Staffords, and Angela his wife. John was adjutant of the Rangoon Auxiliary Force Regiment. They very quickly introduced us to their large circle of friends and we were soon involved in every social activity. Amongst their friends was a Mr. Alsop the divisional forest officer and I immediately began to apprise myself of what shooting prospects there were.

The great jungles of central and lower Burma came to within a few miles of Rangoon and at a place called Wah Net Chaung, 25 miles to the north, there was always a large herd of elephants to be found. The herd of elephants had increased enormously in the last few years, to such an extent that it was decided to thin them out. I was told that, further to the north, there were 20,000 in Myitkyina district alone and 500 of these were to be culled. The same situation applied to many other districts in Burma. Panther were also quite numerous and recently, at Myitkyina, 'Bonzo' Bowers of the 1st 10th Indian Regiment, attached to the Burma Frontier Force, had shot six tigers from the same machan in about a month. This was the gentleman who recently [c. 1973] has been tending Princess Anne's garden, at Oak Grove House, Sandhurst, as a labour of love.

There was very good jungle fowl, snipe and duck shooting to be had, almost everywhere in Burma. We would go to a dak bungalow or a forest bungalow in a country district, and make it a base for a weekend's shooting. When shooting snipe and duck we often got covered with mud and soaked to the skin and when we returned very tired, to the bungalow, a hot bath was always the best thing to indulge in. After my first shoot I stripped off and was lying back contentedly in the nice hot bath in the tin tub when the bathroom door was opened and in tripped a dainty little Burmese girl who smiled and without further ado picked up soap and sponge and proceeded to give me a bath. Later on the bungalow veranda when having a cool beer I remarked on this to my friend who was running the shoot. He said, "Oh that's quite normal; I arrange this on all my shoots".

Kyaikkasan Race Course at Rangoon is very picturesque and in common with all race courses in the East was further embellished by the beauty of so many ladies of different nationalities, in their individual styles of dress. Princess Ma Lat, was married to a Mr. Herbert Bellamy, a bookmaker. Yes, very strange things happened in Burma. Even stranger than that, she was also a very keen racegoer and we always studied the form together and passed on tips, for what they were worth.

On the way to Kyaikkasan from our house we passed the Chaukhtatgyi Buddha. This was an enormous reclining Buddha, about 175 feet in length. The royal lakes, near our hoase, were also very attractive with oriental style pavilions on the small islands and were the home of the Rangoon Boat Club. Regattas both European and Oriental in style were often held there.

In Rangoon, at the time, there were a number of personalities who achieved fame during the war. The best known of these was Bill Williams, 'Elephant Bill', of the Bombay Burma Company and John Edmeads and Bill Farrier, the 'Elephant Masters' of the Steel Brothers Elephant Herd. Firms operating in the teak forests i.e. Steel Brothers and Bombay Burma had large herds of working elephants and as far as I can recollect the Steel Brothers working herd was 5,000 elephants. These powerful and sagacious animals were an endless fascination to me. They are so large and powerful yet they take the greatest care not to injure any other living thing unnecessarily.

The Burmese forests are so vast and consequently elephants are not used for hunting tiger in Burma. In the forests tigers can never be located with any precision. The practice of using and working with shikar elephants was of much interest to the Burma forest people.

One day a Captain Maundy of the Burma Medical Service was being married and Edna and I were invited to the function at the Jubilee Hall near to our house. Several hundred guests sat round in the auditorium and the bridal couple with their families sat on settees on the stage. The bride was in the attractive national dress of Burma, i.e. a white, sheer blouse and a very colourful longyi, or skirt, wrapped tightly round the hips and reaching to ankles. Her hair was piled high in a most intricate fashion and she wore a lot of lovely jewellery.

The bridegroom was in a military uniform and the bride's relations were in national costume. The Burmese wedding ceremony can be conducted by any elderly and reputable male relation.

There were sandwiches and cakes on the tables and tea was served as soon as the guests were seated, followed by spirits and wine etc. The audience was laughing and enjoying themselves whilst the venerable marriage conductor nattered away to the bride and bridegroom and relations. Eventually, he ended by saying, "They are going to go live together, so they are now man and wife". The party went on and when people wished to leave, they waved to the bridal couple and shouted, 'good luck', and then departed. This was an interesting and amusing experience of Burmese social custom.

In one important respect Burma was entirely different to the Middle East and India; with regard to the status of its women. Purdah was unknown and they were not in any way secluded, in fact they ran a surprising number of businesses in Burma, kept all the shops and markets, were contractors and had a very special status indeed. They did not hesitate to enter into conversation with men and the British troops arriving in Burma were completely amazed at the difference they found there, compared with those in India, where women were completely out of their ken and the slightest familiarity could lead to murder and riot.

Many officers of the Civil and other gazetted services had married Burmese women or had

Burmese mistresses, though only a few army officers did so, as this practice was still frowned upon in the army. Sir Spencer Harcourt Butler arrived from India to become the Governor of Burma in 1923. Being a very thoughtful man, he issued an ultimatum that all government officers, (i.e. in the Civil Service) were either to marry any Burmese lady that they were living with or were to resign. The majority of them contracted civil marriages and continued to live happily as before.

I took three months' leave in September to take Brian and Valerie home to school. The journey was from Rangoon to Calcutta by sea and then overland by the Calcutta-Bombay mail [train] to Balapur and then on by P&O liner to England. We placed them in a private school at Poulton-le-Fylde, Lancashire, under the guardianship of their aunt Ida, Edna's younger sister.

I was sad at parting from the children as I returned to Burma, although we knew it was necessary for them to receive a good education and for the sake of their health. They had already, in the short lives, travelled far and had much discomfort and danger which bound them very closely to us. Edna had to make a visit to England in 1939 and in May she completed the journey by the Short Sunderland flying boat service, en route from Australia to England. In those days not a great number of people did such long journeys by air.

The fares were very expensive and the many navigational safety aids, which are now in use, were unknown. The journey took five days. Thankfully the flying boats were air-conditioned. Nights were spent at superb hotels at stops along the way. Among the few passengers on Edna's aircraft was Air Chief Marshall Sir Arthur Longmore, who made the journey interesting for Edna by reason of his great and expert knowledge of aircraft and air travel.

I went home myself in July 1939 arriving in mid-August. At the end of the journey I travelled overland from Marseilles to Dover and passing through Paris one saw train after train with the notices on them, 'Mobilisation National, Reservee'. War clouds were in the air. By the end of the month, being certain that war would break out in a matter of days, I went to Blackheath, in south east London, to see Leslie who was home on leave at the same time. My sister-in-law, Ena, had already moved out of London to Eastbourne. A couple of days after I got to London, I received an order from the War Office to report to Edinburgh by the 1st September for embarkation for India.

I went to Edna's family home, in Preston, the next day. There I packed my kit, made my farewells and left for Edinburgh. I was not to see Brian and Valerie again for six years. A large convoy with a large naval escort had been formed and I was a passenger on the *Duchess of Bedford*. The senior officer was Major General Aukinleck, the beloved 'Auk' of the Indian Army. The voyage to Bombay was really uncomfortable and appallingly hot in the Red Sea and Indian Ocean as the ships were blacked out.

Beer and other drinks were strictly rationed and we ran out of them several days out from Bombay. There were a number submarine attacks on the convoy in the Atlantic and Mediterranean. It was very interesting to see the destroyer escort at work, hounding the submarines and obviously following them with Asdic [Sonar].

Just off Port Said a submarine attacked and a torpedo just shaved the stern of our ship. Some wag said that the Duchess had had a torpedo under her bottom, which was thought to be a great joke. At the end of the awful voyage down the Red Sea there was another submarine scare in the Bab al-Mandab Strait but we arrived in Bombay safely and without damage.

Before the voyage back to India and Burma, while on board the *Duchess of Bedford*, lying at Greenock, I heard Mr. Chamberlain's announcement of the declaration of war, on 3rd September. We sailed on the 5th just a few hours after the *Athenia* had been sunk off the Clyde and naturally there was great speculation as to what might happen to us.

Leslie and Ena were fortunate enough to be given passage together on the *Strathnaver* in September and returned safely to India. Fast ships were at that time being allowed to travel unescorted. Travelling by air was a different matter and it was not until December that Edna was able to return by flying boat, when I was very glad to see her arrive safely.

We had travelled a long way from the war zone and there was no shortage of food and drinks and it was not necessary to curtail social activities in any way, but strenuous efforts were made to raise money to donate to war charities at home and in allied countries. War planning for the army in Burma did not make any appreciable progress, until after Dunkirk, which had caused some consternation.

For several years the United States had been supporting Chiang Kai Shek in his struggle with the communists in China. War material, equipment and supplies had been reaching Yunnan province in southern China via the Rangoon metre gauge railway to Lashio and from there by the rough mountain road ('The Burma Road') to Kunming and onto Chungking.

At Rangoon near the docks there was a vast transit and storage area operated by the Americans containing thousands of crates of equipment, artillery and machine components, and thousands of vehicles. Vehicle chassis arrived in Burma and then they were fitted with their bodies or superstructure by Chinese carpenters using Burma teak and other woods. A large amount of vehicle movement and road traffic had resulted in Lashio expanding into a large corrugated iron shanty town.

The stealing and selling of equipment and the theft of vehicles soon grew to enormous proportions and corruption was rife everywhere. It was said that about every three months a Colonel on the Generalissimo's staff travelled down the whole length of the road from Chungking to Lashio and at the various staging points would select a man who was promptly taken off and shot, on the assumption that they were all in it together and that such an example would thus be effective at reducing corruption.

In 1940/1 the American Volunteer Group (AVG) was formed to assist the Generalissimo's war effort and the Chinese air force. The AVG pilots were all, officially, American civilians and paid by Chiang Kai Shek, including a bonus of $600 in gold for every enemy plane brought down. Consequently, there were a lot of Americans in Rangoon and Lashio before the outbreak of war with Japan.

The AVG was commanded by Col. Claire Chenault and his second in command was Major Harvey Greenlaw who's vivacious and attractive wife, Olga, kept the AVG war diary. The AVG soon acquired the nickname, the 'Flying Tigers'.

On this diary, Olga based her book [first published in 1943], 'The Lady and the Tigers', and in it Edna and I were frequently referred to. We came to know Greenlaws very well, to which I will relate later.

Our army was very short of vehicles and one day when I had taken over a staff appointment at army headquarters Burma, Brigadier J.C. Martin, and another Brigadier showed me a list of vehicles and equipment held at the American storage depot in Rangoon. He asked me to look at them and see if they would be of any use to us, particularly some items called 'reconnaissance cars'. I went to the depot, selected a crate marked 'reconnaissance car' and had it opened. Inside was a German limber type vehicle that is, a box on an axle between two wheels. The wheels were enormous and had metal tyres of solid iron about six inches wide and a quarter inch thick. They dated almost to the time of the Boer War and were meant to be drawn by horses. Our high hopes of new equipment were thus dashed and it became apparent that an enormous quantity of useless junk had been sold to the Chinese.

In May 1940 I went up to Maymyo on the northern Shan plateau, the hot weather seat of the government and where army headquarters was also located, to take over a temporary staff appointment. This business lasted a month and while Edna and I were there, Olga and Harvey Greenlaw stayed in 'Whipsnade Villa' and had our staff of servants look after them.

I still receive letters [c. mid-1970s] from Olga who now has a ranch at Gazelle in northern California. She often refers to, "my lovely house in Rangoon."

Poor old Kurram Khan our wonderful abdur [head-servant] who we had taken from the Pegu Club was quite worn out. Olga and Harvey had thrown parties every night, lasting until the dawn.

Maymyo is a delightful place, situated at an elevation of about 3,500 feet and surrounded by rolling downs, covered with pine forest and lakes here and there. Lovely houses are built round a small lake and the climate is like a warm English spring. In this centre a number of the Shan States ruled by their Saophas [hereditary chiefs] were given guidance and advice by a British officer of the Civil Service, the Commissioner of the Shan States. The town had immense beauty and charm and the Shan tribes were wonderful people, to live amongst.

Before we arrived in Burma in 1938 an eminent member of the Burma Civil Service, Maurice Collis, had written two marvellous books; 'Trials in Burma' and 'Lords of the Sunset - A Tour in the Shan States', a most fascinating story about the Shan states and their Saophas.

We decided to spend the Christmas holiday 1940 at Kalaw a lovely little hill station in the southern Shan States which had a very pretty hotel called the Kalaw Hotel.

The Author's children, Brian and Valerie, by the pool
at one of his villas in Rangoon, 1941/2

Chapter 24

Lords of the Sunset

In a personal story it is better not to become involved in too much detailed history of the past, unless it is necessary for continuity or essential to the reader's understanding. In the 17th and 18th centuries the two major powers in what is now known as the Southeast Asia area were the kingdoms of Ava and Ayutthaya, now known as Burma and Thailand.

Shan tribes inhabit the Shan plateau which geographically is in northeastern Burma and north western Thailand. It consists of a number of native states and the main administrative divisions are the Northern Shan states and the Southern Shan states. They are ruled by hereditary chiefs who are called Saophas [or 'Sawbwas', in Burmese] and are exact counterparts of the maharajas of the Indian princely states. In the East, emperors, kings, khans and other rulers have always had a number of grandiloquent titles that they prize very highly. Amongst those of the kings of Ava were the Lord of the White Elephant and King of the Sunrise. The latter title signified the power and glory of the rising sun and to make a distinction between them and the vassal princes of the Shan states; the Shan princes were known as Lords of the Sunset, which description Maurice Collis used as a title for his delightful book.

It is approximately a 300 mile journey along the Rangoon-Mandalay road to Meiktila, from where a road proceeds almost due east to the Shan plateau and traverses the whole width of it to Kengtung in the largest of the southern states, bordering Thailand and through which the Salween River passes. A branch of the metre-gauge railway runs from Thazi on the Rangoon-Mingaladon line to Taunggyi, the administrative centre of the state, where the Commissioner resides. At that time he was a Mr. Fogarty, who later, in 1943, was killed in a plane crash, shortly after take-off, on a flight to Chungking.

The route climbs up on the plateau through typical Burmese jungle. It is very steep and narrow and has many hairpin bends, but when it debouches onto the plateau there are vistas of beauty in all directions. Green rolling downs are covered with pine woods and low ranges of hills. Picturesque little hamlets are dotted about the downs. Wildflowers are everywhere, and orchids are seen in profusion. The climate is delightful

Kalaw is only a small township with a tiny little bazaar and on a small hill above the town is the Kalaw Hotel, the only sizable building in the place with one or two guest houses and a club. 17 miles away in Yongway State is the large Inle Lake surrounded by pine-clad hills and on the banks of the lake is the town of Yongway. From Yongway the road climbs onto a high portion of plateau through a road junction called Loilem to Taunggyi which is also the end of the railway.

There was to be a big dance on Christmas Eve at Kalaw Hotel at which several Saophas and their parties were to be present. We were all agog to see the beautiful Yongway Princess, a young lady of one of the other noble Shan families, recently married to a Saopha.

After a nice dinner, dancing started and into the ballroom walked a very beautiful young woman. She was about 5' 6" in height with a most attractive figure, shown to perfection in the white blouse and lovely flowered longyi, with a green background. She was fair with a complexion of cream, and an exquisite face of extraordinary beauty. Her black coiffure was embellished with ornaments of silver and precious stones. This was the Yongway Princess, who was even more beautiful than we had the imagined.

Edna and I were introduced to the Saopha and the Princess, and I had the privilege and wonderful pleasure of two dances with her. She spoke English well and her lovely voice, charming manner and vivacity added to the perfection of this wonderful woman. The dancing went on into the small hours. It was a wonderful evening, thoroughly enjoyed by everyone, but the high spot was the attendance of this lovely and charming princess, that made the occasion perfect.

There were many things to do and see in the Shan States. There was a small town called Pindaya, about 17 miles from Kalaw. The town was on the shores of Pindaya Lake and above the lake on the opposite side was a hill about 700 feet high, containing at the top some caves filled with statues of the Buddha, and a Buddhist temple.

When we arrived there with two friends, we saw there were thousands of ducks on the lake but fortunately, we did not take the opportunity to shoot at any, even though there were large formations of duck flying around. A villager, who spoke English, approached us and told us that the ducks were sacred.

We then climbed the hundreds of steps leading up to the temple and a guide took us up to the caves. It was pitch black inside the caves and there was absolute and complete silence. We had hurricane lamps and electric torches with us. In the first cave there were a number of gigantic Buddhas, some 25 feet in height and many smaller ones carved out of the living rock. A passage led steeply downwards into the next cave where there were more Buddhas, not quite as large as the others but more numerous. There were still further caves and the lowest one must have been 200 feet down into the heart of the hill. This vast cave contained hundreds of small Buddhas and the silence was absolute. I knew I was in a very holy place. The aura pervaded everywhere. At that time very few Europeans had visited the Pindaya caves and now that Burma has withdrawn from the outside world there will be fewer still.

On another day we visited Yongway and the Inle Lake. It was surprisingly like Kashmir; lovely vistas of clear water, bordered by pine-clad hills. The houses round the Lake were often built over the water on wooden piles and the small boats, used for trade and travel, were very like the shikaras in Kashmir. The boatmen rowed their sampans with their legs. An upright wooden pole fits into the sampan at the stern and the rower held this with one hand, standing upright in the sampan one of his legs was thrown over the paddle which was held with the other hand at the top of the handle. It was then raised, and the paddle pushed forward and downwards into the water and the propulsive stroke made with the leg pulling the paddle to the rear. Probably a unique form of rowing, it was quite a draw for visitors taking pictures and it also appeared to be very practical.

Young women from the Padaung tribe with the giraffe necks were seen everywhere as this tribe is the largest in the Yongway State. On another day we visited Taunggyi and met the few European residents at the club for tea. The estates varied greatly in size. Some are little more than large farms, while the larger ones at Mong Mit, Kanti and Satemwa were thousands of square miles in area.

An owner's residence or palace is known as a 'haw', again some of these are only large houses while those of the large estates are very like large country houses in England. An amusing story from Taunggyi can be recounted; one of the rare visitors to that remote place was a young American lady and in the club one evening she overheard several of the elderly memsahibs talking. The gist of their conversation was that Satemwa's 'haw' was very beautiful but Mong Pawn's 'haw' was prettier, although smaller etc. Mr. Fogerty, the commissioner, was in the club at the time, so the young lady, being very puzzled, turned to him and said in a loud voice, "Hey Mr. Fogerty who are all these whores they're talking about?"

There was a nice little golf course on the ridge overlooking the Kalaw hotel but it really consisted of a number of greens on knolls. One had steep walks up and down from green to green and if a drive went wrong it was completely lost.

Shans, in all walks of life, had beautiful manners and it was a delight being amongst such people in such a lovely countryside. It was a marvellous holiday, and the memories linger over the years.

Army headquarters was moved from Maymyo to Rangoon in 1941 and I assumed my appointment there. The raising of new units and organisation of new formations was taken in hand and we were all very busy. The Saopha [or Sawbwa] of Mong Mit, the largest of the northern Shan states, offered to raise a battalion of infantry and arrangements were made for him to come to Rangoon with a cadre of Shan officers and NCOs to undergo training and be provided with their first line transport, arms and equipment etc. I was responsible for the provision of their vehicles and the training of their drivers at Sale Barracks in Rangoon.

The Saopha, Sao Hkun Hkio , known as 'Kio', to all his friends had been at Cambridge and while there married a lovely, blonde English girl called Mabel, the daughter of a businessman in Cambridge. The marriage was regarded with apprehension by Kio's family and the fact that the first two children were girls, caused further disfavour.

The young family duly arrived in Rangoon and in addition brought a State retainer and an enormous Great Dane dog. They had a suite in the Strand Hotel, Rangoon, and during the several weeks they were there they either dined at 'Whipsnade Villa' or we dined with them at the Strand Hotel.

One night at the Strand, Mabel appeared wearing some superb jewellery. One piece being an enormous star sapphire in a solid gold necklace. When Edna admired it, Mabel said it was part of the State jewels and was in fact the largest star sapphire in the world.

After dinner in their suite Mabel pulled a tin trunk from under the bed and in it were many more of the State jewels including tiaras. It seems they did not feel worried about the safety of such lovely jewellery. Mabel, nodding at the Great Dane said, "Not with him about and our soldier protecting us".

Kio himself was a very nice person and was very punctilious in his attitude towards senior officers. When Burma became independent Kio was made Foreign Minister and the Minister for the Shan State. Before leaving for Mong Mit, on the completion of their visit, Edna ascertained from Mabel that she was expecting an addition to the family, and that she hoped that it would be a boy and so ease the tension with Kio's family.

In Mong Mit state are the world-famous ruby mines of Mogok and the great silver mine at Bawdwin. When the Japanese forced us to withdraw from Burma the Sawbwas remained in their states, to carry on their administration and, as far as the Japs would allow them, to protect their subjects from oppression as much as they could.

There was no further news of Mabel and Kio until in February 1945 when we were in England, on the first home leave of the war. Headlines appeared in the papers, one day, announcing that Princess Mabel and her family had arrived safely in England. From it we learned that they were both well and that two more girl babies had been born to her during the Japanese occupation.

Chapter 25

Golden Sands and Tropic Seas

In 1941 it had been decided to bring the army in Burma up to divisional strength and another brigade was to be dispatched from India. The brigade was known as 'Force Relief' and was commanded by a Brigadier A.C. Curtis, who I had first met in Peshawar in 1929, when he was a Brigade Major in Peshawar.

After disembarking in Rangoon the brigade moved north and was deployed in the Shan States to watch the line of the Salween River and counter any threat from Thailand and the east. At the same time it was decided to establish a brigade of divisional strength in Moulmein area, which entailed the provision of accommodation for the brigade and also numerous works to enable training to be carried out.

I was a member of the group of officers which went to Moulmein to carry out reconnaissance of the site and make recommendations regarding the location of the barracks, rifle range, etc, and the construction of roads and many other things.

The place selected was a few miles south-east of Moulmein and consisted of undulating ground covered with thick scrub. We completed our task in a couple of days and we were then able to look round Moulmein and the surrounding country.

On one occasion I noticed a grove of bamboos, some of which were nearly two feet in diameter and growing to a height of about 120 feet. This is remarkable considering that bamboo is a grass.

We also visited the old Moulmein pagoda on a spur above the town. Looking over the mouth of the Salween River and the Gulf of Martaban it was easy to imagine a British Tommy and his Burmese girlfriend climbing up to the pagoda and carrying on their courtship looking over the Gulf of Martaban and the great forest area behind the tower.

We also visited one of the timber yards where two gigantic elephant tuskers still carried on their work, piling teak. Moulmein, once a very busy port, became a backwater after the Great War and there was an atmosphere of decay, particularly in the buildings along the waterfront.

I had heard, whilst I was in Moulmein, that there were some very large jheels, (or lakes), on which there were tens of thousands of duck, towards the Thailand border which was about 45 miles to the east. Following a bullock cart track in that direction from a small town called Mudon several of us went there and had some fair shooting.

We also explored Tenasserim, the long narrow tract of country leading from southern Burma down to the Malayan peninsula which was approached by a road from Moulmein and a branch of the metre-gauge railway which runs for 60 miles to a river township called Yebyu. Here the railway ends but on the other side of the river the road continues for a 100miles south to the mining township of Tavoy where a lovely beach called, Maungmagan is located.

At Maungmagan there were several bungalows owned by the mining companies but because the country around is practically uninhabited only people invited by the company managers were able to go there. It was such a lovely place and invitations to stay there were highly prized. Later the opportunity arose for me to take 10 days leave and as we had an invitation to Maungmagan, Edna and I set out on our journey there.

The first part of the journey was by rail from Rangoon to Martaban on the banks of the Salween River. There were dozens of vendors selling cigarette lighters, which worked properly, and some of them were as low as one rupee in price.

The Salween was crossed by a river steamer, taking 30 minutes to make the passage from Martaban to Moulmein.

We stayed over in Moulmein for 24 hours and while there we were invited by John Gunn, the manager of a timber yard, to see the two elephants, I referred to earlier, working in the yard. They were in the Salween River when we arrived and then they walked up the concrete ramp into the timber yard area.

I was able to get a colour cine film of them in the water and emerging from it. They then commenced to work. On one side of the yard was a sawmill, near which there were piles of planks, about 20 feet long, two inches wide and two inches in depth. In the same area were small stacks of teak logs, these were about 18 feet long and a foot square. Their weight must have been very considerable indeed.

The Logs were to be piled on a very large stack on the opposite side of the yard. One elephant would manoeuvre a log into position; so that it could be rolled towards the stack. Dropping the end of its trunk between its toes, to act as a cushion, with a wooden baulk at the base of the stack and then kicked the log, rolling it forward. When it was the right distance from the stack the elephant turned the baulk square onto it. Then one elephant pushed its tusks under the end of the log and lifted the log onto the top of the stack. The other elephant then knelt down and pushed the baulk with its curled trunk onto the top of the stack until the timber was in position and then adjusted the position of the log and more or less smoothed it off in line with the others. When dealing with the planks the elephant dug its tusks into the pile of planks and curled its trunk over the top of the pile of planks to hold them in place. The Tusker gathered up the number of planks that it knew it could handle and carry. Giving its head a jerk and as it did so tightened the grip with its trunk and moved its head in the direction of the point of balance. Then holding the planks in a tidy and balanced package conveyed them to the place required.

One completion of the work the elephants stalked off to a water barrel fed by a pipe with a wheel to turn the water on and off. They turned the water on and having had their drink, by holding their trunk under the water and squirting it into their throats; they then turned the water wheel off, salaamed and were led back to their stables.

I was able to film the whole of this operation and fortunately managed to bring it out of Burma in my pack. [Unfortunately, the film used was a Pathé 9.5mm standard and although popular in the 1920s and 30s, it later became a rare format. Projectors were hard to come by for the showing of this type of film and it was eventually disposed of, after the Author's death. However, as a child, I did have the chance to see this rare film on one occasion, at home, when my father was able to borrow a projector of the right format].

We continued our journey to Yebyu by rail and on the other side of the river a car sent by our host was waiting to take us to Tavoy. The whole journey was through unbroken jungle, with ranges of hills on either side. There were very few habitations or dwellings of any sort. We stopped for tea at a forest rest house built on the road where it ran through a ravine and from the bungalow veranda one looked 500 feet sheer down into the nullah bed below.

Our host was a Mr. Ottaway, a mining company manager. He took us out to the bungalow at Maungmagan, some miles away over the Tavoy River. The beach was about six miles in length, and the sand was very fine and almost white in colour. Behind the beach, for its whole length, was a Casuarina forest and in the bay several small islands, some of them with pagodas on the top. The water was wonderfully clear and it was possible to see to a depth of 15 feet or more. There were thousands of wonderfully coloured tropical fish, a sight to be prized in the days before colour television.

Once we had settled into the bungalow Mr. Ottaway took us to meet some of the other people who were staying on the beach. Amongst them were Hilda and Pat Leigh who were permanent residents on Maungmagan. Pat Leigh had, unfortunately, been paralysed by an accident to his spine some years previously. Hilda was an attractive Austrian blonde who had some unexplained power over animals. She was also a naturist, when the mood moved her.

We spent most of each day bathing and gathered in one or other bungalow for dinner, dance, cards or parlour games afterwards. One place we visited was unforgettable: the beach called Launglon about six miles south of Tavoy and on the other side of Tavoy River.

It was a small horseshoe shaped beach only a few hundred yards across. A narrow sandy beach was backed by a fairly steep and jungle covered hill that rose several hundred feet behind the beach. A small Burmese village, of a few wooden huts was built on the spit of land forming the northern arm of the horseshoe. On the other side was a shallow lagoon of wonderfully clear water full of oyster beds and fish. These oyster beds were producing cultured pearls.

The party consisted of the Leighs, Mr. Ottoway ('Otto'), his lady companion, Lesley Diefenbaker, Edna and me. Otto know Launglon well and the village headman and his teenage daughter came to pay their respects, and were immediately offered a tumbler full of neat gin, which was disposed of quickly and glasses held out for replenishment.

A meal was then prepared in a flagon-shaped metal vessel the centre of which consisted of a hollow cylinder into which hot charcoal was placed, and the meal cooked. The first course was really a soup. When this was finished it was followed by eggs, meat and a variety of vegetables; the main course, all the while, being continually cooked. It turned out to be a really tasty meal; and the gin added to its enjoyment.

The headman's daughter danced and sang. Then, when we had rested, we bathed and lay back on the lovely beach enjoying the whole beautiful view, and cloud-scented air. We returned to Maungmagan in the evening at the end of a memorable day.

One day I was walking along the beach at Maungmagan when out of the Casuarina forest came Hilda walking toward me. She was dressed almost in the minimum. Following her was a small Chital fawn. She had gone for one of her usual walks in the forest and seeing the fawn, called it and eventually persuaded it into following her.

Pat told me that on other occasions she had returned to the bungalow with jungle fowl following her, a squirrel and a mongoose. When the Leighs were forced to leave Burma, by the Jap invasion, they had to make a journey of 1,600 miles and when it was not possible to travel by car Pat Leigh had to be carried on a litter, for another 500 miles.

We saw them on the way out of Burma at Myitkyina and later again at Imphal. They were in good spirits. They eventually got to Kashmir, where we saw them again. We heard some years later that Pat Leigh had died and when the war was over Hilda had returned to Tenasserim and was operating a small rubber plantation.

I visited Maungmagan, once more, during a military reconnaissance in that area. It is so remote that I do not think that its beauty will ever be despoiled, even by modern tourism as we know it. [In fact 70 years on and despite Burma's extended period of international isolation Maungmagan is now an established tourist venue]

Chapter 26

The Japanese Strike and Rangoon is Ravished

"The air situation was even worse, as only thirty-seven aircraft were at first available to meet 100 Japanese – which were doubled by another air brigade in...January."

[Liddel Hart's History of the Second World War, B.H. Liddel Hart, Cassel & Co, 1970, p.244]

In the autumn of 1941 Burma army headquarters moved from the centre of Rangoon to the university estate, an attractive parkland area five miles north of Rangoon. At that time a lovely house on the Victoria Lake owned by a Mr. Brown of the Rangoon Gazette became vacant, and I took over the tenancy. It was a fine modern house with a large garden. The lounge and dining room had a view of the whole length of the lake and on the left was a small creek, on the other side of which was the Burma Oil Company colony. On our right was a fine mansion occupied by two friends Mr. and Mrs. Pope and their 18-year-old daughter. J.C. Martin, of army headquarters, had another house next to the Popes and beyond that there was a Pungi camp at the edge of the lake, surrounded by a large bed of long reed grass.

Olga and Harvey Greenlaw had moved to Toungoo 120 miles north of Rangoon where the American Volunteer Group (AVG) had constructed an airfield. They liked our new house very much and used to come down most weekends, often bringing some of the AVG pilots with them.

A lovely lawn led to the edge of the water on which we had a punt and a canoe. Our bathing parties soon became well-known and popular.

Amongst our friends in Rangoon were Geoff and Gwyneth Dawny-Lowsley. Geoff was a Major in the 4th Gurkhas, seconded to one of the Burma Rifle Battalions. They were a really charming and accomplished couple. Gwyneth, who was very tall, about six feet in height, was a wonderful car driver and knew how to take an engine to bits.

When war with Japan broke out in December 1941 several ladies were appointed as drivers in the Staff Car Pool at army headquarters and in my section of the staff we had Gwyneth Dawny-Lowsley and a young Burmese lady. She had a lovely soprano voice and was known as the Burmese Nightingale.

Together with a Mrs Eden, wife of Alan Eden, director of civil aviation, they volunteered to drive ambulances for the Red Cross and with many other ladies, had spent endless hours in exercises, having training in first aid which they were later to put to good use.

The Japanese Attack

The Japanese had already occupied Thailand and French-Indochina, now known as Vietnam. It was only a matter of time before war would break out. Pearl Harbour was however an utter surprise and when HMS Prince of Wales and HMS Repulse were sunk off Laos on 10th December 1941 Burma and Malaya, with comparatively weak defence forces, were completely exposed to a Japanese attack.

Only a few of us at army headquarters knew the extent of the crippling blow that the American Pacific fleet had sustained. The Japanese opened their first attack on Burma on December 23ʳᵈ 1941 with an air raid on Rangoon. At about 10am the air raid warning sounded at army headquarters and people started to move towards the slit trenches which had been dug in advance.

The Christmas Air Raids on Rangoon

Outside, in a clear sky, could be seen three squadrons of Japanese bombers flying in tight arrowhead formation at about 18,000 feet. They were flying from the south and appeared to be flying along the waterfront. Bombs started crumping, obviously, along the line of wharves and there was also an attack at Mingaladon airfield, six miles to the north.

There was a great deal of aircraft noise and it was clear that the RAF and AVG fighters were up, but they were too high to be seen. Their presence was soon apparent when a Jap. bomber fell out of formation and with a long trail of smoke issuing from it came down in a long curving path and finally exploded.

The raid went on and many more bombers met the same fate. We were anxious at army headquarters to know what damage had been done and I got permission to go to Rangoon and bring back information.

I went in a staff car and Edna followed in her own car. As we entered the Prome road near the university estate a police barricade held us up and we were told that we would not be able to go into Rangoon. I insisted that we must go, as I was a staff officer of army headquarters and Edna had to take up her duties with the ambulance service. The police were obstinate, and a Burmese sub-inspector drew his revolver and threatened me. I lost my temper at this and really let fly at him and we were eventually able to move on.

As we drove down Signal Pagoda Road past our old house we saw several bodies lying on the road but there were no people in the streets. As clouds were building up from the burning wharves I made my way to Booking Street wharf where there were thousands of tons of small arms ammunition, artillery shells, of various calibres, and other weapons supplies. Meanwhile Edna made her way through to Red Cross headquarters.

Explosions from the wharf buildings were continuous and as I got near the gates a British officer climbed out of a slit trench nearby, followed by a few men. They were very white and shaken. I knew the officer; he was a businessman who had been inducted into the Burma Army. I gave him permission to move his troops off and join his parent unit.

Saving the Last Ammunition Supplies

I then went into the wharf shed area. Lying on the ground were two dead Burma Riflemen and on one of the shed walls were pieces of human flesh and another corpse lying in a drain by the shed. At that moment a lone aircraftsman came out of the burning shed pushing a barrow full of steel boxes. I ascertained it was a load of detonators which must be saved if possible.

That he had got the load of detonators so far was miraculous as they are very touchy, and I expected an explosion at any moment. Inside the shed cartridge cases were exploding in every direction, fires were burning, and the heat was terrific. A stack of shells was surrounded by a ring of flame. We knew this was the only reserve stock we had left in Burma, and it was essential that they be saved. The aircraftsman returned and between us we stamped out the fire surrounding the shells and moved any remaining combustible material away from them.

While putting out the fire we were surrounded by a veritable barrage of explosions of whining and ricocheting bullets. Both of us were struck a number of times and each had a number of flesh wounds but miraculously none were serious. Having saved the shells, I instructed the aircraftsmen to return to his unit. It was essential, as soon as possible, to move the shells and other equipment away from the wharf and I went back to Sale Barracks at all speed and reported the situation to the station staff officer and Major Bill Walton, of the 1st Gloucesters, the town major. The Gloucesters were soon on their way and a lot of valuable equipment and the shells were saved.

Corpses were lying in the Strand Road and the streets adjoining the wharves. Tens of thousands of the populace had gathered to watch the planes and a considerable number of 500lb bombs had dropped amongst them. The gutters were literally running with blood. It was difficult to assess the total number of casualties but approximately 4,000 bodies were found and there were likely to be thousands more under the destroyed buildings. In that climate, in a few days, the stench became appalling.

Rangoon was nearly half empty the following day, the Burmese and Chinese having moved to the jungle near the suburbs and many Indians had started the long trek to India. I returned to army headquarters and made my report. I was the only officer from headquarters that actually saw the scene that day.

The Valliant Work of the Ambulance Service

In the evening I awaited Edna at home and she came back after nightfall, her clothing covered with congealed blood and completely exhausted. The other ladies, also, had done magnificent work. Many of the Burmese and Indian drivers went off, once hostilities started. Those drivers who remained at their posts were seeking out and carrying casualties to the first aid centre, while bombs were still falling.

One of the nurses on duty at the headquarters was 18 year old Miss Pope, the daughter of our neighbours, Mr. and Mrs. Pope. Shortly after the bombing had started her father and mother were brought in on stretchers, one dead and the other dying. All the remaining drivers and nurses carried on through that dreadful day and never faltered. Their work was beyond praise.

The Tragic Death of our Neighbours

Later, we walked round to the Popes' bungalow to see if we could help and found out that they had both been killed by a burst of machine gun fire from a bomber flying down Phayre Street, while watching the bombing from the balcony of Mr. Pope's office. All the workmen had fled and two rough wooden boxes had to be used as coffins. Mr. Healey, Miss Pope's fiancé, and two other friends were also at the house.

We covered the coffin lids with black cloth and put their visiting cards on to identify who they were. They were taken away the next day to be buried.

There was a similar raid on Christmas Day but this time the casualties were far lighter. There were not many people left in Rangoon and those that were had the sense to try and take cover as fast as possible.

The New Brigadier

In November a new brigadier arrived from India to take over an appointment at army headquarters. I had met him in Peshawar in 1929. There we had been at loggerheads. After feeling his way for a few months, as he knew nothing about Burma, and was largely dependent on my knowledge and experience he started to become very nasty and a complete obstructionist. His wife however was charming and very popular and has remained a friend over the years.

One night at a dinner party at our house on the lake the brigadier and his wife were among the guests and also Olga and an AVG pilot. Edna had placed Olga next to the brigadier who had fallen for her attractive personality and vivacity. Suddenly Olga said in a very loud voice, "Some man is squeezing my knee." It could only be the brigadier and his discomfiture was enjoyed by everyone. Later he began making advances to Gwyneth who kept him off with a stinging right hander and they were not friends after this.

A prisoner of war camp had, optimistically, been constructed and established at Thayetmyo, a port on the west bank of the Irrawaddy about 220 miles north of Rangoon. In charge of it was a Captain McColl, in civil life an officer in the Burmese Forestry Service. The story of the McColl family was a remarkable one.

I went to Thayetmyo to see Capt. McColl and ask if he needed any help and see how the work was progressing. I travelled by car through Prome and then to Kamma and on to Thayetmyo. The town was on a huge bluff overlooking the Irrawaddy River and had an old fort that was surrounded by dense forest in every direction.

In 1931 during the Saya San rebellion local magistrates had been quartered there and many of their names were carved on wooden verandas. I had an interesting 24 hours with Capt. McColl and we chatted about his brother who I had met in Maymyo earlier. At Prome, the river port on the Irrawaddy 130 miles north of Rangoon was an important communications centre as the western road to the north of Burma runs through to it to Yenangyaung, the oilfield area, and there is also a metre gauge railway line as far as Prome.

Some friends of ours, the Steel brothers, invited us there for a few days. There was a nice club on the riverbank, with a veranda over the water and in the water the most enormous log I have ever seen which was used as a fender for steamer traffic. Mr. Dunbar, the number one of Steel Brothers in Prome, was an enormous 20 stone bachelor whose forte was to prepare a meal of sausages and mashed potatoes. He fried some very large sausages over a primus stove while we sat round drinking and then served the meal which was very appetising.

After dinner we went to the local cinema. This was a ramshackle wooden building, the home of dozens of pigeons whose presence was very obvious on the floor and on the seats. We sat on settees in a semi-circle, a customary arrangement in the east, but the cooing of the pigeons and the noise of their wings and the aroma from their droppings rather spoiled the film. We then went looking round the town. Right in the centre of it, in the main street, and adjacent to a railway crossing was a pond about 25 yards across. Around the pond were sat several men with sieves. They put their sieves under the water gathered up some gravel and earth and then with a circular motion started what appeared to be panning for gold. I asked my host what they were doing, and he said, "They are panning for gold. They make quite a living out of it." This was in the centre of the third largest town in Burma. Burma was a surprising country in many ways.

Chapter 27

The Japanese Advance in Burma

The Japanese had advanced in Malaya and our intelligence sources indicated that the attack on Burma would be in Tenasserim towards Moulmein.

Lt. General T.J. Hutton arrived just before Christmas as the new GOC the Burma Army, to take over from Major General McLeod. In addition the 17th Indian Division, commanded, by Major General Jackie Smyth VC, had also moved to Burma, but his last brigade did not arrive in Burma until 19th January 1942. There were also six more British battalions to come.

Major General Smyth and I were together in Peshawar in 1929. Phillip Gwynn, a GSO 1 in intelligence at army headquarters, who spoke Japanese fluently, was the brigade major in the Bannu brigade in the Waziristan operation of 1936/37.

The direction of the Japanese attack was obvious and necessitated that the units, depots and administrative arrangements for the defence of central Burma and the Shan States should be redeployed with the utmost speed, forward of the Salween River and between the Sittang and Salween Rivers.

As there was only a one metre gauge railway and one road available this was a terrific task; particularly for the newer members of the staff and the supply, transport and ordnance services. In addition there was a tremendous amount of staff work involved of which, by necessity, the heaviest burden fell on the few regular officers. In addition, I had the general responsibility for the supervising, raising and training of the Burma Mechanical Transport Regiment, together with the establishment of a motor transport depot and workshops at Mingaladon.

To add to this there was the need for the raising of a Mule Corps and a total of 42 other smaller supply and transport units. The Mule Corps consisted of Chinese muleteers who lived in the wild hills near the border with Yunnan province and northern Burma. Even for those who knew their language, discipline could not be instilled in to them and on the first Japanese attack on Moulmein they disappeared and were never seen again. It literally broke the heart of the Captain in charge of them.

For political reasons the first Burma Mechanical Transport Regiment had to be raised from Burmese nationals only and because of the pressing military situation recruitment work continued day and night. A recruiting office was open in Sale Barracks in Rangoon, and one day when visiting it to see how work was progressing, a huge Burman came in. He was six feet in height and was in magnificent physical condition. He was only 23 years old, weighed about 18 stone and spoke very good English. I asked his name, he replied, "Mong Sin" which literally means 'Mr. Elephant'. Nothing could have been more appropriate. Mong Sin loved soldiering. He worked with immense enthusiasm in all the training that recruits had to undergo and soon was the smartest and most efficient recruit in the unit. On parade he was a picture, his uniform was well-fitting, always spotless and he looked particularly smart with his impressive physique. All Burma regiments wore the felt broad-brimmed hat worn by the Gurkhas. Within a month Mong Sin was promoted to havildar sergeant and at the end of three months, training completed, he was promoted to jemadar, i.e. a governor's junior commissioned officer, wearing one pip.

In the company there was also another very smart and keen young man, Bobar Tar, who had a Bachelor of Arts degree from Rangoon University. He was promoted subahdar, a GC [governor's commissioned] officer, wearing two pips.

This first purely Burman unit caused great interest in Rangoon and the Burmese politicians paid particular attention to it. The Governor's counsellor inspected the work on Sale Barracks one day, while I was in command of the parade, and it received a terrific report and many photographs in the Rangoon papers. As always Mong Sin looked marvellous. He went from strength to strength in his new army career and was my pride and joy.

As the Japanese attack developed many people started leaving Rangoon again and families of army and other service personnel who lived in the districts outside Rangoon went to their relations, including many in the MT Regiment.

In February 1942, after the "Sittang disaster" [so named by Gen. Smyth; after a four day fierce fight with the Japanese, with heavy losses for British forces engaged, and the loss of control of a strategic bridge over the Sittang River], panic began to spread. One morning at the monthly payday Subahdar Bobar Tar and Jemadar Mong Sin, with an escort, drove into Rangoon to draw the regiment's pay, about 15,000 rupees. Afterwards they promptly disappeared. After withdrawing the money from the bank they had gone off into the delta district. 'Mr Elephant' had sadly betrayed his trust. I hoped that if he survived the war he might have had the chance to rehabilitate himself in the new Burma.

The Japanese advance from Thailand to Moulmein was rapid but I was able to get there a few days before the Japanese captured it. An advance base supply depot had been established. Major Jack Rose of the Rowan Company, a big Rangoon store, was in charge. He had a most efficient show operating and was obviously going to do well if he was spared. I also visited the Mule Corps hidden in the jungle but, as I have said, they were beyond hope.

In his withdrawal across the Salween River, Maj. Gen. Smyth, in common with all other COs, had got rid of the field impress account, i.e. cash; on orders from army headquarters. Unfortunately when the units arrived in India the Indian administrators of the accounts department demanded detailed reports as to how the moneys were disposed of and the correspondence went on for months and months and became a real nuisance.

Chapter 28

The Long Retreat Begins

After crossing the Salween River the Japanese forced the 17th Indian Division to withdraw to the line of the Bilin River. The Japanese then took that position on 18th February. The only line of defence, before Rangoon, was the Sittang River. Two brigades of the division were still on the eastern side of the river when they were heavily attacked by the Japanese. They lost all of their vehicles, guns and equipment and suffered heavy casualties. In the meantime a Japanese encircling force had worked its way through the jungle and attacked the detachment guarding the Sittang Railway Bridge which was blown up before the rest of the two brigades could cross.

Once this news was received, Army Headquarters decided immediately that all European and government civilians should be evacuated from Rangoon. The order was issued at 10.00hrs on 22nd of February and civilians were required to leave Rangoon by 14.00hrs. I phoned Edna and told her to be prepared to leave after lunch. She should put what personal clothing she could get into the car with a stock of tinned food and make her way through Yenangyaung, Meiktila and Mandalay to Maymyo, where there would be friends to accommodate her.

After lunch we bade each other a tender farewell and Edna began her journey to Mandalay. I think that this can best be described by quoting extracts from a letter she wrote on 3rd June 1942 from Srinagar in Kashmir to her parents in England.

Quote

"Dear Mother and Dad,

"It was grand to get your cable and to know that you are all right after all these months. I have cabled you many times from Burma but it is more than likely that the money [for the cables] went into the pockets of corrupt officials. First and foremost, I must let you know that Stanley is safe and in hospital in Dehradun with malaria. There have been many deaths on that awful march through swamp and jungle from Burma to Assam with very little food and untold privations. He is lucky to get out alive. Some others did get through but got killed in an air raid at their first civilised camp. When I go back to the evacuation of Rangoon, Stanley heard a whisper that Rangoon was to be evacuated and phoned me to be ready to leave within a few hours. I was pushed into my Vauxhall with a suitcase, bedding and enough petrol for the journey and tinned stores, to go to Maymyo, and two mattresses and rope to put over the top of the car if we ran into aerial machine gunning. I had no servants as they had run away days before.

"Fighting was going on at Pegu, so I had to take the road through Phyu to Yenangyaung, 320 miles. I met a convoy and tailed on to it for the journey which took us two days and two nights of absolute nightmare and privation. Seventeen of us slept on the floor of one tiny room one night. The traffic was terrible with Chinese lorries doing 50 to 60 miles an hour, cutting in and out of the traffic, trying to get the last munitions and supplies out of Rangoon before it was too late.

"The road was full of car wrecks, military traffic coming in the opposite direction, aeroplanes overhead, waters to ford on bamboo sleepers placed on the river bed, sometimes you made it, sometimes you were stuck with ploughmen jeering at you as you passed through villages. Anyway I made it, to find that Mandalay and Maymyo had suffered air raids the day before.

"I went to some friends of ours, I was lucky, and had a day or two's rest before I could feel normal again. I was hoping to see Stanley, with the rest of army, at headquarters within a day or two but he did not leave Rangoon until 7th March.

[When he did leave] "He was with the first four cars of the column. The Japanese had got wind of the movement of troops and were waiting, 6,000 of them, hidden by the road. They [the Japanese] did not give the show away for the first cars but the next got it and had to fight two days to clear the roadblock. He [Stanley] was posted as 'missing' as he was thought to be in the back [of the column]. But [the column] was joined up eventually and they arrived in Maymyo.

"All the women were being evacuated but I was employed at government house, doing my cipher work, so managed to stay on until the 7th of April. Stanley drove me and Daphne Culatto, the wife of another officer, up to Lashio.

"When we arrived in Lashio people were pouring out in their cars and we were told that the air raid alarm had sounded, so we reversed [changed direction] and carried on with them and then went off into the jungle where we hid. You would do that in Lashio as it was what I call a 'boom town', just sticks and bamboo houses and no protection, except for slit tranches. To our horror we found out that the people who were to have flown out on the 5th, 6th and 7th of April were still waiting and no plane coming for weeks, as the Chinese National Airways Corporation was evacuating wounded. There was no place to stay in. However, Olga and Harvey Greenlaw turned up from Kunming with several AVG pilots and we were given accommodation in the Chinese National Airways Hostel in Lashio. On 12th April after Stanley contacted General Stilwell and Colonel Boatna, American Army, we were flown out in an American transport plane along with a lot of evacuees from Kunming. We left at the crack of dawn having had a bun without butter and a glass of hot water for breakfast.

"Calcutta was a nightmare. Life was [still] normal there. They [still] fired the midday gun. [But] If cars backfired or planes flew over the hotel and dive bombed, in practice, I was either flinging myself on the ground or was sweating blood.

"I got out of there, having done my shopping, starting at suitcases, sheets, towels, pillows and bottles of phospherine [tonic] and arrived in Kashmir and peace. We have lost all of our possessions; Stanley arrived in Assam with only the clothes on his back; and some of our silver in a suitcase following up, behind. I do not know if he eventually got it out, I do not care. We love each other and that is all that matters.

"We were only allowed three pounds of baggage each on the plane but I filled my pockets with money and things which had cost money. We had lost everything else; our crockery and glass, linen, carpets, remaining furniture, a Frigidaire and his blessed tiger skins, [all] went up in smoke.

"Longing for news of the children and all of you. Do you realise that my last letter from you was in November. No Christmas mail, nothing. Write by airmail from now on, now that I have given you the details. When Stanley gets out of hospital he will be re-posted in India. We will get Burma back eventually; there is no doubt about that."

Unquote

While staying in Maymyo, on 23rd February, Captain and Mrs White asked Edna to stay as their guest, pending my eventual arrival in Maymyo. White was one of my officers in Rangoon and his wife had been an army school mistress and knew our children, Valarie and Brian.

On the 6th March in Rangoon a number of us at army headquarters were able to send out messages to our families on the Rangoon radio station and some people in Maymyo heard my message for Edna, which was passed on to her. She listened in at the same time the next night and heard me broadcast my message again. That was the first news that she had had from me and an hour after the broadcast the Rangoon radio station was blown up.

As the hurried civilian evacuation began the Americans let all approved people take Jeeps and cars to make their way to the north. It was a great help to the people concerned but was also a help to the Americans themselves, whose object was to get as many vehicles as possible into northern Burma.

The 7th Army brigade from North Africa disembarked in Rangoon at the end of February. The tanks went forward on their tracks to Pegu and took up positions either to counter attack the Japanese facing the 17th Indian division or to act as a rearguard should the 17th division need to disengage. Reinforcements were pouring into Rangoon with troops, vehicles, stores and equipment. As all of the Indian coolies who provided the labour force at the docks were gone the work of disembarkation was slow. Police services were practically non-existent in the docks and the city and at night Dacoits [robbers, bandits and murderers] came in to loot and do what damage they could. Soon organised bands of looters appeared, some led by Japanese agents or military personnel.

Our Abdar [Indian head servant] Kurrum Khan was still with me as was the Madrasi cook. One day I went home for lunch and as I drove down the drive to the house I saw Mong Sin, my former Burmese car driver, standing on the edge of a patch of reeds and bulrushes between Brigadier Martin's house and the pungi bhikkhu [the pungis' monastery or accommodation]. When he saw my car approaching he ran off into the reeds and disappeared. I went to the porch and found the house locked up. After I blew the horn and shouted the door was cautiously unbarred and Kurrum Kahn came out. He said, "Thank God, you have come Sahib. About an hour ago Mong Sin and several Burmans, armed with iron bars, came to the house and said they were going to loot it. I closed the doors and they abused me and threatened to cut me in pieces. I held them in conversation, knowing that you would be coming soon."

I was so angry at this dastardly conduct on the part of Mong Sin, who had already betrayed the trust placed in him when he absconded with the regiment's pay that I went after him. Seeing him with several other Burmese looking at me from within cover of the reed-bed, I pulled both my pistols out and opened a fusillade of fire at him. They were about 60 yards away and got out of sight quickly. I searched for a short time but they had got right away.

Kurrum Khan told me that some Burmese had been in the Pope's house, so I immediately went there to find out what had happened. Everything in the house had been viciously destroyed. All the furniture, crockery, chinaware and pictures had been smashed to pieces. All the clothing in wardrobes had been torn to shreds and left lying there and carpets had been slashed to ribbons.

Everything in the house had been senselessly destroyed. It was a really dreadful sight.

Returning to my own house I saw a canoe on the lake, about 300 yards away, which was fully loaded with loot and being paddled by two Burmese towards an island in the middle of the lake on which lived Noel Whiting, a wealthy recluse. It was obvious they had been looting in the Burmah Oil Company houses. Seizing my 0.405 Winchester tiger rifle, I ran to the lakeside, shouted and beckoned them towards me. They immediately started paddling with all their might away from me and made their way towards the island, ignoring my continued shouting. I then aimed the rifle at them whereupon they dived overboard and overturned the canoe. They swam to the island where there was a mudflat in front of the jungle. As they staggered through the mud I aimed at the man on the right and fired. He dropped on the mud flat and lay still. I must have killed him with the shot. The other, howling, reached the edge of the jungle and disappeared.

In the direction of the Pope's house I saw several pungi's, in their saffron coloured robes, watching me from the reeds around the pungi bhikkhu.

I moved in their direction and beckoned them but they ran inside the wooden buildings of the bhikkhu and closed all of the doors and windows. It was a distance of a hundred yards and I fired a couple of shots at one of the buildings. The effect of the heavy, lead nosed 0.405, bullets was remarkable. Pieces of wood flew off in all directions as though a shell had hit the building. The pungis ran off and did not return.

The burning of European houses then started on the outskirts of the city. As a measure of safety all officers at headquarters were required to move into the university area under the protection of our company of Burma Rifles. One of my staff captains, a professor at the university, had his house there and I moved in with him.

On 22nd February it was decided that only advance headquarters would remain in Rangoon and the remainder would move to Maymyo to form rear headquarters. The Brigadier decided to go to Maymyo himself and I and two other officers were left behind to deal with advance headquarters operations. All of the war correspondents left at the same time. Apart from the Army the only Europeans left were a few staff of the Burmah Oil Company, Posts and Telegraphs and the Port and Shipping Authorities. It was the intention to deny as many installations as possible to the enemy, especially the oil refinery at Syriam [now Thanlyin]

At the beginning of March Rangoon was a completely ravished city. Shops had been looted everywhere. It became known that barbarous attacks were being made by the Burmese on Indian villages a few miles outside the city.

A most tragic event then occurred at Tadagalay, outside Rangoon, where there was a large mental asylum and prison. There were many hundreds of mental patients and criminal lunatics of all races held there, most of them Burmese and Indians, in addition there were also Chinese, Anglo Indians, and a few Europeans. Conditions in Rangoon deteriorated so rapidly it was not possible to move them out of the city with no transport services or staff to look after them. A civilian officer of the Burma Civil Service had been placed in charge of the hospital and he decided that the only thing to do was to release them. There was jungle all around the hospital and the Burmese villagers became aware of what was going to happen. The patients were released and began wandering where their fancy took them. The Burmese lying in wait began to rob and molest them and the younger women and girls were pounced upon and an orgy of rape and molestation ensued. An unknown number of women were murdered. Once the horrific facts became known the European Officer in Charge committed suicide.

Rangoon was a blacked out city and a full and rigorous curfew was in force. The only people who could go on to the streets at night were the fuel security detachment under Major A. Mains, a detachment of the Gloucesters and officers of Army Headquarters. I went into Rangoon one night with an orderly to accompany me and when driving at a slow pace in a suburb, called Kyimyindain, I saw the movement of a head. We both got out of the car and could have fired without further ado but I ordered, "Hold fire!" When we got close to the person I saw it was a completely naked Burmese woman. She must have been from Tadagalay, as our presence did not upset her and she wandered off into the darkness. A similar incident happened the following night at the Shwedagon Pagoda but on this occasion we were able to lead the woman into an empty house and leave her there.

In an effort to reduce looting I formed, from my own branch of the staff, two officers' parties and we patrolled areas at night where looters might operate. We were successful one night as we had moved to the rear entrance of Roe & Co's store and were lying in wait. We had not been there long when a door cautiously opened and out came seven Burmese loaded with loot. Fire was opened and all seven were killed. In my patrols I came upon an Indian village outside the Chinese market garden suburb. The village headman said that several of them had been murdered in the night by neighbouring Burmese villagers. As there were several hundred Indian villagers, including women and children, in danger I promised to come back the following night and to lay an ambush. I did so and lined-up my party, near a small bank, outside the village and waited right through the night but no Burmese appeared. We had to leave knowing that we would not be able to return again to protect the villagers.

The American Volunteer Group (AVG)[widely known as the 'Flying Tigers'] headquarters had moved from Toungoo up to Kunming in China, although two pursuit [fighter] squadrons still remained behind in Rangoon, and did wonderful work in repelling the Japanese air attacks. After the Sittang disaster a pursuit squadron moved to Magwe and then back to Kunming and eventually the whole group was concentrated in Kunming.

On one of the weekends that she spent with us in Rangoon, Olga [Greenlaw – AVG war diarist] brought a friend. He was a handsome Frenchman in his late 40s and had been a major in the Royal Artillery during the 1914-18 War. He was Count Jacques, of French nobility, and a member of one of the noblest and richest families on the Continent. They had met many years before in Saigon and Hanoi and a deep affection had grown up between them. The Count was on his way to the Middle East to join the Free French in Syria, which he eventually did.

We last saw Olga and Harvey in Maymyo in 1942 at a cocktail party where Generalissimo Chiang Kai Scheck, Madam Chiang Kai Scheck, General Stilwell and many other VIPs were present. Since then Olga and I have corresponded every Christmas and from this I learned that Olga divorced Harvey and married Paul Owsley [in 1946] a businessman, who also owned a ranch in Northern California. Some years later Mr. Owsley died suddenly and so, at long last, the opportunity arose for Olga to marry Jacques. However, one Christmas she told me that Count Jacques had died, so their hopes had come to naught.

Once the Japanese had crossed the Salween, they realised that they had paralysed Rangoon, so that air raids became infrequent and some of the population began to return to the city. One day I was driving down Fraser Street in

Chinatown, when I saw a crowd of Burmese outside a shop. They were obviously looting and stuff was being thrown down to members of the crowd. I stopped, got out of the car and fired two shots over the heads of the crowd at the walls of the building. The crowd dispersed in panic and from the middle came a Burmese police inspector. I asked, "What the hell is going on?" He replied, "Sir, they are looting." I said, "It is up to you to stop it." In fact, he could not do much by himself, so I continued on my way.

Further down the deserted street I saw what appeared to be a little dwarf, about four feet tall or he may have been a youth looking very old. He was a pathetic sight; wearing a Gurkha felt hat, a jacket, shorts, socks and some enormous boots, far too big for him. When my orderly and I went towards him we saw that he had wounds on his legs and in a little bag he was carrying his pathetic haul. When he saw us he started screaming with terror. We tried to pacify him and eventually he calmed down but would not come with us or have anything to do with us, so we left him and he continued walking down the street. His chances of survival were nil and my heart was numb with this experience.

General Sir H.R. Alexander took over command of the Burma Army early in March and after a quick visit to the battle area he decided that the Army must evacuate Rangoon immediately and fight a delaying action northwards to enable the V and VI Chinese Armies to enter Burma and deploy and also to cover the approach to India. Demolition had been carried out in Rangoon by Burmah Oil Company staff and others. Rangoon was to be evacuated on 7 March 1942 and the Army was to withdraw to an intermediate line in central Burma to across the Prome road close to the Irrawaddy River.

Chapter 29

The Last Days in Northern Burma

The Battle of the Taukkyan Roadblock

Army headquarters left Rangoon on the morning of 7 March 1942 and halted at 9.00am where the road divided in two, the western branch running via Tharrawaddy to Prome and the eastern branch through Pegu, Toungoo and Mandalay. The place was called Taukkyan and was in a large rubber plantation. The halt was made to await news of the progress of the 17th Indian Division's withdrawal from Pegu. The division was being heavily attacked by the Japanese; even so the 7th armoured brigade was able to slow down the Japanese advance and enable 17th Division to disengage. General Eric Goddard, the Major General i/c administration, called me over and told me to take a Royal Signal Corps truck with a wireless set and two junior officers with their own cars, to act as messengers, and to proceed to Tharrawaddy, 50 miles to the north. I was to set up advance headquarters and, if possible, contact rear headquarters and the Governor at Maymyo.

Evading the Japanese Ambush

I selected Lieutenants Redhead and Mumford and, with the signal set, went off to Tharrawaddy. I led the convoy with a 50 yard interval between each vehicle. There was a heavy mist lying in the trees of the rubber plantation and it was not possible to see far on either side of the road. We had gone about two miles when there was a long curve in the road to the left in the direction of travel and then about a 100 yards ahead I saw what was obviously a Japanese soldier dive into the drainage ditch along the side of the road and train his rifle in our direction, keeping well under cover. I realised at once it was an ambush and that the only chance of escape was to not let the Japanese know that they had been seen. Up to that time the Japanese had been shooting out of hand all prisoners found with lead nosed bullets in their possession, although our 0.45 service army revolver was the recognised British army weapon. I also had in my car a 0.405 Winchester rifle, a 0.375 Snider rifle and a pair of Webley & Scott 12 bores and was wearing my 0.45 Webley pistol and a 0.32 automatic. I had several hundred rounds of solid and lead nosed rifle cartridges as gun ammunition. The Japanese had been deliberately carrying out appalling atrocities to terrorise our troops. Senior officers, after being tortured to gain what militarily useful information they knew were then either decapitated or cut in half and disemboweled in front of their own and Japanese troops.

All of these thoughts went through my mind in a flash but I kept on driving at the same pace expecting, at any moment, to receive a blast of fire. I hoped that my companions would not see anything. As I passed the spot where the Jap was lying I kept looking straight ahead but from the corner of my eye I could see him lying in the ditch trying to merge into the bank. A short distance further on I could just discern a few yards into the jungle a camouflaged mortar position. I continued without increasing my speed until after about another two miles the jungle opened out and we came into open country, on either side of the road.

Here I increased speed to 50 mph, the maximum speed of the signals truck, and after another four miles I halted and beckoned the others to come to me. I explained that we had been the first through a Japanese ambush and now must go hell for leather to Tharrawaddy. When I said this there were two explosions from where we had come and the battle of the roadblock at Taukkyan commenced. We headed for Tharrawaddy at full speed and then, only a few miles from our objective, several shots were fired at us but fortunately without damage. I heard later that there were several bands of armed Dacoits in the area.

A Warning to Headquarters of the Japanese Advance

I found Major J. Martin, OIC of a company of Burma Military Police, in Tharrawaddy and told him what had happened, which caused him some concern. He then rapidly decided on defence dispositions for the police and made arrangements for the blowing up of the pumping station and the oil pipeline from the oilfield. I selected several bungalows to be used by advance headquarters and then tried to contact Maymyo, about 400 miles away, by telephone. Because of the disturbances caused by the war and the absconding of [civilian] personnel the telephone and telegraph systems were extremely attenuated. Despite this, I was able to get through to Maymyo and spoke to a duty officer there. I told him who I was and what had happened. The report was to be given to the senior officer at rear headquarters and government house at Maymyo. I said that I would be going back shortly to Taukkyan to find out what the situation was and would try and report in the evening by telephone, if possible. This was the first information that Maymyo had received about the Taukkyan incident and there was terrific apprehension.

Reconnoitering the Japanese Attack

At that time Chinese armies were only just entering Burma and the Japanese threat was developing through the Kayin State, from where a road ran north through the Shan States to the Burma Road near Lashio. After a hurried meal I set off again back down the road and when nearing the Taukkyan area I could hear that a large scale battle was in progress. There were also a few Japanese planes bombing and strafing in the battle zone. I got off the road and into the jungle and made my way forward as far as possible towards the battle site. Leaving the car under cover, I went on and eventually found a large tree and climbed it. It was not a great deal of use however, although in one direction I could see about half a mile. The battle continued without halt except for occasional lulls between attacks. Then I saw a Japanese patrol moving northward. I got out of the tree and made my way to the car and started off for the road. The noise and movement gave me away and a few shots were fired at me. One hit the car, through the rear of the roof, but did not impede me in any way. I careered off over the rough undulating ground and eventually made the main road safely. I then roared off to

312

Tharrawaddy. On arrival, I managed to contact Maymyo again and told them that the battle was still in progress. Depending upon the situation I said I would try and contact them again on 8 March. I started off for Taukkyan the next morning and when about half way there I came across the advanced guard of protective troops astride the road and then came upon General Alexander's car and jeeps with the rest of the staff there; Generals, Goddarton, Winterton, Philip Gwyn, Major Brian Montgomery [younger brother of General Bernard Montgomery of Alamein] and others. They, of course, had no idea what had happened to me and my party. They were sure that we had either been killed or captured and we were already posted as 'missing' with 'A' staff. There was general handshaking and congratulations all round.

The Japanese Withdraw from Taukkyan

What had happened should be briefly described. The Japanese GOC intended to drive direct on Rangoon from Pegu and to protect his flank from a land attack, from the west, or a seaborne attack and had sent a force of 6,000 men to provide this cover. This force made its way through the jungles of the Pegu Yomas [mountains] during the night and at dawn was in position across the Prome road at Taukkyan. When the Japanese advance on Rangoon had reached a fixed point and flank protection was no longer needed the flank force was ordered to move straight on to Rangoon. This instruction the Japanese force commander carried out to the letter and the [British] Army in Burma was safe from capture or complete destruction. Little was known of this at advance headquarters until the move to Tharrawaddy started from Taukkyan and the 1st Gloucesters ran into the road block. At the time, the adjutant of the Gloucesters was Captain James Carne, later Lt. Col. Carne VC, of Korean War fame. The Gloucesters put in attack after attack but with very heavy casualties. Forces from 17th Division were also put in but the roadblock held. The Gloucesters lost more than 50 per cent of their strength and Major Victor Morton, my next door neighbour in Sale Barracks, Rangoon, a fine and brave officer was killed. On the morning of 8th March a Gurkha battalion advanced to attack and found that the Japanese positions had been largely abandoned, so the advance continued to Tharrawaddy. It was a very lucky escape for the Burma Army and for me and my companions; indeed a virtually miraculous one as our lives depended on a time factor of a few minutes only. During the night of 7th March, at Taukkyan, the Japanese made continual harassing attacks on all ranks from the general downwards, including from the rear and from barricades of vehicles and equipment. Lt. Col. M.D. Chapman, my colleague on the S&T [Supplies and Transport] Staff at headquarters, had a heart attack. By the time advance headquarters had reached Tharrawaddy his condition was so serious that he had to be evacuated north and to India by air. I was thus left to cope on my own [as General Alexander's Director of Supplies and Transport for the Burma Army and the maintenance of the V and VI Chinese Armies]. Headquarters moved to Prome on 9th March and our offices were on an Irrawaddy steamer tied up along the river bank.

Evacuation of the Wounded Up the Irrawaddy

For the four years I had been in Burma I had come in wider contact with the non-European population than the other officers in the Burma Army Headquarters. Indeed, many British officers had arrived only shortly before the outbreak of war. Lt. Col. Patterson-Knight, the Adjutant General, had been in No.3 Coy at Sandhurst with me and we worked in close liaison. I was called upon to act as a 'trouble-shooter' because of the knowledge I had gained in Burma. About 5th March 'P-K' told me there was trouble at the docks, as several thousand wounded had arrived, to be embarked on one of the larger Irrawaddy mail steamers. He wanted me to go there and see what was happening.

It was dark when I arrived and when I found the steamer I ascertained there were about 2,000 wounded troops, British, Indian, Gurkha, Burmese and Chinese. There was a young Indian Captain in the Indian Medical Service on board, a few RAMC and first-aid orderlies from regiments. He told me there were no food supplies of any sort and there was only a limited supply of drinking water. The wounded were making a considerable noise and all of their clothing was covered with congealed blood. As the cabin accommodation was full, they were lying all over the decks. It was a real shambles and the doctor was at his wits' end.

I found a couple of lightly wounded British officers and a sergeant-major and several NCOs. I told them that they must get some sort of routine organised and instill any sort of discipline that was possible in the circumstances. I said that I would have 10 days' supplies placed on board in a few hours. This resupply was done and then, about three hours later, the steamer pulled away with the medical officer in a happier frame of mind.

At Prome I heard the steamer had arrived safely and moved on up river and eventually reached its destination.

Return to Maymyo

The next day, Major General Goddard told me that my brigadier insisted that I be sent up to Maymyo immediately. I headed for Yenangyaung and the station staff officer there informed me that a Mrs Robins had been flown out to India the previous day. I was very depressed but consoled myself with the thought that she was safe.

Arriving at Mandalay the next day I called in at the station staff office in the port and was told that Edna was in fact in the Maymyo. The lady referred to, and mistaken for Edna, was in fact the wife of another soldier serving in the KOYLI. It was very good to be in Maymyo once again amongst the pine trees and the lovely mountain air and the peace and quiet even if it was only to be for a short time.

Chapter 30

From Mandalay to Manipur

Briefly, Gen. Alexander's plan was to concentrate the Burma Army in the Irrawaddy valley and fight a delaying action in front of the oil fields at Yenangyaung, to give time for the road from India to the Chindwin River to be constructed. South of the Chindwin great efforts were being made to improve the rough track leading from the railhead at Ye-U to the Chindwin crossing at Shwedaung, a distance of a hundred miles. The Chinese V and VI armies were to operate to the east of the Toungoo to Mandalay road, through the Shan States to the Salween River.

In Maymyo life went on quite happily, the Club was full every evening. Tea dances were held and there were moderate amounts of whisky and wines available. After one air raid, one or two of the craters created were very large but there had not been a great number of casualties. Some local residents had vanished and hidden themselves in the forest surrounding Maymyo in every direction. The Americans, as usual, suffered from no shortages; alcohol, cigarettes, vast quantities of tinned food and other stores were to be had at the P-X.

Edna had, amongst other things, taken up cipher work in Rangoon and was one of the staff who operated the top secret 'Drum', used in decoding operations. Members of cipher staff in Maymyo were located in Government House and went there as requested. Cipher work allowed European women to stay in Burma as long as possible and they would not be liable to evacuation at short notice.

The Brigadier was, from the work point of view, glad to see me again but I found it difficult to get information from him about future plans and had to use my own knowledge, judgment and initiative when required. The situation was very confused in the Shan States and towards the River Salween. The VI Chinese Army was still deploying, so I was sent off on a reconnaissance trip to Taunggyi to make an appreciation of the situation and bring back a report. Because, at the time, there was no restriction on ladies travelling in the Shan States, Edna decided to come with me to see again Kalaw, Yongway and Taunggyi. I acquired a Ford station wagon for the journey and took our armoury of rifles, pistols and shotguns.

At Taunggyi the road and rail junction for the southern Shan States road and rail branches started but we found that there had been an air raid the previous day and the station and rail track were damaged. We moved on and were soon climbing through the jungles up the road and arrived at Kalaw in the evening. Kalaw had not been bombed and was as lovely as we had known it in the past. But the hotel staff had begun to disappear and the proprietors, a Mr. and Mrs Sidley, knew that eventually they would have to leave their hotel, home and business.

We returned to Taunggyi the next day, where signs of war were everywhere. The Burma Army field ordinance and supply depots had been established and there were a number of Chinese troops in the area. I was busy all day visiting units and gathering information on Chinese troop dispositions. I spent a pleasant evening at the club with some of the Taunggyi residents and I recall the story of a singular incident, where a Shan had been out shooting and was making his way back home and had to pass through a copse with a small stream running through it. While moving through the copse he saw movement in a tree ahead of him and taking cover proceeded to find out what the animal was. He aimed carefully and had a shot. The animal fell out of the tree and when the Shan arrived at the spot where the animal fell he found it to be a clouded leopard and in its mouth it had a pangolin, the large scaly anteater. This was quite extraordinary, as clouded leopards were one of the rarest animals in the world and the pangolin, not quite as rare but entirely nocturnal and very rarely seen.

Next day we returned to Kalaw, passing by the lovely Inle Lake and bade good bye to our hosts and started the journey towards Mandalay. About 35 miles from Mandalay we approached a village on the road and I saw about a dozen Burmese gathered together. As we came close they waved their staffs and started jeering at us and the situation was very dangerous. I drove straight at them and made them scatter. After about 75 yards I stopped, jumped out of the car and fired warning shots at them with my 0.45 pistol. They immediately dispersed and ran off, yelling with terror. We quickly resumed our journey and were relieved to reach Mandalay without further incident. Thinking about this incident, later, it would have been wiser to drive on. If the car had not started it would have been the end of us.

Meanwhile, back in Maymyo, Gwyneth had joined one of the nursing formations and was also assured of staying in Maymyo for as long as possible. Edna had met Mr. and Mrs. Crosby, in Maymyo, he was the last British Consul in Siam [Thailand].They had travelled out of Siam via the Salween River crossing, thence by road across the Shan States and on to Maymyo. They had only a few suitcases of personal clothing and one of them was a wicker suitcase, very expensive and very strong. When arrangements had been made for Mr. and Mrs Crosby to be flown out from Myitkyina, this suitcase was left with us and eventually I packed some of our best silver in it and bound it with wire and had it sent forward to the Chindwin crossing at Kalewa where an Indian Army unit took it over and it arrived in Calcutta six months later intact. The suitcase is still in my possession. [I can confirm that this was so. In the late 1960s, as a teenager, I can recall seeing the suitcase at home.]

Olga and Harvey Greenlaw who were, at the time, in Kunming in Yunnan [Province] at the 'Flying Tigers' headquarters, as the AVG was widely known by then, visited Maymyo in April and invited us to a cocktail party which was to be held at the American Baptist mission on the outskirts of Maymyo.

When we arrived there we found that the party was in honour of Generalissimo Chiang Kai Shek and Madam Chiang Kai Shek. General Stilwell was also there, as were two other US generals and Major Frank Merrill of 'Merrill's Marauders' fame, Colonel Boatna and others. We were introduced to the Generalissimo and Madam Chiang Kai Shek and it was a very gay [jolly] and pleasant evening. It was also an opportunity of meeting two people who had made their mark on world history. Olga and Harvey were leaving for Lashio the next day and promised to look for us if we should be nearby at any time.

Lt. Gen. 'Bill' Slim had taken over the Burma Corps (or 'BurCorps') on 17 March and the Japanese were relentlessly forcing the Corps to withdraw northwards. They established roadblocks by encircling movements to the rear of the withdrawing troops and each roadblock had to be cleared by hard and bitter fighting and then the exhausted troops had to push on at the utmost speed to avoid further encirclement. In an action at a place called Pin Chaung, north of Yenangyaung, BurCorps had a tremendous battle before breaking out and then only at the cost of losing much of their equipment including, heavy lorries, guns, vehicles and other equipment, for which there were no replacements.

By the beginning of April, I decided it was time to get Edna out of Burma and drove her with Mrs. Daphne Culatto to Lashio. The Culattos were friends of ours in Rangoon and Captain Culatto was serving with the Burma Army Signal Corps. When Gen. Orde Wingate had arrived in Burma, some of his staff had taken up residence in Baker House, Lashio. Edna and Daphne were accommodated in the Chinese National Airways Corporation (CNAC) Hostel, which was full of Americans including Olga and Harvey Greenlaw.

In the evening we went around to Baker House to have drinks with Col. Wingate and the rest of his people there, including the American Colonels, Boatna and St. John, and a Brigadier Hobson, who in civilian life had spent many years in China and spoke Mandarin fluently. Later we had a very good dinner in the CNAC Hostel given by a Col. Lu, a member of the Generalissimo's staff. But, as Edna has related, conditions in the Hostel deteriorated after I departed to return to Maymyo.

My visit to Lashio was also for the purpose of a meeting with Brig. Hobson and with the Quartermaster

Generals of the V and VI Chinese armies with regard to the sharing of military resources and the discussion of outline plans for the withdrawal of the British component of the Burma Army into China, should withdrawal to India become impossible. It was an interesting experience, the Chinese generals sat together at the centre on one side of a long conference table and Brig. Hobson and I sat opposite. On either side were Chinese Staff Officers, about 20 in all. Standing behind them were enormous Manchurian troops each about six feet, six inches tall and with their padded uniforms they looked colossal. They had a great sword slung across their backs and a whole army of other weapons draped round them. At intervals they pushed the dainty china cups of tea, held in their enormous paws, into the officers' faces and glared at them until the tea was consumed. Then their paws were extended again and the cups taken away for refilling. This performance continued during the whole of the conference. Brig. Hobson and I were included and heaven knows what would have happened if we had refused to drink the tea. The conference was fruitless. We talked for hours but at the end achieved nothing.

Mechanical Transport units of six transport companies, each of 130 three ton lorries, had been formed at Lashio under a Lt. Col. Holmes, a Canadian, whose civilian experience was operating a chain of garages. Traffic from Lashio connected with the lorry traffic up to Chunking, along the Burma Road.

From what I had seen, I realised that a withdrawal to China was impossible and impractical from every point of view. The British and Indian units of the Burma Army would have no alternative but to attempt to reach India.

The situation in Mandalay was critical, partly because of the losses suffered at Pin Chaung. To enable the Army to withdraw to Assam, thousands of tons of supplies from the Mandalay Base Depot would need to be transported across the Irrawaddy River, over the Ava Bridge, for fuel supply and ordnance depots to be established back along the route to Assam. I asked Col. Holmes to send a company of three-ton lorries immediately to Mandalay to report to Col. Lewitton the OIC of the base there and to follow it up, if possible, with another company.

In the event the powers that be did have second thoughts about feasibility of a withdrawal to China and thus the movement of supplies across the Irrawaddy was already in progress, when the plan for the withdrawal into India was fixed. I visited Mandalay immediately and stressed the necessity to the OIC Base Depot of keeping movement going day and night. At an Army Headquarters conference the Brigadier told me that he was worried that the change of plan would be impossible to meet, because we had been establishing our lay backs to China. I told him that within a couple of days there would be enough supplies across the Irrawaddy at Sagaing to enable us to get most of the way out of Burma.

In Maymyo we had moved into a fine Bungalow, called 'Race View', just opposite the first tee of the golf course and the race course. The other side of the road was a club where Gwyneth was living in one of the club quarters.

On Good Friday [3 April] 1942 Japanese bombers flew over Maymyo at a great height and delivered a heavy attack on Mandalay. Apart from Fort Dufferin, a few administrative buildings and commercial firm headquarters, Mandalay was mainly a shanty town, made up of wooden huts with corrugated iron or palm leaf roofs, and was almost completely destroyed. A strong wind was blowing and soon the town was an inferno and about 80 per cent burnt out. On news of the attack I went there immediately on my return to Maymyo from Lashio. Many areas of Mandalay were still burning and there were hundreds of bodies in gardens, under houses and by the side of the road. The stench of death was appalling. The terrific heat had made aftermath of the air raid even more horrific. The town was devastated and dead. I had seen the end of Mandalay, to which no British soldiers would ever take the road again.

In one of my visits to see a unit in Fort Dufferin an Anglo-Burman doctor asked to see me. He said that a party of Anglo-Burmans, a total of about 30 men women and children, had decided to stay in Burma and they were going to hide in some dense jungle about 40 miles north of Maymyo with some tinned food and non-perishable stores. Could I help? I gave immediate orders that six months of supplies for the whole party be loaded up in a lorry and delivered to the place indicated by the doctor and then return to Mandalay. The doctor was very grateful, particularly as help was offered on the spot without any 'red tape' delays. I hope that they came safely through the Japanese occupation to enjoy their lives in their lovely golden land. But I have never heard anything further of them.

I had the opportunity during my visit to Mandalay to see the Golden Palace, within Fort Dufferin. The palace buildings were built on a raised rectangular platform, approached by a staircase on the eastern side. The main rooms and halls were enormous in area and very high. The main supports were great teak pillars, lacquered red and gold, some with a gold leaf decorative pattern on them. Some of the buildings were in the attractive oriental architectural style with the upturned eves. The main hall of the palace contained the lion throne, an enormous richly carved ornamental piece the size of a four poster bed. In the queen's apartment was the Lily throne and in the Glass Palace the walls were covered with a mosaic of coloured glassware and mirrors. Exhibits of Burmese court dresses, temple dancer's dresses and other ceremonial costumes were in glass cases. For me it was wonderfully interesting and I felt very close, yet again, to living with history.

While we were in Maymyo we heard the story of the McColl family, one of whom was a Captain McColl that I had met at Thayetmyo. Mr. McCall, in civilian life, had been a member of the Indian Civil Service and had a brilliant academic career at Oxford after leaving Clifton College and was serving in Burma in the judicial branch of the administration. He married a Burmese lady and they had three sons. The sons were all educated in England; one of them became an officer in the Gordon Highlanders, in the Great War and won the Military Cross. He was very artistic and a painter of great talent and was also interested in sculpture and modelling. He opened up a shop in Bond Street after the War but after a few years Burma called him and he returned there and married a Burmese girl.

When we were in Maymyo he lived in a place called Tha Yet Kon in the Jungle about 14 miles north of Maymyo. We went to see him one day and found him with his Anglo-Burmese family. He had some lovely paintings of local scenes and also made wall plaques of the many picturesque tribes in Burma. They were in relief, showing the head and shoulders of the various tribes in their headdresses and jewellery and in colour. It included of course the Padaung or giraffe necked women. The plaques were very attractive and unique. He also had hundreds baby dolls, made out of clay and lacquered in natural colours. He had already started a thriving export business of the dolls to Japan in pre-war days. In one hut he had some wonderful 'Heath Robinson' type machines, made from bits and pieces of old cars he had bought. In appearance, he looked like a full blooded Burman but spoke perfect Oxford English.

His brother, in the Forest Service, came to England after Burmese independence in 1948 and was living in Hampstead with his family. We met, on one occasion, at the Overseas League [a London Club], and talked of the old days in Burma. The other brother joined the Burma Police Service and at the outbreak of war was a superintendent of police in one of the Tenasserim districts. He was captured by the Japanese and a story reached us in India that the Thakhins [or Dobama Asiayone], a political party, which had always been opposed to British Rule had crucified him. Happily the story proved to be untrue and he survived the Japanese occupation. A remarkable story about a family, of western origin, with brilliant cultural and academic attainments, that had been absorbed into an oriental race and become part of its life.

Most of my hunting trophies were lost in Burma, as were nine of my tiger skins and three leopard skins. These could never be replaced and we could never be compensated.

Early in March, before we evacuated Rangoon, I received a message from the embarkation office that the last ship to sail for India would be leaving during the day and if I had any personal belongings which I wished to send they would arrange for them to be conveyed to the docks. I was very busy at the time and although all my possessions were boxed and crated and ready for dispatch, I decided to send them to Mandalay. This was a disastrous and foolish decision. The boxes arrived safely in Mandalay and from there were sent on to Myitkyina and that was the last I heard of them for many years. However at a Burma Reunion cocktail party at the Mayfair Hotel in 1955 I met a Mr. Nelson, of the Steel Brothers Company. He told me that he had been hoping to meet me to let me know that my boxes had duly arrived in Myitkyina and on the last night before the Japanese captured the town he and others had buried my boxes under the Steel Bros. manager's house there. Now I suppose my treasured trophies are embellishing some Burmese or Japanese homes.

Several hundred Europeans, Anglo-Indians and Anglo-Burmans had gathered at Maymyo by mid-April 1942, the majority of them being women and a few children. They had come from Rangoon, Prome, and the Yenangyaung and Chauk oilfields and from other areas in Northern Burma, as well as from Siam and Yunnan Province in China. Evacuation by air had been in progress since the end of February and efforts had been made to increase the rate of movement, as the situation deteriorated rapidly after our withdrawal from Rangoon on 7 March. A number of those women to be evacuated wanted to stay in Burma as long as possible to be near their husbands and not to leave their homes or such of their belongings that they had been able to move to Maymyo or Mandalay.

Gwyneth was carrying out nursing duties at the military hospital in Maymyo but eventually strict orders were issued for all women to leave Maymyo. She had acquired a baby Fiat car and decided to try and make her way out to India via Shwebo, Ye-u and Kalewa, the route that the army was to take on its 'march out'. She realised she would have to abandon her car en route and it was not easy to determine how far she would be able to go by car. The Japanese were advancing rapidly northwards from Loilem, in the southern Shan States, towards Lashio.

On 26 April 1942, I asked her to load her car to capacity with foodstuffs and I arranged for a British NCO to accompany her and be responsible for her safety during the journey towards Assam. The car was grossly overloaded and as they drove off I wondered how far they would be able to go on their journey. The first night's halt was to be at Sagaing, on the western bank of the Irrawaddy, which they would reach by crossing the Ava Bridge, over the river. A house on the river bank was in use as a military headquarters and they were to halt there for the night and then continue their journey to Shwebo, 60 miles to the north, the following day. The communication troops were already moving into position on the withdrawal route and would be available to give assistance to them and to other refugees. Another delaying factor was that there were a number of Chinese troops in the area and they would need to be given a very wide berth.

On the morning of 27 April I had occasion to visit various areas outside Maymyo and on returning to headquarters I found a junior officer of the S&T branch who told me that the Brigadier had left for Sagaing and that he had no further orders. I told him that everybody was to get across the Irrawaddy as soon as possible and to rendezvous at the Commissioner's Residence in Sagaing. I then realised that I had seen very few military personnel and the town was almost deserted. I returned to 'Race View' to collect a few personal belongings and then drove down the hill towards Mandalay.

I drove in my own Vauxhall salon car and 2nd Lieut. Mumford, who had been attached to me ever since Rangoon, had a Ford station wagon. At Mandalay we headed for the Ava Bridge which was approached by a long causeway similar to that at the western end of the bridge in the country near Sagaing. The bridge was of the steel girder type and took the Rangoon to Mandalay rail line across the river, where it continued north to Myitkyina. Road traffic crossed the bridge on wooden beams on either side and between the railway tracks. The bridge was about a mile in length and a vital link in communications. It could be made practically useless for road traffic by bombing damaging the causeways, at either end of the bridge, without interfering with rail traffic.

When we reached the bridge, it was packed with troops and vehicles, as were the roads on either side. Just after we crossed the bridge, three squadrons of Japanese bombers were seen flying very high. There was a terrific rush away from the causeways and everyone dispersed as far as they could in the open country. Cars were abandoned and everyone buried themselves as deep as they could into the ground. With a terrific 'crump', the bombs landed. The bombers did not make a second run and when the dust had settled we found that the causeway had not been severely damaged and forward movement started again. I heard later that casualties were very light.

We found the Commissioner's lovely bungalow on the banks of the river to be quite an enormous place. The Brigadier and the rest of our staff were installed there and Gwyneth with her escort also arrived there. The headquarters were to move to Shwebo the next day, about 60 miles north of Sagaing from where we directed the withdrawal of the Burma Army across the Irrawaddy, together with the Chinese division that was attached to us.

We went on to Shwebo the next morning and when we were about 10 miles away from Shwebo we saw that it was being bombed by the Japanese. We arrived after the raid was over but a certain amount of damage had been done to the army buildings in which we were to establish headquarters. The buildings formed a classic British troop pattern barracks and had been in use since Upper Burma was annexed in 1886 until the Lower Burma rebellion in 1931.

General Stilwell and his staff had crossed the Irrawaddy and the Chinese Division was bivouacked in the Shwebo area and was intending to proceed north to Myitkyina from where they could either withdraw to China or to Assam through the Hue Phong Valley [now Hukawng Valley].

The following day, with Lt. Col. Teddy Tarver, a contemporary of mine at Sandhurst, and the son of a fire-eating old general at Secunderabad, I drove around all of the countryside near Shwebo trying to locate and identify units and take a census of the transport available. The Chinese division was scattered all over the area in a completely discouraged state and couldn't care less about the war. We eventually came across a forest rest house and were horrified to find Gwyneth Downey-Lowsley located there in the middle of the Chinese troops. Her escort had apparently been ordered off temporarily on some special duty and she was completely alone. We loaded up her car and the party returned to Shwebo where we left her in the army headquarters bungalow. We advised her to move on the next day on the road to Ye-U and then continue along the canal bank road to Kaduma where she would doubtless find the line of communication troops who could help her.

When Teddy Tarver and I returned to our branch mess the brigadier and a number of officers were at dinner. As we sat down the brigadier made some offensive remarks, which were quite uncalled for. He implied that I had been out reconnoitering for personal motives. I had had enough of him, with these gratuitous and insulting comments and blew up. I told him he had a hard-working and gallant staff that had carried him on its back ever since he arrived in Burma. He was a coward and he had run out on us both in Rangoon and Maymyo with no thought at all. After these words, uttered in anger, he placed me under open arrest and ordered me to accompany him to General Alexander's bungalow. I said I would finish my dinner first which I did, and then we drove to the GOC's residence. Alexander was in conference with General Stilwell and after waiting about ten minutes the brigadier seemed to have second thoughts and told me to drive the car back to our own branch, which I did.

At about 2am he returned, well oiled with alcohol and said, "Robbie, we are finished. The army troops have to move at dawn and push on as fast as they can towards Ye-U and we have no transport to move them." I told him that Tarver and I had got details of all transport available in the area and of its location. I then, with some difficulty, ascertained the route which was to be taken by the troops, because they were all Burmese names that he was unable to pronounce them properly. I was then able to issue orders for the movement of the army headquarters echelon, to start at dawn. The brigadier thanked me and the incident in the mess was not mentioned again.

The next day General Stilwell and his staff moved to a river port about 14 miles away and embarked on the steamer to take them up to Katha from where a rough fair weather road travelled 150 miles through hills and jungles to the Burma Frontier Force post at Homalin on the River Chindwin. The army advance headquarters also moved to Ye-U the next day and opened up a temporary officers' mess, in some jungle, adjacent to the road running from Ye-U to Monywa, a port on the Chindwin River.

I had to go back to Shwebo the following day and when beginning the return journey, I saw a squadron of Japanese bombers flying north. Shortly afterwards, heavy bombing started. Some miles ahead on the road was a railway station called Khin-U. When I arrived there I found a train which had been bombed and left burning on the track and the station was demolished. The train had halted at Khin-U and was full of

Anglo-Indian, Anglo-Burmese and Indian personnel who were being sent to Myitkyina. The passengers became aware of the approach the bombers and had time to run off some distance from the train and hide themselves by taking cover in the jungle. As a consequence there were, fortunately, very few casualties.

To secure help I rushed off to Ye-U and passed the information of the bombing to the appropriate quarters and a relief train was on its way within two hours. The train's passengers eventually reached Myitkyina safely.

In the morning while we were away from our living bungalows and our headquarters offices our Chinese allies paid a visit and completely ransacked the bungalows taking everything away: boots, clothing, razors, cameras and anything that they could transport without difficulty. As a result of this some of us grew quite wonderful beards. My own was mixture of grey, brown and red hair about a quarter inch long and I was a dreadful sight. Others looked like bearded patriarchs and prophets. Professor Mayitt, a staff captain of mine, who I saw weeks later had a magnificent grey beard reaching down to his waist.

On the second night at Ye-U when I returned to the mess, at a late hour with Lt. Mumford, I found it deserted. I had no idea where everyone had moved to. We decided to have a sleep on some charpoys [light bedsteads] that had been left there but were woken up at about 2:30am by troops moving up the road in the darkness, towards Kaduma on the Ye-U Canal.

A number of army units had also moved from Ye-U to Monywa, on the Chindwin, to proceed upriver by steamer and while embarkation was taking place Japanese forces that had crossed the Irrawaddy further downstream and made their way north to arrive on the opposite river bank had started shelling and bombing. Our troops immediately withdrew at full speed towards Ye-U. They knew the Japs were following close behind in the darkness. We also moved on and were relieved to regain headquarters by dawn and also to regain our headquarters mess facilities.

The route of withdrawal was from Kaduma through a number of jungle villages to the eastern bank of the Chindwin about six miles south of Kalewa. On the other bank the road was through thick jungle most of the way and several ridges of approximately 5,000 feet had to be crossed. The temperature was as high as 120 degrees [Fahrenheit - 49 degrees Celsius] in the shade on some days.

I had scarcely left Kaduma when I came across Gwyneth standing by her little Fiat car on the side of the road. It had been losing power and had finally stalled. She said a field security section knew her position and had promised to give her assistance shortly. In those nerve-wracking and truly frightful conditions that the journey entailed, it was a wonderfully brave effort for a woman alone to make.

We quartered for the night at Pyingaing, where the track crossed over several miles of sand which, in some places, caused vehicles to sink up to their axles. In a patch of jungle through which the road passed there were many abandoned vehicles. I saw one lorry which, amongst other things, contained a large Frigidaire.

There were still thousands of Indian refugees travelling towards India. The terrific heat, constant pall of dust and appalling terrain made the journey a nightmare. There was also very little water in the area and many thousands had died of sheer physical exhaustion and hardship. The odour of death was everywhere and day by day got worse. At one crossing of a dry river bed where it was expected to get water from a well that had been sunk by the sappers there were only a couple of feet of liquid mud in it. After a couple of hours rest the exhausted and thirsty troops had to march a further ten miles before water was found.

After leaving Pyingaing I came across a wounded British subaltern and three wounded sepoys lying under the shade of a tree. I stopped to see if they needed help and asked the subaltern if he could drive. He said he thought he could so I told him to get into the Vauxhall and drive it as far as he could towards Shingbwiyang and if it had to be abandoned; he must either burn it or damage the coil or the distributor, anything to make it unusable. He and the three wounded sepoys got into the car and he drove off and I continued my journey in the station wagon with Lieut. Mumford. I never saw the Vauxhall again.

We stopped for the night at a small detachment camp about eight miles from Shingbwiyang and moved on there the next day. At Shingbwiyang the track debouched into a circular basin about two miles in diameter ringed round with hills a few hundred feet high and at the opposite side the cliffs of the riverbank about 100 feet high down which a narrow steep track zigzagged to a small wooden jetty. There were thousands of troops in the basin and a small river steamer commanded by a Captain Moody of the Irrawaddy Flotilla Company was loading up.

The steamer had been doing some invaluable work running between Shingbwiyang and Kalewa six miles to the north on the right bank of the Chindwin. At Kalewa a fair-weather road ran along the Kale Valley to Tamu, on the Burma border, a distance of about 120 miles.

Edna had given me a lovely little French bulldog for my birthday present in August 1941, which I called Agnes. I had brought her with me from Rangoon, but she had got hookworm and become very thin. It was also difficult to obtain food for her and at Shingbwiyang. I decided I would have to have her put down this being the kindest thing to do. I asked the sergeant of the security section to do this and he said, "What a lovely little dog, sir. It is a shame, but it must be done".

Within an hour of my arrival at Shingbwiyang the signal section found me and handed me a message which said I had to proceed immediately to Kalewa on the first available steamer and report to my brigadier at army headquarters in the jungle near Kalewa.

I gathered up our belongings and went to Kalewa. By now Japanese bombers had begun to pay attention to the Chindwin and a heavy attack had been made on a river boom, about four miles south of Shingbwiyang. [A boom had been established across the Chindwin to stop the Japanese moving up the river by boat, and this measure was successful until it was broken by shelling on the 7th of May]. Attacks were also made on troop movements.

I had not seen the brigadier since advance headquarters at Shwebo and he said I must now remain with him until we reached Tamu. In the morning, while looking around the Kalewa area, which was only wooden houses and a small bazaar in a copse of immense trees, I found, in a patch of long grass on the riverbank, several crosses, marking the graves of soldiers of the Manchester Regiment who had been killed or died during the Burma rebellion of 1931. It was very lonely and there, once more, I thought of the remote and wild places, in many parts of the world, where the graves of British soldiers marked the tide of Empire.

I later returned to Shingbwiyang to collect my rifles and found that during the night, while Mumford was away from the station wagon, it had been ransacked. I lost a cine camera and some film that I had taken and some clothing, but the weapons had been left. The station wagon was now abandoned as only four-wheeled drive vehicles were allowed to move on from there to Kalewa. The brigadier and I had a Jeep from Kalewa and after about 60 miles we came across Captain White and his detachment stepping briskly along the rough boulder-strewn road. We wished them good luck and drove off.

We then went on to Tamu and I decided to stay the night en route to keep in touch with the progress of the withdrawal of the S&T units. After my stay, while completing the last six miles to Tamu on foot, I came across a Colonel Acton of the 10th Baluchistan Regiment, standing on a jungle track. He hailed me and said, "You look pretty tired. I've got some cold beer for you."

Col. Acton was commanding a battalion of pioneers, working on the road, and his headquarters was three hundred yards up the track into the jungle. He had the beer immersed in some clay pots full of water and it was wonderfully cool and refreshing. Leaving his mess tent to continue my journey I heard a gibbon calling and looking up saw a green gibbon in a tree. Col. Acton said it had been abandoned by somebody and kept in the vicinity of the camp. I called to it and it came down the tree and leapt onto me, its hind legs round my waist and its arms round my neck, and there it remained. It would not be put down and cried pathetically when I tried to do so. It was a lovely little animal so I took it with me and having found our mess at Tamu the gibbon settled down in one of the trees there.

Tamu was packed with refugees and there were piles of personal baggage and clothing everywhere. There was also a graveyard of vehicles, hundreds of them in fact. Tamu's situation was very attractive; it was set in a wide valley with plenty of water in the river that flowed down from a ridge of hills beyond which, to the north, was the plain of Manipur.

On the morning of the 7th April I went back in a jeep down the road towards Kalewa where, near a place called Indainggyi, Japanese bombers suddenly appeared and scattered some bombs. There was a pall of dust everywhere. I heard a loud explosion and felt a blow on my left thigh. A bomb splinter had hit me causing a flesh wound. I was able to bandage it up and carry on without much discomfort. I returned in the evening and as I walked into the mess the gibbon howled out at me and came down the tree and leapt onto me as before. The brigadier said that it had been a perfect nuisance and I had better keep it with me in future, which I did.

We went on another reconnaissance the next day by which time the majority of the troops had moved northwards with only the rear guard in contact, followed by the Japanese reconnaissance patrols. On making my way back to Tamu I saw a British officer and three sepoys propped round a tree. I could hear rifle and mortar fire to the rear and saw occasional small detachments of our own troops. The military situation was confused and dangerous, which was not helped the fact that the jungle was dense and the dust was heavy.

I stopped and discovered the officer was Lieut. Neil, who I knew, and three of his men. They were all wounded, not seriously, but in no condition to march any distance. I knew that I must get them moving immediately and that they all must get into the Jeep. The last two wounded had to be carried bodily onto the Jeep and one of them had to be propped up against the windscreen sitting astride the bonnet. Mortar bombs exploded quite close and the rifle fire was getting nearer.

Once we set off we could only proceed at a very slow pace with a heavy load of wounded men. About four hours later I drove into Tamu and passed the wounded soldiers to a field ambulance.

Many years later in 1972, at a Burma reunion cocktail party in London, Mr. Neil came up to me. I had not seen him since that day in May 1942, and he said to my wife, [not Edna, but the Author's second wife, 'Margery', née Whelan] "The Colonel saved my life Mrs Robins, and three of my men, after we had been abandoned. I will never forget it." I had, over the years, not recalled this incident and had not mentioned it to Margery. I was very pleased to know that Mr. Neil and his men had come through it all safely.

The 23rd Indian Division had concentrated in Manipur state to oppose a Japanese advance towards

India and to assist the Burma Army in its withdrawal. The division was also tasked with improving the road between Dimapur, the rail head of the Bengal-Assam metre gauge railway and Tamu. It was here, in a range of hills 40 miles south of Imphal, through which the road crossed into Burma by the Lokchao Bridge, that two regiments of the Royal Nepal Army at Tamu were positioned; the 'Brave Tiger Regiment', and the 'Brave Kali Regiment'. This was the first occasion on which the regiments had served outside Nepal since the Indian Mutiny. They were both smart and were obviously very fine regiments.

The brigadier had moved north to Imphal and the rest of the staff, piecemeal, the next day, to Pallel, a small town in the Manipur district, near Imphal.

Before leaving Tamu I looked over the abandoned car dump in the town and found a Ford V8 car in reasonable condition. Another reserve officer, over 60 years of age, had arrived in Tamu and I decided to take him with me and get him to India as soon possible. We did not leave Tamu until the evening and were on a very difficult hill section at 8pm that night. The gradient was very steep, there were sharp hairpin bends and the road surface was crumbling badly. At one sharp hairpin bend we came on a halted lorry with several people gathered round. It appeared that one of the lorries ahead could not take the hairpin bend and had gone straight over the edge. They were making up lengths of cordage from webbing equipment and baggage ropes to enable them to get down the steep cliff side. A small party went down in the darkness and found the lorry some hundreds of feet below. The vehicle was completely wrecked but the driver only had a broken nose and several cuts and bruises. Nevertheless it took some time to get him up and then we then moved on. By this time my companion and I were very tired and as I had no lights on the vehicle we halted off the road further on and went to sleep. At dawn we crossed the Lokchao Pass and reached Pallel.

The following day we drove on to Imphal where army headquarters were located in a school. Imphal, the capital of Manipur state, was at a height of 4,500 feet. It was a pretty place with neat bungalows and flower gardens and the valley was surrounded by wooded hills. Parts of the Dimapur road had been turned into landing strips and the following morning General Wavell, Commander in Chief India, flew in for a conference with General Alexander.

We were on standby at the conference, and it was obvious that there was a difference of opinion between the two commanders. The outcome was that the Burma army should withdraw to India and there re-organise, re-equip and re-arm and train for active operations as soon as possible. In my mind there could have been no other course of action, given the conditions of complete physical exhaustion of the troops of the Burma Army. They had been marching and fighting continuously since January and had fought a rear guard action for a distance of a 1,000 miles in terrific heat, over some of the worst terrain in the world. They were riddled with dysentery and malignant malaria, and the majority of men had lost several stones in weight.

The commander of the Burma Army headquarters moved to a new location, at a forest rest house, at a place called Kanglatongbi on the Dimapur road six miles north of Imphal.

341

Chapter 31

The End of the Retreat

I had been accompanied from Rangoon by our Madrasi cook as a personal servant. He had looked after me very well and was loyal and faithful. When a move to Kanglatongbi was decided, I took him into Imphal and arranged a point of rendezvous later. When I returned, he was not there and although I waited two hours he did not appear. I went on to headquarters. I was medically evacuated several days later. I looked for him on a number of occasions without success. I was very stressed about this as he had reached comparative safety and throughout these terrible months he had been of the greatest service to me.

At Kanglatongbi we slept on the concrete floor under mosquito nets. It was alive with bandicoots, a type of giant rat. One even got under my mosquito net one night and tried to drag one of my 'ammunition boots' away. [the standard footwear for the British Army from the late 1880s until the late 1950s.]

The Indian Tea Planters Association had set up a refugee organisation in Imphal in the charge of a Mr. Blennerhassett, a tea planter. Gwyneth had arrived in Imphal and was helping Mr. Blennerhassett with his work. We all had dinner one night, it was very pleasant, but she had still had no news of Geoff. Days later, when I was on the road outside the forest rest house, Geoff and Gwyneth drove up in a car from Imphal. They were both ill with malaria and were going to Dimapur en route to India. We arranged to make contact in the future and said our goodbyes.

On a visit to Imphal I saw Pat and Hilda Leel. It was miraculous that they had got so far safely. It was their intention to try and get to Kashmir. The dangers of their journey were demonstrated the following day when the refugee camp in the centre of Imphal was bombed and the European manager, his wife and about a hundred of the residents were killed.

I had had dysentery since early April, which was unpleasant and a weakening disease, but one simply had to keep going no matter what. There were bags of mail which had accumulated over several months and had been sent forward to Kanglatongbi. It formed piles of about seven feet high and we just had to search for our mail and hope for the best. None was for me and I felt rather low and depressed. I was then struck down by a most virulent attack of cerebral malaria. I was very ill indeed and had a temperature of over 106 degrees [Fahrenheit]. The nearest field hospital at Dimapur was 120 miles away on the mountain road. The monsoon had broken and at that height it was bitterly cold at nights. The Medical Officer ordered my immediate evacuation when an ambulance was available.

A few hours later an ambulance reported in and it loaded up me, another British officer and two Indian troops. I was delirious and have only a hazy recollection of the journey. We halted at Kohima and were given medical attention and then drove onto Dimapur. The monsoon had broken and it was pouring with rain. The field hospital, a tented unit, was located in a park-like area round a very ancient

Hindu temple in Dimapur. The other people with me in the ambulance were found dead on arrival.

After waiting some hours on a stretcher in the rain I was moved into a four-bed tent. The casualties already there included a subaltern of mine who was a rugger international. Within in an hour they were all dead. The bodies being removed, three more casualties were brought in. This procedure was essential because of the shortage of beds. When dawn came I was the only one still alive. The wounded and sick were coming in at about 2,000 a day. Lorries continually reported in, to be used for evacuation of the wounded and sick. As soon as it was physically possible for casualties to be moved on they were put into trains and taken forward to Guwahati, on the south bank of the Brahmaputra River, a distance of 200 miles.

Scores of planters' families had gathered and we were given tea and packets of sandwiches for which we were very grateful. I still had a raging fever and must have had a temperature well over 104 degrees. The Guwahati platform was about three quarters of a mile in length and this had to be traversed before we boarded a steamer to make a 30-minute crossing of the River Brahmaputra to Amingaon

At the hospital in Dimapur all weapons were taken from casualties, but I refused to hand over my sporting rifles. After I reached the steamer at Guwahati, hardly able to stand up, I found I had left the rifles in the railway compartment. I turned round, staggered the whole length of that interminable platform and eventually found my rifle cases. I tried hard to hurry back, the cases weighed about 11lb each and in my condition they felt like a ton. I could only just crawl up the gangway and my heart seemed to be about to burst. At the top of the gangway a field security troop tried to take the rifles. I played hell and would have shot anyone who tried to take them away from me. I eventually saw Major Tony Mains of the allied field security section who I met at Rangoon and the matter was settled amicably.

We crossed the river by steamer and then journeyed on from Mangaldoi in Assam where there was a metre gauge railway, the East Indian Railway, then a broad gauge line and finally to the cantonment of Dimapur in Bihar, where we were admitted to the British military hospital. After a few days we were moved on in a properly equipped hospital train to 17 Field General Hospital at Dehradun in the north of the United Provinces.

When the train passed through Lucknow, we were given small khaki bags containing a pair of pyjamas, toothpaste, a piece of soap, flannel, etc. A godsend as we had nothing but the worn khaki clothing we were dressed in. We travelled another 10 days by train and although 17 Field Hospital was a tented hospital it was very comfortable and the young English nurses, with their friendly natures and sympathetic attention, gave us great care and were a wonderful tonic as well. We knew we would not be discharged until we were well enough to travel.

I had at long last received a letter from Edna saying that she and Daphne were in a houseboat on the Nigeen Bargh in Kashmir. A few days later, at the end of May, I persuaded the OIC of the hospital to discharge me and I started off on the long journey to Kashmir.

Chapter 32

A Paradise on Earth

A few days later I arrived on the shore of the Nigeen Bargh and a shikara took me to the houseboat 'China Astor', which was on the far side of the lake. I had not sent a telegram and Edna and Daphne were surprised and delighted when I walked onto the houseboat. The houseboat owner exceeded himself that night and we had a wonderful dinner and talked on and on and on. I told Daphne that Louis had called in to see me and that was the last news we had of him before we left Burma.

The next day I was felled with malaria again having a temperature of 104 degrees and the civilian doctor ordered me to have complete rest for several days. Daphne began to worry and fret not having any news of Louis and decided that she would go and stay with some friends in Calcutta, as being a more likely place to get news that filtered from Burma. Daphne left the next day on the road to Murree, Rawalpindi and Calcutta.

The next morning a letter arrived on the houseboat for Daphne from Calcutta, signed on the back by Major Haycroft, the OIC signals to which Louis Culatto had been attached. The letter was to tell her that Louis had been killed accidentally at Byainggyaing in the Yingkiong valley during the march out of the Burma. We relayed the information to the friends she was going to in Calcutta, but they could not bring themselves to break the news to her for 48 hours. When they told her she retired to her bedroom, became ill and died three days later from meningitis. Daphne and Louis were a nice couple and close friends of ours. It was very sad to think that fate had ordained that their graves should lie so far apart; one of them in a most remote area where it would probably never be seen again.

Quite a number of people from Burma had arrived in Kashmir, include Nora Healy, daughter of our friends the Popes in Rangoon, and her husband, the Sidleys, from the Kalaw Hotel, and Hilda and Pat Leel We were very glad to know that the Leels had arrived safely after their long and dangerous route from Tenasserim to Kashmir despite the physical stress caused by Pat's injured spine.

When I recovered from my bout of malaria I was once again able to enjoy the pleasures and beauty of Kashmir. Swimming parties on the Nigeen Bargh, visits to the Srinagar, lunchtime drinks at the club on the Bund, and of course innumerable fishing trips. It was sheer heaven to spend days on the banks of Sind River at Gangabal Lake or at Ninglegull on the bank of the Wular Lake where the river Jhelum issues from it. We had wonderful sport, getting huge catches of fish.

Other visitors to Kashmir were the Prince and Princess of Bohra. The prince was the Nizam of Hyderabad and his wife was the daughter of the last sultan of Turkey. She was very tall, had a fair complexion and blue eyes, enhanced by beautiful dark hair. She always wore gorgeous saris. She enjoyed the dances at the lake club, firmly kept in place admiring American officers who attempted to take advantage of the cheek-to-cheek mode of dancing, popular at the time. She had great charm and manner, combined with vivacity and humour. At that moment I recalled the Yongway Princess that I had seen at the Christmas Eve dance in 1940 at Kalaw and I knew that I had been fortunate indeed to be in the presence of two of, arguably, the most beautiful women in the world, at that time.

The Adhoos Hotel in Srinagar is a lovely place in the green park-like area; trees everywhere and adjacent to it the polo ground, on which some of the finest polo in the world could be seen. Many of the maharajas brought their polo teams up to Kashmir and there were many teams from the cavalry and infantry regiments of the Army. One of the characters in Kashmir at the time was an elderly lady called 'Billy', living on a Queen Mary-sized houseboat on the Chinar Bargh. She was of Anglo-Indian birth but claimed a connection with Spain. 'Billy' did a lot of entertaining and was particularly proud of drawing attention to the signed photographs of two European crowned heads, in beautiful silver frames. The day after a party on 'Billy's' houseboat some guests were asking who she was and somebody said, "Oh don't you know? Her mother was a Spanish dancer and her father was a subaltern in the Guards."

The Shalimar and the Nishat gardens were in their full glory of flowers. The sides climbing steeply behind the vistas of clear water and the scent of the pine woods made it indeed a land for lotus eaters. The drawback was that money was running out. Most of the Burma service people had not received any pay for three months. It had been customary for many years that European visitors must settle all debts before leaving Kashmir and tradesmen were asked to report to the Resident [the senior British diplomat in a princely state] details of any sums owed by them. When the Resident became aware of the circumstances affecting people from Burma, he immediately took action with the government of India and the dilatory Indian military accounts department was galvanised into unwanted activity and we received our back pay.

In August 1942 I had to go to Murree, 160 miles away, to see a medical board and I was given another month's leave and thereafter was to report for duty at the Burma Army camp at Hoshiarpur, in the northern Punjab.

Chapter 33

Back in Harness

Hoshiarpur was about 30 miles from the military cantonment at Jalandhar and as there was no accommodation for families there Edna and several other wives stayed at a small family hotel called 'Parry's', in Jalandhar.

Hoshiarpur was the worst possible place that troops, in the low physical condition of the Burma Army, could have been sent. The area was the most malaria ridden in the Punjab and there were no amenities for the troops. There were millions of flies everywhere. All plates and dishes of food were covered by mosquito nets, and we ate our meals by putting our heads under the nets. There were no punkahs or other facilities for cooling our tents and the temperature remained steadily at about 118 degrees [Fahrenheit] in the shade. It was an incredible decision and I am of the view that it was done to prevent the true condition of the Burma Army becoming widely known in India.

After a short time in Jalandhar, Edna had managed to get accommodation at a hotel in Lahore. It was a first-class hotel with every comfort and where, on the occasional few days of short leave that I was able to visit, one could lead a good life. Unfortunately, I was soon ill again with malignant malaria at Hoshiarpur and it was decided I should go to the British military hospital Colaba, Bombay where an Australian doctor had started a new course of drug treatment for the disease. On completion of the course, I returned to

Hoshiarpur and in November I was transferred back to the Indian army, to be second in command of the reinforcement centre at Deolali, about 110 miles from Bombay.

On my way to Lahore, to join Edna, I had dinner at Parry's Hotel with Gwyneth and Geoff Downey-Lowsley. We talked far into the night of all the times we had enjoyed together and the experiences we had had in Burma. I was sad at parting from them, as they were good friends. I never saw Geoff again. He later joined the 4th Gurkhas and one evening, while cleaning his weapons, was killed accidentally.

At Deolali, after a few days residing at a small hotel there, Edna and I were given married hut accommodation in the camp area. The recruits at the centre consisted of eight battalions of sepoys totaling 10,000 men in total. Having completed their initial training at other centres, they were equipped, given further training, and finally moved forward to their units in the Burma operational theatre.

While we were in Deolali we went down to Bombay on several occasions to enjoy the life there and spent Christmas with Brigadier J.C. Jones, the embarkation commandant. He and I were on the embarkation staff in Bombay together in 1926-1927 and he was at our wedding in October 1927 at St Thomas's Cathedral, Bombay. He had been divorced from Cathy Stanton, his American wife, and had re-married. At one party was Major Ernest Simpson, of the embarkation staff, the former husband of the Duchess of Windsor [the former Mrs Wallis Simpson], and we went to several parties given by him at the Taj Mahal hotel, Bombay. He was a pleasant, likeable person and promptly put in place anybody who attempted to refer to his former marriage.

My brother Leslie had been seconded to the Indian political service and while we were at Deolali he was assistant resident in the Central Indian State Agency and lived at Indore. He was also in charge of the criminal investigation departments of all the native states in the agency, which included Indore and Rewa States, as well as several others. He had, amongst other things, to visit a European internment camp a few miles from Poona, the inmates being mostly German, Hungarian, and Austrian. It was in a huge hill fort. Married couples were in one pound and the single men and women in two other segregated camps.

As Leslie passed within a few miles of Deolali on his inspection visits he would often meet us after his visits to the camp. On one occasion, he related one of the problems at the camp. In such conditions the single women and men had become quite frustrated and one very voluptuous Austrian blonde had made several requests to be transferred to the men's compound. This was refused and when Leslie arrived, she had taken off all her clothing and climbed a tree saying she would not come down until her request was met. Eventually she had to be forcibly removed from the tree. In some matters involving misconduct, of both the maharajas of Indore and Rewa and the Indian government, Leslie had to take a leading part.

In February 1943 I was transferred, as assistant director supplies, to the headquarters of the Eastern Army at Barrackpore, 14 miles from Calcutta, on the banks of the Hooghly River. We were fortunate enough to get a lovely flat on the top floor of the Army and Navy stores in Calcutta on Chowringhee overlooking the Maidan and close to the racecourse. I, however, had to remain in Barrackpore and officers of the Eastern Army were only permitted to spend the Saturday night in Calcutta with their wives. This was a disgraceful affair, particularly for personnel who had served in Burma. We were the only people, with a few exceptions, who had seen any active service and we had already been separated from our wives or families for many months and had been through exceptional hardships.

Edna joined the Chief Census Office in Calcutta but later was to take up a role in the American Red Cross, which established and operated clubs for the US forces in Calcutta and the eastern theatre. She also had met Dr Ronnie Senior-White and Mrs White. The doctor was chief medical officer of Bengal-Nagpur Railway and had a lovely house in Garden Reach on the banks of the river, a little way south of Fort William and we spent many pleasant weekends there.

At Barrackpore another officer and I were billeted with a Mr. and Mrs. Ford who had a nice modern style bungalow and they made us very comfortable and very welcome. Duties at headquarters Eastern Army included regular tours to all the forward operational areas of the Army, from Ledo, in the far north of Assam; where work on the 'Stilwell Road' in the Hukawng Valley was being carried out, at the utmost speed, to the forward areas in Manipur State and the Arakan, and southwards to Cox's Bazar. There was a terrific workload to carry out but in doing it I was able to visit many tea plantations and meet the tea planters at their clubs and I got to know something of their lives and work. On occasions I travelled on the big river steamers on the Brahmaputra; it was a pleasant interlude of good food, drinks and comfortable beds, complete relaxation in often beautiful scenery.

On one occasion I had to halt for the night at a forest rest house on the south bank of the Brahmaputra, in a rhinoceros sanctuary at Simla Guri. Driving into the bungalow compound I saw a Naga head hunter standing on the veranda and lights were burning in the bungalow. As I walked towards the bungalow an Englishman came out and said, "Very glad to see you. I am Barron the chief game warden of Assam." I introduced myself, delighted at this unexpected meeting, having heard of his reputation. When I had settled in Mr. Barron said, "We must celebrate our meeting on Her Majesty the Queen's birthday [HM Queen Elizabeth, consort to George VI], which is tonight, the 4th August 1943", and I replied, "Nothing would give me greater pleasure as it is also my birthday".

We had quite a nice dinner, cooked by the bungalow orderly, and after offering a royal toast to HM Queen Elizabeth went and sat on the veranda in long chairs and drank and talked for hours. We could just see the mighty Brahmaputra, through the tall trees on the riverbank. There was complete silence except for insect noises. Barron had albums of wonderful photographs of the animals of the IFS jungles, particularly elephants. They were of immense interest to me especially as I knew Mr. F.W. Champion of the Indian Forest Service and had his wonderful books, 'With the Camera in Tigerland' and 'The Jungle in Sunlight and Shadow', before I lost them in Burma.

We had not been talking long when a rhinoceros whistled in the jungle, followed by others. It was obvious that there were several of the animals about.

It is an unusual sound to come from such a large animal. A short time later, in the distance, we heard the great booming 'AOO AOO' of the tiger. Suddenly complete silence prevailed; even the crickets and other insects ceased their noise. Presently, my Punjabi orderly brought us drinks and very gradually the insect noises recommenced. Mr. Barron had a short-wave radio set which was a boon to him in the jungle, and although it lay in bits and pieces about the room it worked when he went up and touched one of the knobs. In the early hours a tiger called again and with that marvellous sound in our ears we retired to rest.

Each group of tea gardens [tea estates or plantations] had a club and on specific nights club members would act as hosts, to all who wished to come. In the dry season there was usually a polo match or in the afternoons tennis and cricket matches, followed by cocktails, dinner, and a gramophone dance. Different nights of the week would have different themes for their entertainment. Although the tea gardens had communicating roads, horses were necessary to enable the planters to supervise the garden areas properly and of course they were popular for sporting purposes. These events were very jolly affairs and I went to a number of them during my tours.

At Dibrugarh the Brahmaputra River is several miles wide and on the northern bank lay the Sadiya frontier track. This was the tribal territory of the Abor head hunting tribe. The region consisted of a belt of dense jungle, stretching from the river to the Himalayas, varying in width from 25 to 75 miles. A political agent lived at Sadiya, with a company of Assam Rifles as escort. The tribe, as with the Nagas and other head-hunters, was allowed to pursue their own way of life, provided they did not harm Imperial subjects or the nationals of other countries. Hunting among the tribes, which was part of a fertility rite, was not interfered with. The agreement with the tribes meant that in Dibrugarh, on a Saturday evening, there could be a European style dinner dance with those attending in smart evening attire or fashionable dresses, but only five miles away the Abor head-hunters might be on one of their headhunting expeditions.

In those days in India, Malaya, Burma and the Far East nearly all Europeans, without exception, were generous in the matter of hospitality, especially in isolated areas, and in such places, travelers arriving at any time of day or night were made welcome and given any assistance they might require. On one occasion, at dawn, a planter at Tinsukia went downstairs to go for a walk and found on the bungalow veranda an American major with an attractive young lady. They were both completely naked and held out two bundles of clothing and said, "Can you dry these for us and give us some breakfast?" The planter, without batting an eye, agreed to the request. It was in the monsoon and the visitors had been drenched and in the darkness stopped at the first bungalow they came to on the tea garden plantation.

On one of my tours I visited Shillong, a hill station in Assam, located at 5,500 feet. It was a pretty little place, somewhat reminiscent of the Shan States terrain amidst extensive pine woods. However the road was rather hazardous, and the traffic flowed in one direction only for six hours and was then reversed, and the road was completely closed at night.

356

I made an extensive tour of the Arakan Area where the Japanese had established themselves on the Myu peninsula and fierce fighting had failed to dislodge them. To approach the Arakan was done by rail to Calcutta and then on the Brahmaputra by river steamer to Chandpur, a journey of several hours. There were about 1,000 troops on board the steamer and it fell to my lot to be OC troops. At Chandpur the route was again by rail to Chittagong, a port that was of great importance to the maintenance of our troops in Arakan and later for the 14th Army thrust into Burma.

It was then full steam from Chittagong to Cox's Bazar. On the way part of the voyage passed between several islands lying on occasions so close to the coast that sometimes branches brushed the superstructure of the steamer. Also on board was Lt. Col. K.M. Cariappa, of the Indian Army, who later, after independence, became the Commander in Chief of the Indian Army. He represented a very fine type of Indian officer.

While in one of the narrow passages we heard some Japanese bombers approaching overhead and soon they appeared directly in line with us. There were two squadrons of bombers and we felt completely naked as we could not change course in any direction and had to go straight ahead. Soon we were able to heave a sigh of relief because they reached a point too close to hit us. They went on and bombed Kidderpore docks in Calcutta, creating a colossal panic.

During these tours vast quantities of tour notes for information and action had to be prepared quickly, to be effective, and detailing individuals or branches of headquarters staff, responsible for taking action. On one tour I had to investigate the progress of the cattle supply organisation dealing with the provision of fresh meat to troops in the forward areas. The cattle were sent by rail to the Brahmaputra and then taken over the river by flat bottomed rafts. Once ashore the cattle were formed into herds and moved forward by men on horseback to successive staging camps until they reached the forward areas.

In charge of cattle organisation was a Lt. Col. Edwards, who in civil life was a rancher in Argentina. Thousands of cattle were involved in the supply of fresh meet to the troops in forward areas but it necessitated a long and strenuous journey and resulted in a great waste of animals.

The tigers were not slow to start following the herds and must have thought it was a real bonanza. Kills were numerous in most places through which the cattle passed. On one or two occasions the tigers had entered the camps and wrecked equipment and frightened the troops. As for the rhinoceros at Simla Guri; the rhinos had come into the camps but they went up to the cattle pounds just to be friends, as they apparently liked cattle.

Eventually what had been feared did happen. At the last staging camp, that held 1,500 head of cattle, anthrax broke out. They began to die in hundreds. I was ordered to make an immediate visit and initiate such action as I could and report the situation to army headquarters. The conditions of the camp were appalling. Hundreds of dead cattle lay over the site, some had been dead for days and in the sheds the carcasses were a crawling mass of maggots and liquid putrefaction which we had to walk through.

Many animals I saw also had foot and mouth disease and the poor beasts were in agony. I ordered the OIC to segregate all animals that appeared to be fit and move them several miles away and watched carefully for further cases. I also ordered the immediate shooting and destruction of all other animals and the burning of carcasses where they lay. Assistance from the neighbouring army units was to be asked for as a priority measure. I then signaled the line of communications to divert the cattle supply route and sent a brief 'sit rep' to army headquarters. The shortage of tinned meat reserves in the forward areas caused anxiety for a time but the action taken was effective.

In October 1943 Brigadier Leclerc-Fowl held a 'comms meeting' at army headquarters and said it was to be about re-organisation of the lines of communications to deal with the plans for the advance into Burma. He announced the formation of the 14th army, to be commanded Lt. General Sir William ['Bill'] Slim. The new army commander had appointed the brigadier to his staff and the brigadier, in his turn, gave the names of those who were to accompany him, which included me. The newly formed Barrackpore 14th Army headquarters would move to Comilla in east Bengal.

As the brigadier was talking about this his phone rang and he asked us all to leave the office. When we returned, he said it was a confidential call from general headquarters Delhi. An effort was to be made by the Americans to keep Chiang Kai Shek in the war and make the Chinese efforts more effective. Amongst the measures to be taken were: the building of a pipeline from Calcutta to a port on the Brahmaputra, the operation of a fleet of tanker barges on the Brahmaputra and increasing the number of petrol tanker trains to airfields in Assam to ensure the delivery of an increased quantity of petrol to the various airfields, together with other measures to greatly increase the number of flights over the 'Hump' into China. In order to do this a composite force was to be formed of: an area supply regiment, some garrison battalions, a pioneer battalion, an American railway operating regiment and American and Indian army sapper units. The Southeast Asia Command headquarters staff link in Calcutta, known as ACFUEL, would keep in touch with our operations and act as a link in all directions.

I was to be in charge of the area regiment to be based at Parbatipur, 140 miles north of Calcutta, where the broad-gauge line linked with the metre gauge line of the Assam areas. The railway operating battalion and the pioneer battalion were also to be located at Parbatipur. I was pleased to learn that the pioneer battalion was to be commanded by Colonel Echlin, my friend in the Baluchs Regiment. My unit controlled the operations of the force and kept in close touch with the headquarters in Calcutta, reporting daily the tons of petrol distributed from Parbatipur.

I did not really like this appointment and the Brigadier said although he did not want to lose me the general had insisted that no other officer was acceptable for the position. Relations between the Americans and our forces in Assam had not been too happy. Amongst other things the officers selected to do this work had to be able to handle the Americans and, if necessary, kick them in the pants as often as was required.

Chapter 34

Lifeline to China

Parbatipur in northeast Bengal was a dreadful place. It was only a Bengali village but it had a rather important railway junction. The broad-gauge line from Calcutta to Siliguri, at the foot of the Himalayas, and the metre gauge line from Brahmaputra eastwards, through Assam and Bihar in the United Provinces, met at this junction. All our forces and American and Chinese allies operating in the Burma theatre were largely dependent on this single railway line. Work was in progress in doubling the track from Calcutta to Parbatipur and also in two sectors of the Parbatipur - Aminagar metre gauge section. This was continually subject to interruption or serious damage by the monsoon and climatic conditions. Bridges over the rivers were dangerous weakness as they only carried a single track and if traffic was interrupted or reduced, even for a short period, the operations of our fighting formations were immediately affected, as they only held very small reserves; on occasions as little as only two or three days supply.

All the capacity of the lines of communication and supply of rail, road and river were required to meet the daily requirements of food, necessary equipment and stores and thus the building up of reserves was a slow process. A large number of American and Canadian metre gauge railway engines and railway stock began to arrive in the area and the American operating regiment made great efforts to increase the daily movement of tonnage. Unfortunately, American methods soon resulted in trains being derailed almost daily and when this occurred movement was severely curtailed or halted in both directions on the single line track.

The Parbatipur unit was housed in tented type camp in palm groves. The country surrounding was completely flat, malaria was rife and there were snakes everywhere. The Americans had very good, hutted accommodation two miles away on the other side of the town and the pioneer battalion was on the eastern side of the railway track. Brigade trains arrived from Calcutta daily loaded with packed petrol and oil lubricants; the majority of packed fuel was in 44-gallon barrels. These barrels were unloaded from the broad-gauge wagons and re-loaded on the metre gauge trains standing on the opposite side of the platform. These trains then left on the same day for north Assam and the airfields on route.

Trains of bulk petrol tank wagons arrived daily from Calcutta and these were pumped into 350,000-gallon storage tanks. Metre-gauge bulk storage tanker wagons were filled from the bulk installations, and formed into trains and again sent forward.

Eventually a petrol pipeline was built from Calcutta to Parbatipur and also along the length of the Assam trunk road to the airfields, in the far north of Assam. Pumping stations on the pipeline were located approximately every 15 miles, operated by American forces. On the Brahmaputra, a fleet of tanker barges operated and these filled up at floating pumping units on the river and then sailed upstream, calling at the various airfields en route to unload their petrol.

The operations were carried out and made possible by about 18 hours sheer hard physical labour every day by the troops. Amenities or comforts of any sort were in short supply for our troops. US troops were fortunate as they had the Post Exchange [P-X] where everything could be bought and they were much better off in all respects, including the opportunities for going to Calcutta as frequently as they wished.

Operations had always to be kept at a maximum effort. Leave in Indian units was restricted to a very small percentage. Returning late from leave was a serious offence as it prevented another man going on his leave. I was very severe on such men, and equally so for the officers. In India where men may be long distances from their homes journey time was added to the leave to enable them to have a full leave quota at home. In some cases, e.g. in the case of Gurkhas and men from other parts of the Himalayas, they might need to take up to 20 days to get to their homes.

When each leave list was completed, it was brought to me, and in my office in the presence of the adjutant, the subahdar major and the quartermaster, a fine old Sikh soldier, I marked in myself the number of days journey time being given to each name on the list. I usually went through the list, without referring to a journey guide or map. The Indian officers were greatly impressed as no one else could do this and it engendered a feeling of competence and security in the men, that the commanding officer knew something about the country and the conditions in which they lived.

I had two companies of Punjabi Mohammadans and Pathans in the unit and I ordered that foot drill, weapon training and ceremonial drill should be kept to as high a standard as possible. This fact had been noted by the

Americans. The 1st railway battalion was commanded by a Col. Emmanuel, from Illinois, a railway man in civil life and his second in command was Maj. Truden, a West Point officer of the US engineers. The men under their command were however, hillbillies, from Kentucky, and on one occasion of a train derailment Maj. Truden, in anger and frustration shouted, "These goddamn cowhands never saw a train before they were drafted".

A character named 'Tex', because he obviously came from Texas, disliked one of the 'flat-top sergeants' and one day, fuelled with alcohol, hit the sergeant and was placed under arrest. In due course he was arraigned in front of Captain O'Neil, the adjutant, who proceeded to read out the charge. Tex suddenly hit the adjutant and the flat-top sergeant also and then dashed in to his hut and came to the door with 0.45 automatic pistol in his hand and sat on a camp stool, daring any "goddamn Yank" to arrest him. The US army held the arrest at bay and then Col. Emmanuel phoned me and asked if I could help. He did not want to risk a tragedy, which would have happened if he'd sent his own troops in. With my adjutant I paraded a section of Pathans and told them to follow me to the US lines where an American soldier would be sitting, armed with a pistol. They were to drive right up to him in their truck and leap out and disarm him. The huge Pathans grinned when they heard what they were being ordered to do.

I drove down, followed by the truck of Pathans, to the US lines and there was Tex sitting on the camp stool surrounded, about 25 yards away, by a circle of American troops, including Col. Emmanuel and his staff. I drove close up to Tex and just beyond him, and the truck followed me. As it stopped the two biggest Pathans jumped out and were on Tex in a flash, wrenched the pistol from his hand and then one of them picked him up by the scruff of the neck and handed him over to the Americans. That was the end of that little contretemps.

American troops moving to the forward areas in Assam used to shoot at vultures and kite hawks flying around, and prairie dogs and where there was nothing else to shoot at they shot at the porcelain insulators on the telegraph lines. They ignored all warnings about this and one day a six-year old village boy was killed near Parbatipur. All of our units were very angry about it, and the Anglo-Indian population and Indian population threatened violence.

While stepping into my bath, one evening, a bullet came through the roof. I immediately phoned the adjutant and told him to turn out the Bren gun team as quickly as possible and fire a few bursts in the vicinity of the American post on the pipeline but be careful not to injure any personnel. A few minutes later several bursts of fire occurred, and that was the end of firing by the trigger-happy Americans. Afterwards Col. Emmanuel phoned and angrily protested about the matter. I told him that I was determined to stop this reckless behaviour by American troops and if any more shooting occurred, aimed at my camp, the American piquet would be hit next time.

The next morning Horace Ekland came round to see me and said he was very worried as Col. Emmanuel had reported the incident to General Wheeler, the commanding general at Delhi. I said, "Don't worry Horace; they won't move me from here". The incident was not pursued officially and as the senior officer the settlement of the affair was left to my discretion.

I was doing tours of inspection continuously, from Parbatipur, visiting all the American airfields in Assam. These were situated on the either side of the Brahmaputra along its whole course between Bengal and the Assam-China border in the far north, a distance of 700 miles. This enabled me to get to know the entire theatre of war and also to experience some unusual incidents.

On one occasion when travelling between Chabua and Ledo, accompanied by Major Arnold Segal of the American Quartermaster Corps we came across a long row of coffins, about 60 in all, lying outside the cemetery. I asked him if there had been an air raid and he replied, "There's no reason for the Japs. to raid this place while this bunch is here." He explained that a squadron of Liberator bombers were coming into land as another squadron was about to take off. The bomber taking off was hit by one of the returning bombers and both blew up. Another returning bomber overran the runway and hit a second bomber exploding one more plane nearby. The result was the long line of coffins waiting to be repatriated to America.

On another occasion, a visit to the American officers' mess at Ledo was pleasant and surprising. The camp buildings were wooden and asbestos huts, mosquito proofed, with electric lighting and Frigidaires etc., coloured tablecloths and curtains and good crockery. It was a pleasure to see such relative luxuries again and in addition there were pretty American girls everywhere; the officers' secretaries, telephonists, administrative clerks and even hostesses to care for the welfare of the men and write home to their people for them, if required.

At Parbatipur I had another miraculous escape from certain oblivion. A naik, (i.e. corporal) in charge of the quarter guard, had deserted in the early hours one morning and taken with him a pistol and a quantity of ammunition. As a set procedure for desertion in the Indian forces the civil police are immediately informed and given details of his personal appearance, his home village, district etc. The same information is wired to the superintendent of police of his home district and also the railway police. In a land of 800,000 villages of different religions, many castes and sub-castes anyone who is away from his village is a stranger even if the next village is only a few miles away and his presence is noted immediately. The naik was apprehended by the railway police as he got off the train at Delhi and he was back in my quarter guard within a few days, under arrest awaiting court martial.

It is impossible in tented accommodation to maintain a proper standard of security and within a few days, in the early hours of one morning, the prisoner escaped and again took a 0.45 calibre pistol and some ammunition. My orderly, who had had a restless night, came back early to my tent at about 4.30 am and saw a figure near my bed, with a pistol pointing at me. He shouted and the man ran off into the darkness. I was woken up by this and a few minutes later it was reported to me that the naik had escaped. The next day at 2.00pm he was in a village about 14 miles away when he was challenged by the village constable. He fired six shots into the policeman's chest and killed him.

At his trial for murder the naik said he had made his way to my tent to kill me. I was sleeping in the compound under mosquito nets, and he aimed at me as I lay sleeping. His finger was on the trigger when my orderly arrived at that God given moment and challenged him. The naik was found guilty and hanged. Only the arrival of my orderly saved my life because this murderer would have had no hesitation in carrying out his plan, if he had not been disturbed at that moment.

On a visit to Dispur, a river port on the Brahmaputra, and the centre of a large number of tea garden estates. The company commander of one of my companies on the airfield told me that he had a book given to him by a US Officer, the book was called 'The Lady and the Tigers' and the authoress was Olga Greenlaw. Of course, I was very interested to see the book and the US officer kindly allowed me to keep it. [This book was retained by my father, over the years, with various footnotes and corrections included in it, in pencil. I now have this rather dog-eared copy of the 1943 edition].

Olga mentioned Edna and me in the book on a number of occasions, including our last meeting at Maymyo. Later it helped me to regain contact with her and we have corresponded and exchanged Christmas cards with each other ever since, although we have not actually met since 1942, i.e. 32 years ago [at the time of recording]. Olga kindly sent me an autographed copy of her book and last year [1973] the sad news that Count Jacques had died. She was a widow after her second marriage and they had planned to get married themselves, but it was not to be.

Horace Ekland and I were the only two regular Indian Army officers in the area and having known each other for many years it was our habit to meet on alternate evenings; one night in my tent and one night in his tent, when I was not on tour and operations permitted. He spoke Pashtu fluently and he had chosen as his personal orderly an enormous Afridi named Afzal Khan, of the Adamkhel tribe, although aged only 21, he was about 6' 4" in height, powerfully built and had very handsome features.

The worldly-wise weather beaten tough little colonel sahib who spoke his own language so well was literally worshipped by Afzul, he mothered Horace day and night and spent all of his time in looking after his master's needs. He slept outside Horace's tent at night and Afzul's terrific presence was sufficient to prevent anyone trying to interfere with his sahib. He regarded me as his sahib's number one friend and Afzul and my own orderly, who was a fine-looking young Punjabi Mohammadan also, got on very well together.

One night when going over to the lines to have curry with Horace, I saw as I drove down the line of tents the whole battalion squatting in a vast semi-circle and looking into the officer's mess cookhouse. I drove to Horace's tent and Afzul brought me a whisky. I enquired what the troops were looking at. Afzul replied, "Colonel Sahib is cooking a curry for you." I strolled over and saw inside the cookhouse Horace, clad only in a singlet and Khaki shorts, preparing what was a delicious curry. The sepoys, who also thought the world of Horace, could not miss the sight of their colonel making a curry with his own hands for his friend another colonel sahib. It was a delicious curry and with good drinks and interesting talk made a pleasant interlude in that awful, dreary place. The Jawans, (i.e. the young soldiers), also now had a topic of conversation, which no doubt they would relate for years to come in their villages.

Good organisation, efficient planning, and the sheer hard physical work of the troops had resulted in a great increase in the tonnage of petrol, oils and lubricants flown into China over the Hump and the wagons handled had increased from 25-30 per day in the early stages, to 120-130 early in 1944. The air transport available was used to maximum capacity and better relations with the Chinese were achieved. A high rate of movement, however, began to have an increased number of adverse effects. Train journeys lasting sometimes weeks and iron wagons in which the barrels were crashed about in a dreadful manner combined with the terrific heat and the rough handling of loads, weighing 350lbs or more, gave rise to leakage of petrol. During one flight these leakages contributed to the concentration of petrol vapour causing an explosion, resulting in the loss of vital cargo and the death of all of the plane's crew.

After the first incidence several more planes exploded, and this gave rise to a most serious situation. A number of United States air force officers were sent to Parbatipur to carry out the inspection of all barrels being transshipped for onward dispatch to China. All barrels showing the slightest signs of leakage were rejected. This slowed down operations considerably and it took a long time and prodigious efforts to return to our previous daily tonnage.

While this was happening, I paid a visit to the US Tenth Air Force group at Chungichuk in Assam, probably at the time the largest air group in the world. About half a mile from the aerodrome the smell of petrol vapour was very strong and on arrival there, accompanied by my company commander, I saw hundreds of barrels scattered all over the place and to our horror from one of the wagons out stepped a black US serviceman smoking an enormous cigar. Major Tetlar, the US officer with us, acted immediately to prevent a disaster and ordered my own officer to withdraw all Indian army troops, to a safe distance, and not to return until further orders were received from me.

When I was in Ledo having lunch with the US officer, Brigadier Arrowsmith, a message arrived to say that a petrol train going to Chungichuk had caught fire and was completely destroyed with hundreds of thousands of gallons of petrol. The situation was then made more difficult by the derailment of a train while crossing a large girder bridge over the River Teesta which resulted in a number of wagons being broadside across the track, completely blocking all movement to the 14th army areas. The situation really was serious. It would need heavy breakdown cranes and equipment to clear the line and it might take a number of days. After confidential discussions of the position between Col. Emanuel, a Royal Engineer officer and myself, examination of the site of the accident showed that the wagons could be tipped into the river with only slight damage to the superstructure of the bridge. This was done and the daily deliveries of fuel by train were resumed in less than 24 hours.

When visiting 14th army headquarters at Comilla I was invited to stay with the Delaunay Brothers in their magnificent house there. The two Delaunay Brothers were zamindars (i.e. large landowners), in east Bengal and in addition to thousands of acres in the Comilla district they owned Sandwip Island in the Brahmaputra – Ganges Delta. This island is approximately 60 miles by 30 miles in extent and may well have been the largest private island estate in the world. It suffered grievously in the cyclone disaster in 1973 in Bangladesh.

The brothers offered to try and arrange some tiger shikar for me but as important matters prevented me from being away too long, I visited some of the jungle areas myself and spent some relaxed and happy hours looking for spoor and watching the bird life. There were two tigers in the area, a leopard, several types of chital, and the odd bison.

There was a very nice swimming pool in the Delaunay garden, lined on either side with tall palms and a border of grass; altogether a lovely and pleasant place. Unfortunately, I do not know how their fortunes have fared since the partition of India and the creation of the state of Bangladesh.

General Dougie Stewart the GOC 303 LFC area inspected my unit at Parbatipur in 1944. I had my best quarter guard mounted for the occasion and after inspecting them he said, "It is the finest quarter guard I have seen in the whole of my service". I was very gratified to hear this, especially as we were old friends. He had been Staff Captain of the Secunderabad brigade when I joined the North Staffords there in 1924.

A week later General Maine, GOC Eastern Army, paid a visit and after inspecting the quarter guard, he said, "It is one of the finest guards I have seen". Major Harold Fisher, my second in command, and the unit's adjutant deserved a large part of the credit for this excellent effort.

Chapter 35

The World's Greatest View

*"I have trod the golden sand that leads to fabled
Samarkand and sailed the seas to far Cathay, and
watched dawn break red on Himalay."*

[Unattributed, but possibly: Armenius Vambery,
Travels in Central Asia, New York,
Harper & Brothers, 1865]

I was given a week's casual leave and joined Edna
on the Darjeeling mail from Calcutta at Parbatipur
and we continued our journey to Siliguri the centre
of a large tea garden area at the foot of the Darjeeling
range. At Siliguri a narrow two-foot gauge railway
[now known as the Darjeeling Himalayan Railway]
runs up to Darjeeling at 7,000 feet above sea level.
The ascent is very steep and at one place the
railway zigs-zags up the steep mountain side, a few
sections of the track being immediately above those
below. In another place it runs out on an isolated
spur and round the spur back again onto the
mountain side, and during this the engine travels
in one direction and passes the rearmost carriage
moving in another direction, with only a few yards
between them.

Two of the most notable halts were at Kalimpong,
a missionary centre, and Ghum, where a restaurant
on the station served meals and the wonderful Orange
Pekoe tea for which the Darjeeling tea gardens are
famous. The railway ran right through the main
streets of these two places, and if one wished one

could put one's hand out of the window and take things from the shop stalls along the side.

At Siliguri the route traverses dense, heavy rain forest and as it gains altitude rhododendrons cover the whole hill side. The motor road runs alongside the railway for much of the journey with road and rail continually crossing each other. Cars held up by the train at one point, will, after the train has passed, speed up to the next crossing in order to get ahead of the train. The journey through forest is a delight and is full of wonderful tropical birds.

Pines appear on the higher slopes of the mountain side. The last half mile of the line is level, and the station quite spacious. If the visitor is lucky and there are no clouds, the enormous white mass of Kanchenjunga can be seen when approaching Darjeeling station though that does not happen very often.

We stayed at the Mount Everest hotel right on the top of the ridge, on which Darjeeling is built. There are wonderful views in all directions from the limitless Turi forest below on one side to the great 25,000 foot ranges on the other. On the third day, as we walked on the hillside, the sky was clear and we saw the most tremendous and incomparable sight on earth, the vast white face of Kanchenjunga gleaming in the bright sunshine, reaching to a height of 28,260 feet. It appeared to be only a few miles away yet it was 45 miles away, and although we were standing at a height of 7,000 feet we had to look upwards at a sharp angle to see this unforgettable sight. We saw it three times more before we left.

Mount Everest can only be seen from Tiger Hill at the other end of the Darjeeling ridge, but Everest is

120 miles away with many high ranges intervening, so it only appears as a small cone just above the far ridges. We rode to the far end of the ridge and looked upon Everest.

The Darjeeling Club was spacious for a hill station, where space for building is often at a premium. It was very comfortable and the centre of quite a hectic social life. While we were there a Buddhist religious festival took place which was most interesting and picturesque. The lamas were there in their dark brown and salmon coloured robes with high conical hats. With them was a procession of boys carrying the Buddhist scriptures, wrapped in cloth, on their backs. There were 18 foot-long curved horns, resting on boys' shoulders for support that were being blown vigorously by the lamas. This particular festival was only held at very rare intervals, it was said every 100 years but I cannot say if that was correct. It was however very fortunate that we had the chance to see it.

The rest of our leave was spent in Simla. Neither of us had visited Simla before. It is a very pretty place and the associations with Kipling were everywhere. With friends whom we had known in Rangoon we went on some delightful picnics to Jakhu Hill, to Narkanda, about 35 miles away, on the Hindustan-Tibet Road and elsewhere. Each time we had morning coffee or tea in the afternoon at 'Bellitas', the ghost of Mrs Hauksbee appeared to be present, and there were ladies there who must have been identical with Rudyard Kipling's original character. The interesting and famous little antique shop, kept by Logan Sahib in Kipling's stories, was also to be seen.

Groups of muleteers were met in parties along the Hindustan-Tibet road and views of the vast ranges of

20,000 foot snows were always there to uplift the soul. We found this delightful and the wonderful days passed all too quickly. We completed the journey down to Kauka by rail car, which is a small 10 to 12 seater carriage mounted on railway wheels. Some days after we had come down in the rail car it was ambushed by two deserters from the Indian army and all the occupants killed or wounded.

On my return to Parbatipur the "stiff leave" [special army service] scheme to England was announced. The officers selected were given four months' leave including journey time. The journey was to be carried out by ships in convoy or in a few cases by warship passages. This resulted in us having approximately two months leave in England. We were given a passage on the *Monarch of Bermuda,* sailing from Bombay in January 1945.

On the day I left Parbatipur, on arrival at the station, I found nearly the whole of the regiment drawn up on the platform under Major Fisher the second in command. I bade the men farewell and then had a few words with all the Indian Officers. When speaking to the Subahdar Major, I told him how much I appreciated this gesture because I had had to drive them very hard. He replied, "You had to Colonel Sahib but you have been invariably fair to all ranks, and we have always felt safe with you".

On one of my weekends in Calcutta before sailing we went to the Saturday Club to the usual Saturday night dance and we were all delighted to see Noel Coward walk onto the ballroom floor. We enjoyed a memorable hour of entertainment by that great artist. He was in the process of making a tour of the Burma operational theatre.

Chapter 36

England's Shores Once More

We had a comparatively uneventful voyage in convoy through the Red Sea, the Mediterranean across the Bay of Biscay and finally to our home port of Greenock. We arrived one evening in February at Edna's sister's home in Poulton-Le-Fylde in Lancashire. We were greeted by Valerie and her aunt Ida. Brian was at the Rossall School at Fleetwood and was coming home the following day. Valerie was only six years old when we had last seen her, six years previously. Now just approaching her teens, she was really lovely, with all the promise of the very beautiful woman she was to become. It was a wonderful reunion after long years of separation.

The next day I saw Brian running down the village road and then at last we were all together. There was so much to say, so much to share with each other before the time for another parting drew near.

Only a week after our arrival Edna's father, Thomas, was taken ill and died in a few days. It was a tragic homecoming for her, after the long years of separation. After the funeral I went down to London to see my mother who was then living at Carshalton, having been bombed out of her home in Blackheath. Leslie was also at home on leave and I arranged to go down to see him as well. It was a Sunday and I was staying at the Cumberland Hotel, Marble Arch. I usually went for a walk to Speaker's Corner before breakfast when staying there. When I was in the hotel porch, just about to go for my morning walk, I realised that there was no regular train service running and I had better start early in case of any delay and so went back into the hotel, without my usual walk and sat down to breakfast. A few minutes later there was a terrific explosion and the whole hotel shook. There was surprisingly little panic and the waitresses in the hotel were marvellous. They went round calming people, saying, "It's all over now, don't worry, eat your breakfast".

A V2 rocket had struck the copse at Speaker's Corner leaving an enormous crater. Many trees had been blown down and all the windows in the buildings around Marble Arch were shattered. If I had gone for my regular morning walk, I would've been on the exact spot where the V2 had landed; yet another very, very lucky escape from oblivion. [The 'West End at War' project reported the incident thus, "At 9.31am on 18 March 1945 a V2 rocket hit Speakers' Corner at the north-eastern end of Hyde Park, close to Marble Arch. Three civilians were killed and 81 others injured. Fortunately, the rocket landed at a time when relatively few people were walking through the park."]

Later, I went to Carshalton, and enjoyed a very pleasant family reunion. The following day I met Gwyneth Downey-Lowsley, who was then living in Sloan Square. We went to see 'Perchance to Dream' and afterwards had supper at the Cumberland Hotel. She then told me about Geoff's death and asked me to take a photograph of his grave if I should ever get to Chakrata.

The leave had of course already been marred by the tragedy of my father-in-law's death which also distressed the children. It was wonderful being together again with them but I knew my leave time was passing all too quickly and although the end of the war in Europe could be anticipated, I also knew that headquarters, SEAC [South East Asia Command], were planning for a further three-year campaign against the Japanese. Families were not permitted to go back to India, so it was possible I would be separated from my family for several more years.

I eventually received instructions to embark on the *RMS Maloja*, a troop ship sailing from Greenock early in May, to take over the command of No 3 Reserve Base Petrol Depot at Paragarh in Bengal on arrival in India. This was the largest petrol base in any theatre of operation.

Chapter 37

The Last Days in India and the End of the Raj

I was at sea in the Bay of Biscay on 8th May 1945 when the war in Europe ended and VE Day was celebrated. Alcohol was in short supply on ships in convoy during the war years. As far as I recollect, it was two bottles of beer per head on the *RMS Maloja*. The ship was packed with passengers and the ship's staff was under-strength, so many junior officers had to take their turn as waiters during dinner.

We did not get out of range of German submarines very quickly and we had a scare in the Bay of Biscay and another off Algiers, but the rest of the voyage was uneventful, and we arrived in Bombay in due course. [A considerable number of German U-boats were at sea at this time, on their way to home or to neutral ports to surrender but if sighted by Allied ships the possibility of a U-boat attack could not be ruled out.]

Srinagar was a great reserve base area, providing for the operations of the 14th army in Burma and the Logistic Support Corps (LSC) areas sustaining it. It was about 40 square miles in extent and various areas were allotted to the stores and equipment concerned: the base petrol depot, the base supply depot, the engineering depot and medical hospital, reserves, etc. I wasn't particularly enamoured with the job and was therefore very excited when I heard, in September, that I was to be posted to the headquarters of the Lucknow district, where my brother Leslie was Senior Superintendent of police, as he had finished his secondment to the Indian political department. This was the first time in 20 years when we had been stationed together or even within 100 miles of each other.

Leslie's appointment had extremely heavy responsibilities. He was superintendent of police of the Lucknow, the capital city of the United Provinces, now Uttar Pradesh. He had, under his charge, 5,000 city police, three squadrons of mounted police, two battalions of armed constabulary and the hundreds of police in the stations in the district. The central jail of the province was also located in Lucknow city. My own appointment was Officer in Command of all RIASC units and installations in the District.

Leslie's official residence was in the city civil lines area in Shah Najaf Road. It was a very large house and set in a spacious and lovely garden. There was a police quarter guard mounted on the bungalow day and night. Only 100 yards away was one of the great historic buildings of India, the Shah Najaf Tomb, around which a terrific battle was fought in the Indian mutiny.

My sister-in-law, Ena, Leslie's wife, was in England and was due to return to India just before Christmas. In addition to his office at police headquarters in the city Leslie had an office in his house, where each morning the station officers from the police stations in the district gathered to give their reports and apprise him of all happenings in their areas. Inspectors and sub-inspectors of the city police station were also there, and he had an official interpreter and legal clerk.

His routine was to go to the police lines at dawn and watch the training in progress: physical training, arms drill, equitation etc. Returning to his house he then held a conference, after which he had breakfast and went to the city headquarters or toured various areas of the city or visited one of the stations in the district. Work continued after lunch. In the evening, there would be games with the men, polo or tennis, or perhaps some small game shooting, of which there was a lot in most parts of the district.

The political situation in the city was always very delicate and trouble was liable to erupt without warning at any time. There were large numbers of Mohammadans in the city. Under the rule of the kings of Oudh and the Moghuls the Mohammadans had held the political power over the numerically larger Hindu indigenous population. To manage the precarious political situation Leslie was in touch with the governor, Sir Francis Wylie, almost daily and other members of the state government, as necessary.

Hindu and Mohammadan religious festivals created a terrific amount of work for the police who were required to keep order at festivals such as, Holi, Dussehra, Eid al-Adha, Eid al-Fitr and Muharram. If rioting occurred at these festivals peace had to be restored and the rioters dealt with. As a consequence, every senior police officer in India risked assassination. To guard against this danger in Lucknow senior officers had a plain clothes shadow in attendance, 24 hours a day. Threats to harm Leslie were received daily. However, this was not allowed to interfere with the normal course of work or our social activities, which were very extensive. There were dinners, investitures, and dances at Government House, and at a number of Lucknow clubs in the cantonment.

A number of maharajas of states in the United Provinces had palaces in Lucknow and we were often invited to dinners at these palaces. The palace of the Maharaja of Mahmudabad was very reminiscent, in one respect, of the Rajgir palace in Srinagar. It had several large rooms, crammed full of Victorian furniture, clocks in glass cases, display cabinets etc.

One evening when I got back from the cantonment Leslie said, "Mahmudabad wants us to have dinner with him and go to the cinema with him afterwards." We duly went to the palace, and when we entered the dining room the table, which could seat 100 people, appeared to be covered with a coloured tablecloth of a rose flower pattern. Three places were laid at the end of the table and a number of the maharaja's staff, dressed in wonderful livery were in attendance. When we sat down, I saw that the flower pattern consisted of tens of thousands of grains of rice, dyed in various colours, and arranged in the pattern. The work entailed was enormous and must have been taken hours to do and it was just for this dinner arrangement.

On one occasion Lord Wavell, the Viceroy, was scheduled to pay a four-day visit to Lucknow. Prior to this visit Leslie handed a book to me, that was about an inch thick. It contained his police arrangements, orders and instructions for the Viceroy's visit, to ensure his safety during the tour. It entailed a vast amount of work and responsibility.

A reception was held at Government House in the Viceroy's honour, and it was a great privilege for many, who had not met this famous soldier. Reception lines had been arranged on the lawn in front of Government House and the Viceroy and Governor took up a convenient position to receive the line of guests. The Viceroy shook hands with each guest, had a word or two with people he knew, and then we went off to sit at a table, where the tea was served by the Government House servants in their traditional uniform.

For the four days the Viceroy was in Lucknow and United Provinces, every yard of each journey by railway and car had to be under surveillance, with military or police protection.

The administration of India and Burma was organised on a district basis and the two officials responsible for the administration of the area and enforcement of law and order were the deputy commissioner, an officer of the Indian Civil Service, and the superintendent of police.

At the time the Deputy Commissioner in Lucknow was Humphrey Trevelyan, later Lord Trevelyan, who was to so ably handle the Aden crisis later, in the mid 1960s. In the dry season these officers spent a lot of time touring the district meeting and advising their subordinate officials on various matters, inspecting works, land surveying, etc. Tours offered splendid opportunities for game shooting and they were generally used to the utmost advantage.

In a district with tigers, a traditional Christmas tiger camp was often held. When Leslie suggested a weekend's small shoot in the district, I was very surprised at the great preparations made for this. The area of the shoot was only about 30 miles away. A large lorry was loaded up with two 600lb tents, about 24 feet by 18 feet, with bath tents attached, camp furniture, boards and carpets for the tent floors, cooking equipment and stores, camp office furniture etc. In addition, we had our car and there was also a truck for the police escort for the area and its paraphernalia. I was very amused at this performance and told Leslie of the contrast with the North West Frontier, where we were only allowed 10lbs of kit per man and might be away for six weeks or more. On the other hand it could be fairly said that many of the officers were obliged to tour for several months every year and had to make themselves as comfortable as possible to make life bearable and to allow them to carry out their work more efficiently. These weekend shoots were very pleasant and often there was a nearby canal or tank to bathe in.

While playing polo one evening Leslie had a fall and broke his left arm, which was placed in splint. It was hot weather, and we were sleeping outside the house, on beds under mosquito nets. At about midnight when an orderly was helping Leslie undress three pistol shots went off. They were quite close and seemed to come from the road junction about 75 yards from the house.

I said, "They sounded like .32 automatic shots". We went to bed, and I was soon asleep. I was woken up by the sound of voices and in the light of a Petromax Lamp [Tilley lamp] Leslie was being helped into his uniform by the orderly and an Indian inspector was talking to him. They told me that two British other ranks had been shot dead at the crossroads and they were starting investigations.

The police officers returned shortly before dawn and told me that the two murdered men were Major Richardson and Lieutenant Masters, both of the Army Special Investigation branch, A number of people had been brought to the house for interview, including a captain in the Indian Engineers, whose bungalow was only about 25 yards from where the bodies were found, and an Indian businessman, who was keeping an Anglo-Indian girl, who was also a friend of Lieutenant Masters and a number of others.

Within a few days several anonymous letters were received threatening Leslie's life and four Indians were murdered in Lucknow city. The next night two ladies, Mrs Kay Richardson and Miss Claire MacPherson of the SSAFA, dined with us and we all went to the cinema. We had a lorry load of police following us and when we arrived at the cinema, we did not get out of the car until the police had cleared the foyer and assured themselves that it was safe for us to enter. After the cinema the ladies returned to their hotel under police escort, and Leslie went to view the scene of the murder and pursue investigations at the time of the night that it occurred. Wherever we went at night the same precautions had to be observed. It was very interesting for me to see how the police investigation was conducted and how far and wide they spread their net. In one case an Anglo-Burman Captain was brought from Bombay, 1,100 miles away.

Some weeks went by after the shooting and then one evening a British other ranks deserter was involved in some trouble at a local railway station. He was arrested and evidence came to light that led to a charge of murder of the two officers. He was brought to trial, but some technical ballistic evidence submitted by the police was found to be inadmissible and soldier was sentenced to two years of imprisonment for desertion instead of the capital charge of murder.

By custom Hindus and many Oriental races distinguish between brothers by calling the elder one the 'Bada', the big sahib or big brother. The younger brother is the 'Chota' sahib, or small brother. It is general, irrespective of the actual position, status or rank that the two brothers might hold. Although Leslie was the most powerful person in Lucknow and had the authority to issue any orders he considered necessary in the course of his duties, or permit or refuse any activity at his discretion, in his area of responsibility, I was the 'Bada' sahib to all of the house servants and the whole of the police force. In actual fact our ranks of Lieutenant Colonel and Senior Superintendent of Police were equivalent but I came under the special care of the police force, and was given preference over all other people, short of the Governor of the province in my daily comings and goings. This, on one occasion, resulted in an embarrassing situation. The District Commissioner of Lucknow, General Curtis, my old friend of Peshawar days in 1929 and force relief in Burma, was returning to the cantonment in his staff car with pennant flying and two military police motorcycle outriders, while I was returning, on my motorcycle, to Leslie's house from the cantonment. Some police constables stationed at a junction with Shah Najaf Road promptly held up the general and his outriders but turning to me, gave a magnificent salute, and waved me down to Shah Najaf Road. A short time later I phoned the General to apologise but he replied, "Oh that's quite alright. Everybody knows that Leslie's big brother must be given priority".

Leaving the house one morning I came across a group of Indians standing around a handcart. I stopped to see what the centre of interest was and saw, to my amazement, a very large pangolin, the scaly anteater, which is very rarely seen, as I have noted previously. Making enquiries I ascertained that during the night, the night-watchman in the house next to us, had seen an animal which in the darkness he thought was a jackal. He hit it with his wooden staff and stunned it and saw then that the animal was in fact a pangolin. He tied it up and was, at the time, taking it to Lucknow Zoo. There was a very old cemetery behind Leslie's house which had been used since the first Europeans arrived in Oudh and evidently the pangolin had a burrow there. This cemetery was in the heart of the Lucknow, the capital city of the province, and the animal must have been there for years but being nocturnal in their habits they are very rarely seen.

The Rama Navami festival came round during which two enormous figures made of bamboo, about 100 feet in height would be the centre of attention. They represented figures of the gods and were filled with combustible materials and fireworks. As part of the festival the figures were burnt to great acclamations by the crowd. The event was held in a large open area on the outskirts of Lucknow. Leslie and I were invited to join some eminent Hindus, who organised the festival. Staying with us at the time was the young daughter of another superintendent of police, so we took the young lady along with us to see the festival. The route lay, for several miles, along narrow streets which were densely crowded by the thousands of people going to the ceremony. We were in Leslie's official car, preceded by a line of six mounted police moving at a fast walk or slow trot. The crowd, parting smoothly, allowed the car to be driven slowly without being held up at any place. Occasionally, individuals in the crowd would need a touch from a lance point to clear the way but never at any time was the crowd anything other than in good humour.

We saw the ceremony from a special enclosure during which the gigantic figures were ignited and blazed away accompanied by rockets, shooting stars, and all kinds of fireworks. After the ceremony was over, we returned to Shah Najaf Road without any inconvenience.

Of Lucknow, William H Sleeman has said,

"Not Rome, not Athens, not Constantinople; not any city I have seen appears to me so striking and so beautiful as this..."

('A Journey through the Kingdom of Oude in 1849-50', London 1858)

In Lucknow there were a great number of beautiful and historic buildings and also many beautiful gardens and park-like areas with numerous trees in the city. The sight of Lucknow in the early morning has been described as one of the most beautiful in India, which is high praise indeed. Near our residency there was a sacred place for British visitors, set in a lovely garden near to the River Gomti, and on a lawn surrounded by flowerbeds was a small stone cross erected as a memorial to the heroic dead and to the many deeds of valour that occurred during the siege. [In the Indian Mutiny, 1857]

The [old British] Residency Gardens were all kept in beautiful condition and the Union Jack was kept flying day and night on the tallest tower ever since the Indian Mutiny, until midnight on August 14th 1947 when with due ceremony the Union Jack was lowered and placed in the hands of my brother Leslie, for safekeeping and later to be presented to the General Officer Commanding (GOC) Lucknow District for its final disposal.

The Kaisarbagh, was the main palace of the kings of Oud, and alleged to be in those days the milieu of every kind of depravity, debauchery and evil. A lovely part of the palace, in the Moghul style, was built to accommodate the ladies of the harem and had a picturesque garden with the River Gomti flowing alongside. After the mutiny it became the Lucknow Club and was so until Independence in 1947.

La Martinière College was an enormous building, built by Major General Claude Martin, a French soldier of fortune, who took service with the Nawab of Awadh, Asaf-ud-Daula, and made enough money to live in quite an imperial style. In front of La Martinière College lies an attractive park holding the tomb of Major William Hodson, the officer who raised 'Hodson's Horse', an irregular cavalry unit, and who shot the Moghul princes, after the surrender of Bahadur Shah II, [last of the Moghul emperors] at the siege of Delhi, during the Indian Mutiny. He was also an ancestor of Colonel Hodson of my old regiment, the 1st North Staffords. Claude Martin's own residence was the 'Dilkusha', which means, 'House of the Happy Heart', a lovely and palatial residence in a park quite close to La Martinière.

As Christmas 1945 approached preparations for Christmas tiger camps were put in hand and I was invited to the one being organised by Mr. Parsons, the Deputy Inspector of Indian Police, at a place called Katarniaghat close to the northwest Nepal – United Province border. A metre-gauge railway from the United Province ended at Katarniaghat, the border being marked by a river, about a mile away at the forest rest house compound, at which we stayed. This was surrounded by a vast forest in all directions holding every kind of game, including tiger, panther, elephant, bison and every variety of deer.

Accommodation and cook tents were pitched in the rest house compound together with a large shamiana. The party consisted of Mr. and Mrs Parsons and their daughter, and Mr. and Mrs Aldridge of the Indian Civil Service and Colonel Johnny West of the Baluch regiment and myself.

The Quarter Guard was on duty at the camp and we had a forest department ranger on site and forest guards to help us with the shooting arrangements. We were fortunate in having the use of four elephants from the forest department and police at the camp. There were three female elephants and a fine young tusker bull, 24-years-old, showing about a yard of ivory outside his head. The forest rangers said the tusker got excited at the scent of tiger and panther and became difficult for the mahout to control and so only the men in the party were allowed to mount him and, in the event, I largely appropriated him as my own personal mount.

In the evening we sat down to dinner in the dining tent and were chatting merrily when there was a terrific uproar from the cook tent, shouts and yells and people running about. We rushed outside to see what had happened and the cook, trembling with excitement, said: "I looked out of the tent and saw a big panther and shouted to frighten him. He has gone off into the jungle".

A high fence surrounded the rest house compound and on one side there was a patch of dense jungle which the panther had come from. The next day, when we had returned from a 'ghum' on the elephant, that is a tour round in the jungle, the guard said that during the morning two panthers had walked out of the jungle, crossed the road and gone in the direction of the Nepal border.

The following morning, before leaving the camp area, we decided to put the elephants into the dense thicket, which was practically impenetrable to human beings. The three female elephants and mahouts and the rest of the party advanced towards the thicket from one side, and I approached from the opposite, on the young tusker. As we moved in the tusker suddenly struck the ground with his trunk, boom boom, and then made a terrific trumpet. He then ploughed forward, with upraised trunk, trumpeting and bellowing. When he was almost in the centre of the thicket a few monkeys ran out but nothing else. The tusker had obviously got the scent of the panther in the thicket, which had been using it for cover and from which it had ventured to the cook house

There was plenty of small game in scrub jungle about a mile from the forest rest house and we formed a line to beat through the area. The Parsons were on the left line, I was in the centre and the Aldridges and Johnny West to the right. Looking towards the Parsons I suddenly heard a shout as Mr. Parsons leapt up into the air still shouting. The Parsons often indulged in these acrobatics. Right across our front ran a large sounder [a group of feral hogs or pigs] led by a big boar. They were so close to Mrs Parsons that she had to jump to avoid being run down by the pigs. Fortunately, the sounder belted out of sight. As we were only armed with shotguns and had ladies with this party, it would have been very unpleasant incident, had pigs really meant business.

The animals that we had tied up for tigers were not taken for several days. The reason for this was probably because there was such a large amount of wild game in the area. On a very cold and misty morning, we set out with the elephants to visit the big baits and when moving along the fire line heard ahead a noise which was like a buffalo's bellow. The elephants were halted and then I moved forward on the tusker alone. As my tusker mounted a gradient in the fire line, I saw the buffalo standing there bellowing and half dozen wild dogs feeding on its entrails. I took a shot at the dogs from the elephant and they ran off. I then dismounted immediately and shot the buffalo, to put it out of its misery. I waved the other elephants away so that the rest of the party should not see this harrowing scene. As it turned out, I did not hit any of the dogs but this was an example of the cruel and merciless killing that is just one aspect of the 'law of the jungle.'

It could be argued that the fault lay with us who had tied up the buffalo, but foxes behave in the same manner with lambs and chickens. Had a tiger come across the buffalo its death would have been almost certainly instantaneous, with a broken neck, the normal manner in which a tiger would dispatch such prey.

In the afternoon a beat for game was organised, through the jungle towards the river boundary with Nepal, with the four elephants formed in line abreast, with beaters on either flank, and between them. The line was moving steadily through the jungle when up went the tusker's trunk and he trumpeted and went off through the undergrowth at a very fast pace, bellowing and trumpeting for all he was worth. Sitting on a pad, i.e. a mattress tied onto the elephant's back behind the mahout, I was struck sharply by branches on several occasions. Using his ankus or goad the mahout with all his strength hit the tusker on the head, producing a reverberating, hollow noise. Eventually he caused the tusker to slow down and then took him away from the beat. It was an exciting experience but if a tiger had been disturbed things would have been extremely dangerous as we would most likely have been shaken off the elephant or had to face an attack on the elephant by the tiger.

At the end of the camp I returned to Lucknow the day before the rest of the party. The journey back to Lucknow was on the metre gauge line passing through a very large estate called Balrampur. The line ran through very extensive and dense jungle and in many sections of the line the way was on embankments with many sharp bends and steep gradients to negotiate. The speed limit was restricted to 15 mph. In my compartment was an Indian railway official and while we chatted the train gathered speed and soon it was careering along at about 35 mph lurching as it took the sharp bends which was quite alarming. The Indian railway officer got very worried, and he said, "Oh God what to do, the driver must be mad".

When the train pulled up at the first station, we hurried down the platform to the engine to see what had happened to find the driver as drunk as a lord and singing at the top of his voice. He was a Christian and had been celebrating Christmas for several days already. There was no relief driver at the station and having made the driver a little more aware of his responsibilities a man with a large spanner in his hand was positioned to stand by the driver. He had instructions to knockout the driver if necessary. The fireman knew how to halt the train in an emergency so we considered the situation as sufficiently under control to continue the journey, which we did to Balrampur. At Balrampur the driver was promptly arrested by the police and taken to the local lockup.

After a meal had been served, I changed trains and proceeded to Lucknow. It was an unusual and happily not a very common experience, to be a passenger on a train when the driver was very drunk.

My sister-in-law, Ena, returned from England in mid-December 1945 and it so happened that trouble had broken out in Lucknow and Leslie was not able to go to the station to great her, so I went down in his stead. Travelling with Ena was Mrs Thompson, wife of the manager of the Imperial Bank of India in Lucknow and her 19-year-old daughter, Kathleen.

On Ena's arrival our social life became very hectic and active. On each day of the week there were dinner parties at Shah Najaf Road or we dined out at friends' houses or attended social functions of which there were many. On the official side there were receptions at Government House and the many regimental functions of the large garrison station. One evening, in company with the Thompsons, Sir Frank and Lady Ware and Mary their daughter and Mr. and Mrs Cantley, of the Pioneer newspaper, I visited the room in which Kipling used to work.

Police Week was perhaps the most important and enjoyable week of the year in Lucknow. During it, the Indian police headed by Sir Frank Meadows the Inspector General of Police were host to the station.

During the day there were entertainments and social functions, sports etc. and the work of the Indian police was demonstrated to the public.

There was a parade in the police lines in their large parade ground and it was a most impressive spectacle with Leslie in command. We watched the parade from shamianas. The police were drawn up in two long lines, with three squadrons of mounted police, the two battalions of armed police and then the city and district police. They all looked very smart.

The commencement of the parade was under the command of the senior inspector of police of the city. Leslie then rode onto the parade ground on his beautiful grey Arab. It was the most marvellous horse I had ever seen. It had a classical Arab head, short and broad and was in wonderful condition. There was a gasp of admiration from the spectators. The parade gave Leslie a salute and command was handed over to him by the inspector. When the Inspector General of Police rode onto the parade, he was given a general salute, followed by a salute to the Governor and then the full ceremonial of the parade and march-past took place. It was very smart and a credit to Leslie and his officers and men. After the parade there were a number of events; a polo tournament, tent pegging, show jumping, etc. and mounted sports to follow, it ended with a ball at the Chuttar Manzil club.

Later, a court of inquiry took me to Lansdowne, a hill station on the United Provinces border, in an area known as Himachal Pradesh. It was the regimental headquarters of the 18th Kohal Rifles and, being a purely military and official station, was only known to very few Europeans. The European population normally comprised only military officers of the regiment and civilian government officials, who were stationed there from time to time. Lansdowne is located at a height of 7,000 feet and is approached via Najibabad, the headquarters of a forest division. The surrounding jungle was the hide out of the notorious Indian dacoit, 'Sultana', until he was brought to book by Freddie Young of the Dacoiti Police and Jim Corbett, as related in Jim's book 'My India'.

The Rifles regimental mess was a fine building, right on the top of the ridge and has a magnificent view of the snows that stretch in a huge semi-circle round it. In the garden of the mess was a plinth on which there was a brass plate, marked with veins pointing in the direction of the most famous peaks, and there was also a vast pointer which could be rotated, and one could take a view in the direction of the peaks and identify them.

By 1946 the majority of the Indian troops that had gone over to the Japanese and become known as the Indian National Army (INA) had been brought back to India, about 20,000 in all, and were in prison or detention camp awaiting the decision of the government as to their fate. The situation was critical as the men were all trained soldiers and large numbers of arms and ammunition were spread all over India because of wartime operations.

Congress Party politicians praised the members of the INA as patriots, fighting for their country, and demanded their release and complete freedom for all. The Government of India and army headquarters could not overlook the treason and sedition of the leaders of the INA. It was, therefore, decided to make plans for the protection and movement to safe strongholds of the Europeans and Anglo-Indian population in the event of a rising by the INA. This plan included the protection of the strategic roads and railways, vital services, military depots and posts etc., and the concentration of the Europeans in strongholds. This was known as 'Scheme Asylum'. It was top secret and exercises were held to deal with the possible situations and emergencies that might arise.

I was involved with our district scheme at Cawnpore [Kanpur]. While there, we lived in the circuit house on the banks of the Ganges. Although things were very busy, it was a pleasant station and we enjoyed the stay and I went on a visit to the memorial gardens to see, once more, the well of the Bibighar Massacre of the Indian Mutiny.

In 1946 another leave scheme was brought into operation, which was known as 'Long Leave', and as I was eligible, I left Lucknow in June 1946 for England via Deolali and Bombay.

On returning from leave in England I was posted to Number 10 MT regiment in Calcutta. My headquarters was based in Alipore and the regimental companies were located in the outskirts of the city. Communal rioting and political demonstrations were a daily occurrence and a dusk to dawn curfew was in force. The amount of staff work required in headquarters at Fort William and of the unit commanders was terrific. Duties in aid of the civil power, enforcement of the curfew, demobilisation of units, preparations for the anticipated reorganisation of the army and withdrawal of United States forces, stores and equipment from Assam.

The continual breakdown of public order allowed no let up on the part of all senior officers. On top of this I had an unusual situation to deal with in Christmas week. One morning two young subalterns of the company located in the southern area of the city commanded by a long-service major, who had been promoted from the ranks, arrived at regimental headquarters in Alipore and asked to see me. They were nervous and embarrassed, but I ordered them to tell me why they had come to see me and to withhold nothing. This was their story. The major had, for several days, been going into Calcutta after lunch and had not returned until the early hours of the morning in a very merry mood. At 3am that morning they were woken up by a couple of revolver shots from the officers' mess, and when they got to the mess a naik (or corporal) was in a very agitated state. The major sahib had walked into the mess stark naked and ordered bacon and eggs, and when he was having the meal something upset him and he fired a couple of shots at the naik. He had then left the mess and gone to his quarters. The other officers went to the major's quarters and found him asleep. The major appeared at breakfast and then went into Calcutta and they decided to come and see me and tell what had happened.

I ordered them to go back to the company and notify the provost marshall what had happened and ask him to put out a military police net to apprehend the major. I then proceeded to the company lines but when about halfway there I came across a truck in which I saw the major sitting. I stopped the truck, and in the presence of my second in command, Major Paddy Field, I placed the company commander under arrest and ordered him back to his unit and to remain confined to his quarters until he received further orders from me.

I followed him down to the lines and entered his quarters and went over to the dressing table. I opened the drawer and in it I found a 0.45 pistol and two empty cartridge cases. The other chambers held loaded rounds. The major had earned a pension and he would lose it all if he were court-martialed and found guilty. I gave him the strongest ticking off I was capable of and impressed upon him not to make a fool of himself if he wished to save his pension and to carry out my instructions to the letter. He was really aware of the trouble he was in when I left, and I felt sure that he would co-operate to the fullest.

I sent a written report to the general officer commanding (GOC) and he decided to deal with the matter himself. Three days later I arraigned the major in front of the general, who had the reputation of being a fearsome tiger of a man. When the major came out of the GOC's office his face was white and his knees trembling. He said to me, "By God. I never want to go through anything like that again." The GOC in his wisdom had severely reprimanded the major and put the fear of God into him but the officer's pension was safe.

I knew that my posting to Calcutta would be a temporary one as the demobilisation was proceeding at a pace and the regiment was due to complete demobilisation by the 10th of January. I was then posted to headquarters, Northern Command India at Rawalpindi, in charge of a training team.

On arrival at Rawalpindi, I obtained accommodation at the well-known and comfortable Flashman's Hotel, which of course I had known well over the years.

Communal Violence

My duties necessitated me touring of the whole of the northern command area, which included a number of journeys to Lahore. The decision that 14th August would be the date of the partition of India was made in February 1947 [and announced in June 1947] and rioting, murder and looting broke out along the Punjab, United Provinces' border and the Delhi province border.

In Lahore and Rawalpindi the situation was appalling. Nearly every Hindu and Sikh house in the two cities were burnt to the ground, people were slaughtered in the thousands, as I witnessed in my journeys up and down the line. There were riots in Rawalpindi at Saddar Bazar, and one morning when leaving the hotel I heard two shots in the road just outside. I ran down to a crossroads a few yards away and round the corner found two bodies. They were Mohammadans and they were both dead.

I reported the matter immediately to the police for action, and also to the provost marshall as I had seen an Indian officer, a Sikh, walking away down the road.

In early 1947, the great fear of riots and violence, amongst the general population, was evidenced by a peculiar and touching incident that happened to me at that time. One day, when standing on the station platform at Wazirabad, a man rushed up to me, knelt down and kissed my feet, shouting, "Do not leave us sahib. There will be no one to protect us and our children and to give us justice."

The number of people who were murdered has never been accurately disclosed [at the time of writing] but the opinion of many people like myself, are that over one million died and probably up to 10 million were injured in these dreadful riots. This was the price that Lord Wavell had refused to pay for the independence in 1947. As a result Wavell was replaced as viceroy by Lord Mountbatten, who was willing to speed-up Indian independence, as much as possible.

My younger brother, Leslie, had a very heavy burden to bear during this period as he commanded a force of patrol battalions of armed police, on the Punjab - United Provinces border. Leslie had been promoted to Deputy Inspector General of Police and, while occupied on military duties, was also a full colonel in the army

In one border township there was a mixed population with a large Hindu majority but communal rioting was unknown and both communities were on the best of terms. As soon as the partition was announced an immediate change in attitude occurred, agitators arrived and began to incite and provoke the two communities. The communities ceased all contact with each other and rioting between them started. The police force was predominantly Mohammadan but carried out their duties impartially. Then one day a bazaar brawl, started by bad characters, quickly developed into a bloody riot of appalling savagery. The Mohammadan inhabitants ran to the 'Godwale' that is police headquarters, which was surrounded by a high wall and offered the only hope of protection. The mob surrounded the godwale and eventually broke down the gates and streamed in to complete their dreadful work. Every Mohammadan man, woman and child and the whole of the police force were murdered and mutilated, and the bodies set alight.

When news reached Leslie he rushed a force of police in lorries at full speed but they arrived too late. The crowd was dispersed and first aid given to any survivors of the massacre. A new police garrison was established in the township. These brutal events were to be repeated again and again. The exact number of people killed in this incident was not established but several hundred bodies were collected.

One day I was travelling on the Frontier Mail from Lahore to Rawalpindi when the train came to a halt about six miles from Rawalpindi in the open country. I walked down to the engine and found the driver and guard in an argument with a crowd of small boys and girls who were squatting across the track. The children said they were stopping the train because it would cause the government trouble. Many of the villagers had gathered and were laughing and encouraging the children in their work. I picked up a stick which happened to be lying to hand and gave one or two of the small boys sharp snaps on their posteriors which quickly resulted in movement away from the train and the driver and guard and several passengers joined in with me. The villagers saw that our action was not vicious, and we returned to the train which got moving to Rawalpindi without delay.

Later, I told my Punjabi bearer about the incident and what it would mean for the future. He said it would be a bad thing for the people of India. I pointed out that Indian politicians had been campaigning for independence for many years and it must come some day. I also said independence would result in many other European nations being able to come to India, in larger numbers. He shook his head and said, "They are not sahibs".

Last Days

On my return from my long tour, I saw a medical officer about the rather bad pains in my stomach and severe indigestion which I had had for many years. He ordered me into hospital for an investigation. A large number of x-ray plates were taken and examinations carried by two surgical specialists. At the end of it they told me I had a growth in the stomach and should proceed to England as soon as possible to take further medical advice. It was a worrying situation as I was approaching the end of my career and could not just go home as the doctors suggested. I was however placed on a diet and given medicine which eased the pain enabling me to return to duty.

We reorganised the station, as necessary, to reform the Indian Army units into units of a new Pakistan army and a new Indian army. The withdrawal of British troops to England, caused a lot of personnel moves to take place. As part of this reorganisation I was informed in March that I was to be commander of the RIASC Area Regiment at Kamptee in the Deccan district of India. I was very pleased with the new assignment as Kamptee was in the middle of a marvellous jungle area and was the cantonment for Nagpur, capital of the Central Provinces. In addition Secunderabad, my first station in India, was also in the district, as were the cantonments at Mhow, Nasirabad, Jabalpur and Pachmarhi.

In April I boarded the Express which ran from Rawalpindi in the far north right through the centre of India to Bangalore in the south. My journey to Kamptee was one of 1,750 miles and after taking over my new job, and moving into a nice bungalow, I began to tour the district. I was very eager to see Secunderabad again. When I got there I was put in a club quarter and happy to find that the club secretary was a Captain Mark Cuilin who had served with me in Agra. The amenities of the fine club had been improved by the addition of a very good swimming pool. As I sat on the lawn having drinks my thoughts went back to the evening when Carman Watts had driven in with two panthers in the back of the club car.

When I went into the breakfast next morning an elderly club bearer came out and said, "Salaam, Robins sahib". I asked how he knew me and he replied, "You were in the North Stafford Regiment sahib". I left Secunderabad in 1928 as a first lieutenant, weighing 11 stone. I returned 19 years later as a lieutenant colonel weight 14 stone and I thought it was quite remarkable that the bearer recognised me in the circumstances. I enquired about my old bearer, Baloo, the hero of the panther shoot at Bhongir. Baloo was well and still doing bearer's work but was in Poona and so, to my great regret, I did not meet him again.

In Secunderabad I met Major Johnny Barham and Betty Barham, his charming wife. Johnny was posted to Kamptee, as my second in command, in a matter of a few days. They had a young family, a small boy Nicky and two little girls, Jilly and Ginny. They were pleasant, charming people and a close and loyal friendship was formed which has continued to this day [late 1970s, at the time of writing], though we have not seen each other since 1947, when they emigrated to New Zealand, direct from India at the end of our service.

Like a number of stations in India Secunderabad had expanded greatly during the war but the older places also remained and I enjoyed my stay there. The Commander in Chief (CIC) of Southern Command at the time was Lieutenant General Eric Goddid, who I served with in Burma, and the General Officer Commanding (GOC) of the Deccan district was Major General Philip Gwyn, my old friend of Bannu and Burma days. The brigadier at Kamptee was Brigadier Thakur Nadir Singh, a Rajput chief. Because of my determination to prevent any unfair treatment of Mohammadan officers we had several differences of opinion.

I also visited Nasirabad, it too had expanded during the war, but the old pre-mutiny bungalows were still there and the club and the regimental lines. The cemetery was kept in good condition where Lance Corporal Murray and Private White and many of their predecessors lay awaiting the 'grand reveille'.

I had some leave in May and went up to Nainital where Leslie and Ena were also on leave. One afternoon walking along the lakeside road I met Jim Corbett, who was being carried in a litter, toward the club. Poor old Jim looked rather frail. He had been on a fishing trip with the governor of the United Provinces and had been struck down with pneumonia. He had been very ill and at his age recovery was slow. I am glad to say he got well again and after the end of the Raj went to Nyeri in Kenya. I had a letter from him in 1955 in which he said he had been greatly disturbed by the exploitation of big game shooting in Africa and the disgraceful methods being used by rich tourists: chasing game in jeeps and four-wheel drive cars, shooting at the animals in safety from a few yards distance, often leaving the dangerous wounded game to be finished off by alleged 'professional hunters', many of whom had little experience and perpetrated some dreadful cruelties. Jim died shortly afterwards. It was Jim who also seconded me for membership of the Shikar Club, the big game hunters club. Jim was a wonderful person; it was a privilege to have known him.

Also while in Nainital I climbed up the hillside to Freddie Champion's bungalow to see the latest of his wonderful photos of animals of the Indian jungles.

There was a forest rest house about 40 miles from Kamptee in typical Central Provinces jungle near the Pench River which had always held tiger. The area around was reserved for the Kamptee garrison and to me it was wonderful to be able to go out every evening when in Kamptee and roam around the jungles. I was usually accompanied by Johnny and Betty Barham and another lady, who was touring India. We saw a number of tiger pugs in the sand by the river and on every visit we saw some samba, chital and barking deer, occasionally a bison and bear were also seen. During this period I did not make a serious attempt to bag a tiger as my absences from Kamptee were too frequent, because of my work commitments.

I had to visit Jabalpur, about 145 miles from Kamptee, the road traversing some fine Sal forest almost the whole of the way. It passed through Seonee, where I had stayed in 1929. The small jungle township was unchanged and the magic of Kipling was reawakened in me. The memories of that time being more poignant knowing that my stay in India was rapidly drawing to a close. Kamptee was a typical and delightful Indian cantonment. A well made road, with an avenue of trees on either side, ran through the place. The bungalows were spaced well apart in large compounds, with carefully tended gardens. On most mornings packs of langur monkeys could be seen in the bungalow compounds or in the trees along the road.

The club was located on the bank of the River Pench, some 75 feet above the river, and had a small swimming pool in the garden. The flame of the forest trees added colour everywhere.

There was a large Anglo-Indian population in Nagpur. It was an important railway centre, and the Saturday night dances of the Railway Institute were very popular. It was my birthday on 4th August and Walter Purcell, a Gurkha major, and ADC to the governor of the Central Provinces, had arranged a party for me at his quarters at Government House, Nagpur to which Betty and Johnny Barham and several other friends were invited. We drank and played cards surrounded by beautiful tiger skins and when I at last reached the haven of my bed in the early hours of the morning I felt a good ten years older.

Regrettably, as Independence Day approached, the underlying religious antipathy between the Hindu and Mohammadan officers became obvious. The partition plans provided for officers to be moved to their own respective countries, if possible before Independence Day, and a definite responsibility to ensure this and prevent unfair treatment devolved on senior British officers.

The provost martial in Kamptee, a Hindu, had been paying special attention to a unit of mine, commanded by a Pathan officer. The military police had been found in the unit's lines without the CO's knowledge. He was very angry at this as it was contrary to regulations and I ordered the CO to refuse access to the military police until he received my assent. Any military police caught inside the lines were to be arrested forthwith. The provost martial was also anti-British and the brigade commander became involved in this affair. I would not however agree to any procedure that was not correct and did not accord with the proper regulations. After some dispute, I won the day.

A short time later when the Brigadier was on tour the Pathan officer came to me and asked for leave to go to his home, which was in the Mohmand tribal territory, near the Afghan border 2,000 miles away. I had him flown out, but he did not return, presumably having arranged with the Pakistan army to see to this. I also had another confrontation with the Brigadier on his return from tour with regard to the matter, but no further complications developed.

After a recurrence of my stomach trouble I had further examinations by several medical officers. They said I should go home as quickly as possible and get immediate medical advice. Headquarters India had asked all British officers of the Indian army to volunteer for another year's service in India and the general officer commanding chiefs of all commands made personal requests to this effect.

General Dorrel, who was in Kamptee, asked me in particular to stay on. I said I would like to but I told him about my physical state and he agreed I should go home as early as possible. Because my name was not on the list of those who volunteered I was not awarded the Indian Independence Medal but an RAF friend whom I knew who arrived in India for the first time in August 1947 and left in November of the same year now proudly wears this medal.

The danger of mass bloodshed on Independence Day in Nagpur is averted

Independence Day was celebrated by a programme of sport, parades etc. in Kamptee on 16th August 1947 and in the historic Sitabuldi Fort in Nagpur on 14th August by the flag hoisting ceremony in the presence of official guests, including the new Indian governor of the province, the Indian Prime Minster of the Central Provinces [now part of Maharashtra] and the outgoing British GOC, Major General Philip Gwynn. A crowd of 40,000 or more surrounded the fort and were packed in the approach road to the inner keep, which is flanked on either side by very high walls.

Also at the hoisting ceremony was a Gurkha battalion, commanded by British officers. The army unit garrisoning the fort was the 3rd Battalion, Sikh regiment that also had to guard the gates of the inner keep. The crowd was very excited and nearly all the men in it had knives, swords, lances or cudgels. They started stoning the Sikh guards at the gate and several men were carried away wounded by stones, after which the gates which had been left ajar were closed.

The hoisting of the new flag of India was completed with due ceremony, but it was not possible to leave the fort because of the hostile action of the crowds outside the inner keep and all around the fort. Desperate appeals were made by Indian politicians and the police but it was to no avail and the Indian governor, the state Prime Minister and GOC could not make their departure.

About 4pm standing at the top of the inner keep with Lt Col. S.C. Middler, the DSO 1, I said "Why not tell the crowd they can come in, now, but make them promise to behave and not to damage their own property". This was done and the crowd started streaming in. One man passed me waving his spear and looking right for murder. At this point I had had enough and taking Captain Prince, my staff captain and a lady who also wished to come with us. I led the way out of the inner keep and towards the outer gate, outside which our vehicle was parked. The crowd was solid, and I had to push my way, shouting in Hindi, "Give us room". The stench from the pressing crowd was quite horrible.

I kept moving forward and as I did so I said, "It is your big day, it is your fort, good luck to India". Suddenly a man started clapping, others took it up, they patted us on the shoulders and then there were cries from all sides, "Thank you very much, sahib, good luck to you". We reached our vehicle and drove back to Kamptee. If I had trodden on anybody's foot or anyone had been hurt during our progress we would probably have been hacked to pieces. The Indian governor, the state Prime Minister, and Philip Gwynn did not get out of the fort until 10pm that night.

Our task was nearly done and every British officer of the civil service, the army and the other government gazetted services had done their duty to the British Empire and doubly so to India.

I do not think anything can illustrate more clearly the long devoted and valiant service to India by a comparatively small circle of families and social groups, generation after generation, than the following announcement on the programme of the Independence Day celebrations at Kamptee.

"Light music will be played by the band of 3ʳᵈ battalion the Sikh regiment, 'Rattray's Sikhs', by kind permission of Lieutenant Colonel P.H. Rattray."

On Independence Day 1947 the great, great-grandson of the Rattray, who had raised the regiment, was commanding the same regiment. What an inspiration to the men of 'Rattray's Sikhs' and how great was their 'Izzat', (i.e. 'honour'). To know that across the generations a single family should be so faithful to them and so proud to devote their life's work to the Indian soldier and to India itself.

APPENDIX A

Lt. Col. Stanley C Robins: Military Honours, Decorations and Medals

Honours

Member of the British Empire (MBE) – Military Division

For Distinguished Service

Decorations

Mentioned in Dispatches, Waziristan 1936/37

For gallantry in the Khaisora Valley operations

Mentioned in Dispatches, Burma 1941/42

For distinguished service in the allied withdrawal from Burma

Medals

Indian General Service Medal with Clasps (1929/30) (1936/37) & (1938/39)

Awarded for campaign service in India

1939/43 Star [later changed to the 1939/45 Star]

Awarded for operational service in World War II

Burma Star

Awarded for serving in the Burma campaign 1941-45

Defence Medal

Awarded for at least 3 years service with one or more campaign stars

War Medal

Awarded for military service in World War II

APPENDIX B   RECORD OF SERVICE   *Page 01*

OF

LT-COLONEL S. C. ROBINS. M. B. E.

DATE:	APPOINTMENT. NATURE OF DUTIES etc.
Jan: 1922 to Dec: 1923.	Cadet at the Royal Military College, Sandhurst. Obtained prizes for Organisation and Administration at the Final passing out examination.
31 Jan: 1924. to Sept: 1928.	Commissioned 2nd Lieutenant 1st Battalion N.Staffordshire Regiment, Secunderabad, India. Regimental duties as Platoon Commander and Machine Gun Platoon Commander. Passed Machine-gun Course, Range-finding Course, Physical Training Course (a) and (b) promotion examinations for Captain. Promoted to Lieutenant 31/1/26. Captain of Regimental Rifle Eight. Passed Course of Embarkation and Staff Duties, Bombay. Dec: 1925 - April 1926.
Oct: 1928. to Apr: 1929.	Attached to Royal Indian Army Service Corps on probation. Passed Courses in Supplies, Animal Transport and Mechanical Transport.
Apr: 1929 to Oct: 1930.	Section Commander 15th M. T. Coy, R. I. A. S. C. Peshawar. and Rawalpindi.Took part in the Khajuri Plain operations against the Passed "Urdu" qualifying Language examination. Afridis '29/30
10. Oct. 1930.	Transferred to the Indian Army.
Mar: 1931 to Nov: 1931	Adjutant, Base Supply Depot, Rawalpindi.
Dec: 1931 to Mar: 1932.	Brigade Supply Officer, Abbotabad Brigade. Took part in several small expeditions against the BLACK MOUNTAIN TRIBE. N. W. F. P.
Mar: 1932 to Sept: 1932.	Section Commander 5th Motor Ambulance Convoy, Bareilly.
Oct: 1932. to Mar: 1934.	Officer in charge Supplies, Agra. Promoted Captain 31st Jan. 1933.
Apr: 1934. to Nov: 1935.	On furlough in the United Kingdom.
Apr: 1935 to Dec: 1935.	Section Commander No. 14 M. T. Coy, Mir Ali, Waziristan. O. C. No. 10. A. T. Coy (Gurkha) Wana. S. Waziristan.
Jan: 1936. to Feb: 1938.	Officer Commanding 25 Animal Transport Coy, Razmak, Waziristan. Took part in the operations against Faqir of Ipi over a period of 18 months. Mentioned in Despatches for Gallantry.
Mar: 1938. to Oct: 1940.	Seconded to the Burma Army as Officer-in-charge Supplies, Rangoon, and Embarkation Staff Officer. Was responsible for the maintenance of the Lower Burma Mobile Column operating against Rebels from Apr: '38 to Dec: '38.

DATE	APPOINTMENT, NATURE OF DUTIES.
Oct. '40.	Appointed Deputy Asst: Director of Supplies & Transport Army Headquarters, Burma. Promoted to temporary Major. Passed promotion examination (d) for Major.
31. Jan '41.	Promoted to substantive rank of Major.
Dec. '40 to Apr: '41.	Officiating Director of Supplies & Transport Army in Burma. Was responsible for the expansion of the Burma Army Service Corps, which involved the raising and training of 40 Field Supply Units: 26 Mechanical Transport Coys: 1 Animal Transport Coy: Provision of vehicles and spare parts for all Units of the Burma Army: also responsible for preparation and costing of budget estimates concerned.
Nov: '41.	Appointed Asst:Director of Supplies & Transport Army in Burma.(Lt-Col).
Dec: '41 to May: '42.	As Asst:Director of Supplies & Transport on General Alexander's Staff: was largely responsible for the maintenance arrangements of the Burma Army during the withdrawal from Rangoon to Imphal in Assam, and all the operations involved over difficult and unknown terrain. Was also responsible for the maintenance of the V and VI Chinese Armies, strength 120,000. Mentioned in Despatches for Distinguished Services.
Jun: '42 to Sep: '42.	Casualty. In hospital and on sick leave.
Oct: '42.	Appointed Commander, Burma Army Service Corps to re-organise and train B.A.S.C.Units for further operations. Returned to Indian Army on completion of this task.
Dec: '42. to Feb: '42.	Second in Command "B". M.T. Reinforcement Centre, Deolali. 10,000 Recruits under command.
Feb: '42 to Oct. '42.	Asst:Director of Supplies, (Lt-Col) Headquarters Eastern Army and 14th Army.
Nov: '43 to Jan: '45.	Officer Commanding Reserve Base Petrol Depot, Parbatipor, Assam. This Unit was responsible for the provision, distribution and storage of all type of petrol, Aviation Spirit, Oils and lubricants for the 14th Army. L of C.Troops, U.S.Air Forces and the China Base. It included the handling of six trains per day of packed petrol, four trains of bulk petrol, the operation of bulk installations all over the Assam area, and control of fourteen tankers operating on the Brahmaputra. Awarded M.B.E. for Distinguished Services.
Jan: '45 to Oct: '45.	Officer Commanding Reserve Base Petrol Depot, Paragarh, Bengal, (Lt-Col). Largest petrol base in any theatre of operation.
Nov: '45 to Jan: '46.	Commander R.I.A.S.C.Regiment (Lt-Col) Lucknow District. Held command of all R.I.A.S.C.Units and installations in the District.
Nov: '46. to Jan: '47.	Commander 13th M.T.Regiment, Calcutta (Lt-Col). 26 M.T.Coys under command, comprising 2560 Vehicles. Engaged in duties in aid of the Civil Power.
Jan: '47. to Apr: '47.	Officer Commanding R.I.A.S.C.Training Team. (Lt-Col) Headquarters, Northern Command, India. Responsible for the training and efficiency of all R.I.A.S.C.Units in the Command.

......2000

--3--

DATE:	APPOINTMENT, NATURE OF DUTIES etc.

Apr '47
to
Oct '49

Commander R. I. A. S. C (Lt-Col) Deccan Area, Kamptee Central Provinces. Duties as above at Lucknow.
I proceeded to the United Kingdom on leave, pending retirement in Oct:'47 owing to the constitutional changes in India.

HONOURS, DECORATIONS, MEDALS etc:

i.   M. B. E.

ii.   Mention in Despatches, Waziristan. 1936/37.

iii.   Mention in Despatches, Burma. 1941/42.

iv.   Indian General Service Medal with Clasps,
         1936/37: 1938/39.

v.   1939/43 Star.

vi.   Burma Star.

vii.   Defence Medal.

viii. War Medal.

SPORTS:

Have played several games well in the past, i.e. Hockey, Tennis, Golf, Squash.

Established record 300 yds Swimming Championship, P. M. C. Sandhurst, 1922.

Have done a large amount of Big Game shooting and have bagged a considerable number of Tiger, Panther and other Big Game.

APPENDIX C

The Shikar Club

From 1955 to his death in 1976 Stanley Robins was a member of the Shikar Cub, which took its name from the Hindi word for 'Hunter'

The aim of the club with regard to hunting was [As originally worded in 1907]:

> "To maintain the standard of sportsmanship – it is not squandered bullets and swollen bags which appeal to us; the test lies rather in a love of forest, mountain and desert; in acquired knowledge or [sic] the habits of animals; in the strenuous pursuit of a wary and dangerous quarry; in the instinct for a well devised approach to a fair shooting distance; and in the patient retrieve of a wounded animal."

The club was founded in 1907 and its Patron was HM Queen Elizabeth II.

The Chairman was Brigadier, The Lord Lovat.

The Committee included Wilfred Thesiger

In 1974 the total membership of the Club, British and international, was 202 plus 31 honorary members (including HRH, The Duke of Edinburgh).

In the club's 1974 membership book Stanley Robins had the largest entry for any member for, "Districts Shot in", as follows:

> "India 1924-29: Hyderabad State – Adilabad, Bhongir Central Provinces - Chanda, Raipur, Khariar Zamindari, Bastar State S. India: Kanara

1930-37: Kashmir - Sind Valley United Provinces – Pilibhit, Kumaon, Champawat, Nundhaur, Hildwani, Kheri, Lilitpur Burma 1938-41: Pegu Yomas, Shan States, Tenasserim India 1943-47: East Bengal – Comilla, Assam-Dibrugarh, Silghat Nepal – Katarnian Ghat Central Provinces – Kamptee, Seoni"

For his membership application to the Shikar Club Stanley Robins was seconded by Jim Corbett, one of the most renowned big game hunters in India and world-wide. Stanley and Jim were lifelong friends after a chance meeting in India and both strongly supported wildlife conservation and condemned the rise of, as they saw it, commercialised and 'unsportsman like' big game hunting after World War II.

APPENDIX D

Administrative Map of India Prior to 15th August 1947

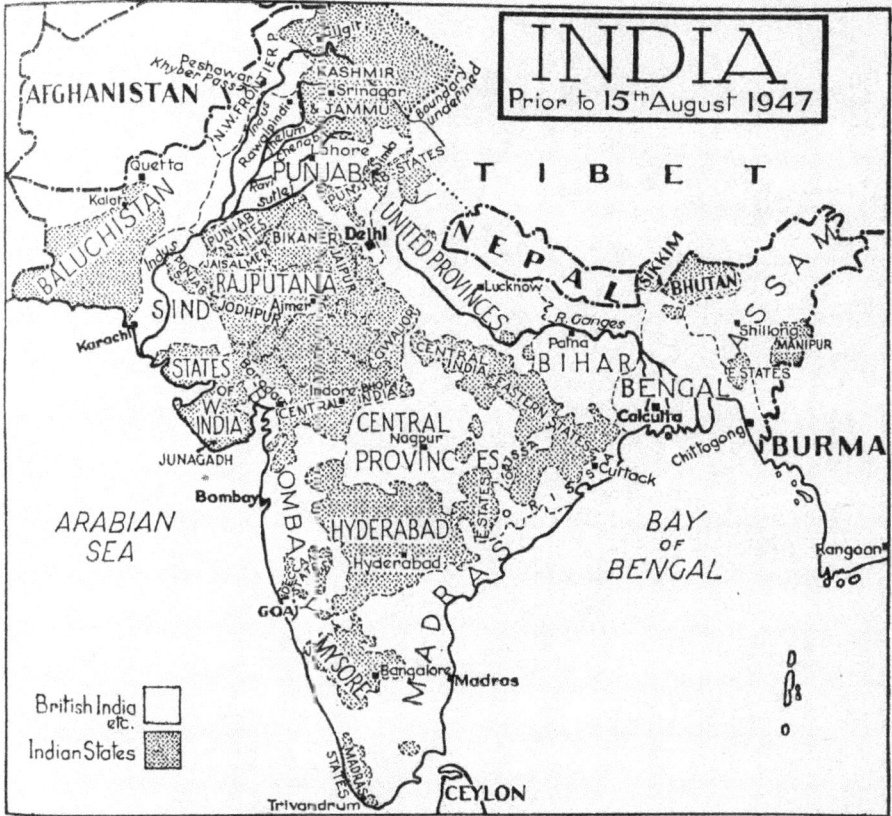

Image ID: G1CBF0
World History Archive/Alamy Stock Photo

APPENDIX E

Outline Map of Waziristan – 1930s

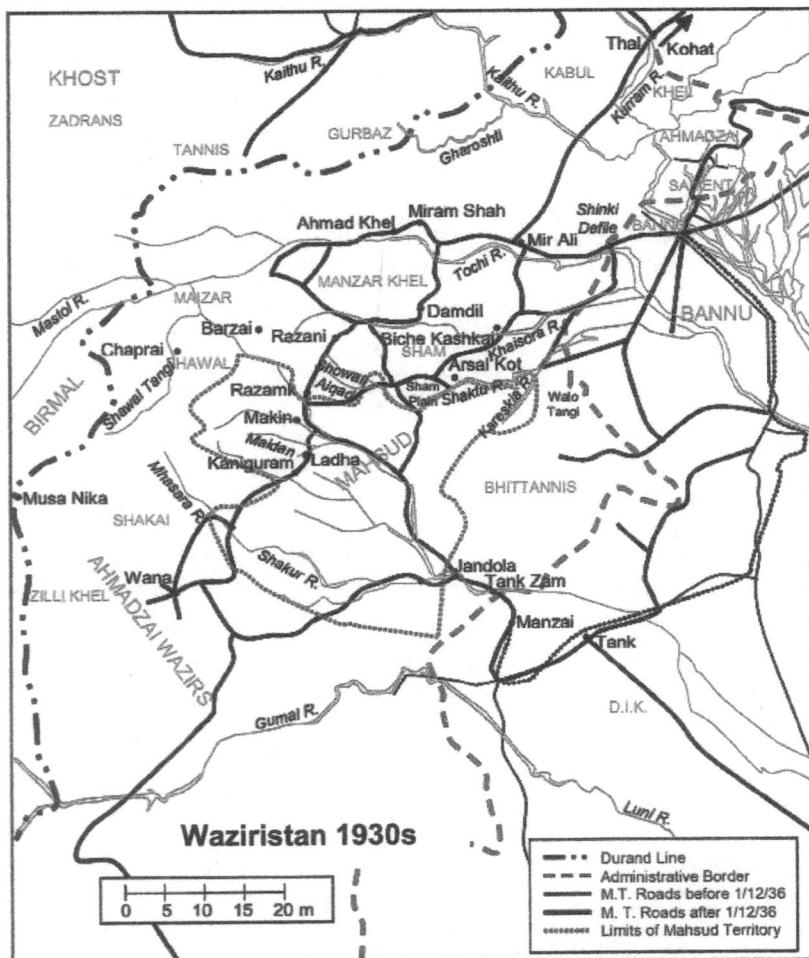

Credit: Matt M. Matthews

An ever present danger: a concise history of British military operations on the North-West Frontier, 1849-1947, CSI Press, 2010. Public Domain [note, 'Razamk' on map should be 'Razmak']

APPENDIX F

Outline Map of Burma – 1941

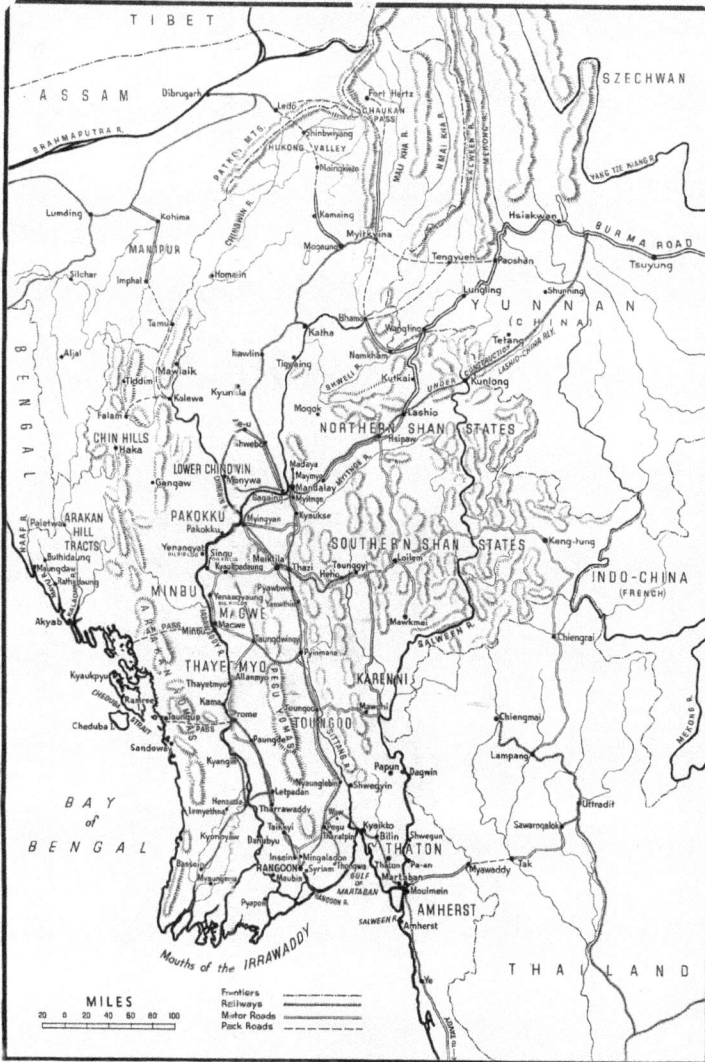

APPENDIX G

Japanese Advance in Burma,
20 January – 19 March 1942

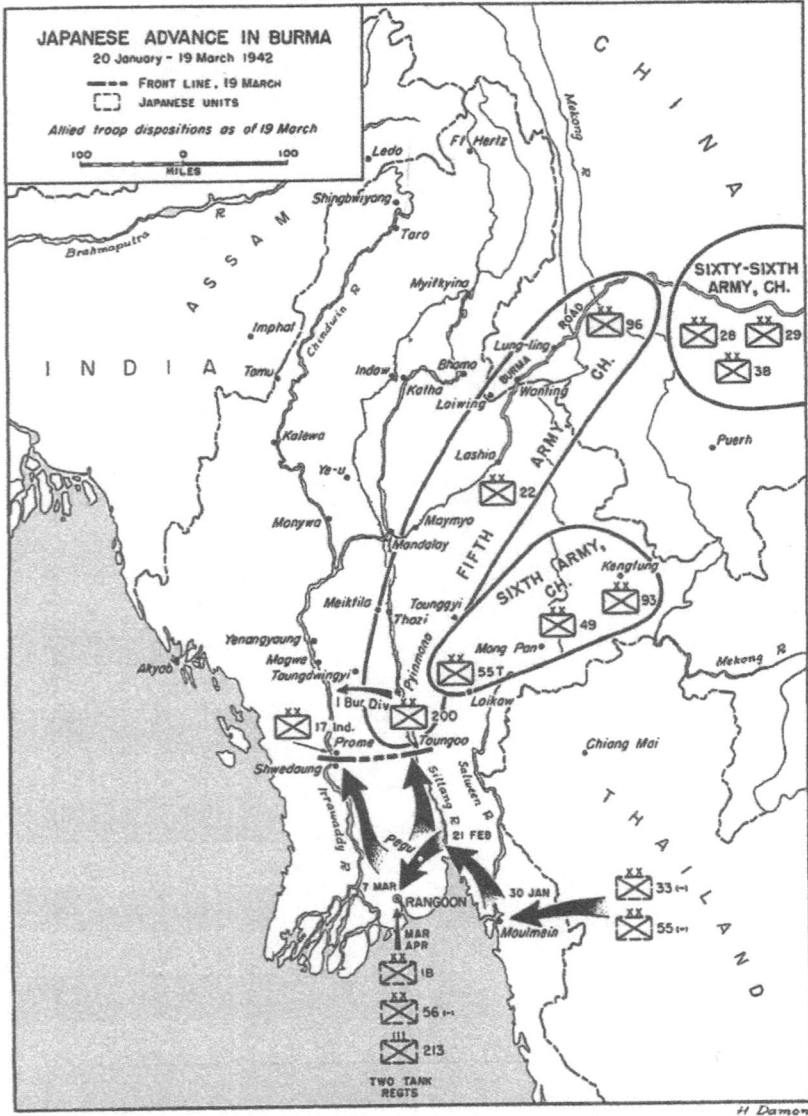

Credit: Charles F. Romanus, Riley Sunderland, Public Domain

www.ingramcontent.com/pod-product-compliance
Lightning Source LLC
Chambersburg PA
CBHW021210090426
42740CB00006B/176